# Libya's Foreign Policy in North Africa

# Libya's Foreign Policy
# in North Africa

Mary-Jane Deeb

Westview Press
BOULDER • SAN FRANCISCO • OXFORD

*Westview Special Studies on the Middle East*

Published in 1991 in the United States of America by Westview Press, Inc., 5500 Central Avenue, Boulder, Colorado 80301, and in the United Kingdom by Westview Press, 36 Lonsdale Road, Summertown, Oxford OX2 7EW

Library of Congress Cataloging-in-Publication Data
Deeb, Mary-Jane.
Libya's foreign policy in North Africa.
    (Westview special studies on the Middle East)
    Bibliography: p.
    Includes index.
    1. Africa, North—Foreign relations—Libya.   2. Libya—
Foreign relations—Africa, North.   3. Qaddafi, Muammar.
I. Title.   II. Series.
DT197.5.L75D44  1991   327.61′2′061     87-14179
ISBN 0-8133-7244-5

Printed and bound in the United States of America

The paper used in this publication meets the requirements
of the American National Standard for Permanence of Paper
for Printed Library Materials Z39.48-1984.

10    9    8    7    6    5    4    3    2    1

# Contents

# Acknowledgments

I wish to express my profound gratitude to Professor I. William Zartman, director of the African Studies Program at the School of Advanced International Studies (SAIS), The Johns Hopkins University. This work could not have been done without his unwavering support and encouragement throughout my four years of doctoral work and beyond. I also thank Professor Michael C. Schatzberg, of the African Studies Program at SAIS, for his perceptive criticisms and good advice, always given with humor and kindness.

I wish to express my appreciation to all those who took the time to share their ideas and insights on Libya with me: Ambassador David Newsom, director of the Institute for the Study of Diplomacy at Georgetown University; Rosemary O'Neil, desk officer for Tunisia at the Department of State; Ambassador Richard Parker of the Foreign Service Institute and former editor of *The Middle East Journal*; Joseph Montville of the Center for the Study of Foreign Affairs at the Foreign Service Institute; John Ruedy, professor of history at Georgetown University; Peter Bechtold, chairman for Near Eastern and North African Studies at the Foreign Service Institute; James Blake, who was deputy chief of the U.S. Mission in Libya at the time of the 1969 military coup; Steve Savage, of the Egypt desk at the Department of State; Michael Dunne, former editor of *Defense and Foreign Affairs*; and Ibrahim Shehata, vice-president and general counsel for legal affairs at the World Bank. Ambassador Clovis Maksoud, permanent observer of the League of Arab States at the United Nations, and Ambassador As'ad al-As'ad, the assistant secretary general of the League of Arab States, in Tunis, were most helpful to me in my research. I also thank Ambassador Habib Ben Yahia, minister of state for foreign affairs of Tunisia, and Ambassador M'hamed Bargach of Morocco for their assistance and encouragement while I was preparing this book.

While doing research in Tunis in 1986, I had the privilege of meeting members of the Foreign Ministry, the Parti Socialiste Destourien (PSD), and the University of Tunis, retired national political figures, and others who were interested in inter-Maghribi relations. I particularly wish to thank Ambassador Rachid Driss of the Ministry of Foreign Affairs, who

x                                                              *Acknowledgments*

represented Tunisia at the United Nations and in Washington for a
number of years, and Bahi Ladgham, ex–prime minister of Tunisia, for
their insightful discussions of Libyan-Tunisian relations and of the role
of Libya in North Africa. Others were also most helpful, especially Faraj
al-Chayeb, chargé of foreign relations of the PSD at the time; Omar
Fazzani, then secretary-general of the Ministry of Foreign Affairs; Mohammed Jniffen, director of Arab political affairs at the Ministry of
Foreign Affairs; Redha Bin Slama, adviser to the prime minister; and
Mohammed Ghareeb and Zouhair Allagui of the Ministry of Foreign
Affairs. Members of the Faculty of Law, Political Science, and Economics
of the University of Tunis were most generous with their time and their
ideas. I express my gratitude to Habib Slim, director of the department;
Sadok Belaid, ex-dean of the school; and Mohammed Charfi on the faculty
of the school and also president of Rencontres Maghrebines. Khalifa
Chater of the Institute of International Relations and his wife, Su'ad
Chater, consultant for the United Nations, provided me with illuminating
insights about Libya's relations to its neighbors, as did Khemais Chamari,
director of the Institute for the Financing of Development, and Lotfi
Karim Charfi. I am also indebted to Jean Mrad, Director of the Centre
d'Etudes Maghrebines à Tunis, for her help while we were in Tunisia,
and Ambassador Peter Sebastian, who put Libyan-Maghribi relations in
a historical and geopolitical context that was most useful for my work.

I am indebted to the many institutions whose services I have used
extensively, including the U.S. National Archives, the Library of Congress,
the Arab League documentation offices in Washington, D.C., and in
Tunis, the World Bank, the Middle East Institute, the Defense and Foreign
Affairs Institute, the Centre d'Etudes Maghrebines à Tunis, the Institute
of International Relations of Tunisia, the Institut National de la Statistique
in Tunis, and the libraries of the Faculty of Law, Political Science, and
Economics of the University of Tunis, the University of Georgetown,
and the School of Advanced International Studies of The Johns Hopkins
University. I also acknowledge with gratitude the grant I received from
the American Institute for Maghribi Studies to do research in Tunisia.

I express my thanks and my deep appreciation to Lisa Hajjar, who
is a Ph.D. student at the American University, Washington, D.C., edits
*The Merip Report*, and yet was able to type this whole manuscript and
make a splendid job of it.

Last but certainly not least I dedicate this book with love and gratitude
to my husband, Marius K. Deeb, and our son, Hadi, for their unfaltering
patience, support, and encouragement throughout the period of research
and writing.

*Mary-Jane Deeb*

# 1

# Introduction

Since 1969 when Colonel Mu'ammar al-Qadhdhafi came to power through a military coup, Libya has been the focus of a great deal of attention. Its experiments with nation building have been viewed with curiosity and its foreign policy with dismay by Western analysts. Much has been written to explain Libya's international and domestic behavior, but despite fascinating insights into Libya's society and political system, there have been few attempts to create an overall framework to explain Libya's policies.

This book is an attempt to create such a framework. Rather than viewing Libya as unique, this book looks at it as yet another small developing nation facing much the same problems other small developing countries are facing. Only by dispelling the myths surrounding Libya's leader and by viewing Libya in the general context of the region of which it is a part can one begin to understand the country's political evolution since 1969.

## Foreign Policy and the Nation-State

This book analyzes Libya's foreign policy in North Africa between 1969 and 1989, addressing two main questions: What have been Libya's foreign policy objectives in North Africa since 1969? And what means have been used to achieve those objectives?

I have used a neorealist approach to examine these questions, a natural offspring of the earlier political realism of Hans Morgenthau, George Kennan, Reinhold Niebuhr, and others.[1] Neorealist advocates, such as Kenneth Waltz,[2] make many of the same basic assumptions as did the founding fathers, but neorealists qualify and refine their concepts in answer to the major criticisms that were leveled against Morgenthau and others.

The first assumption of realists and neorealists is that the nation-state is the most important unit of analysis. This book deals with Libya as the principal focus of analysis, viewing Libya's foreign policy from its own perspective—that is, in terms of its own perception of what constitutes its interests.[3]

The second assumption of traditional political realists is that international politics is a struggle for power and that states seek to maximize their power.[4] Neorealists contend that definitions of power by theorists such as Morgenthau are murky because they fail to distinguish between power as the capacity to influence the behavior of others and power as a resource.[5] The concept of power that will be used here is that of the neorealists who see power as a resource or as a state's national capabilities.[6] How those capabilities are then used to influence others and achieve national objectives will vary in time and place.

Power will be used in this analysis to refer to a *means* to reach certain goals, not as an end in itself,[7] and states will be viewed as seeking to maximize their capabilities in order to achieve or defend those goals. National capabilities include territorial, military, economic, and demographic capabilities; level of development; strategic location; and natural resources.

A third major assumption of realists and neorealists is that a balance of power exists in any regional context. The concept has been so broadly used, however, as to have become inconsistent and at times even contradictory.[8] Neorealists have refined the concept in order to explain objectives, means to those objectives, and changing patterns of alliances within a regional context. Within a balance-of-power framework states are perceived as unitary actors within a larger system. Each actor within that system seeks its own preservation at the very least and hegemonic domination over the other actors at the most. In order to achieve those goals, states use internal and external means. Internal means include efforts to develop economic resources and increase military capabilities; external means involve "moves to strengthen and enlarge one's own alliance or to weaken and shrink an opposing one."[9] In this framework Libya is viewed as a unitary actor within a broader system of North African states pursuing the goals of self-preservation of its regime and territorial integrity and using both internal and external means to achieve those goals.

I will use the term *balance of power* to mean a dynamic process by which states seek to prevent any one state within a system of states from becoming so powerful that it could dominate others politically and/or militarily.[10] The aim of that process is to adapt constantly to the changing external and internal environments of the region and by so doing to preserve the independence of the constituent elements of the system.

The concept of balance of power in turn assumes the existence of a system within which the process takes place. For Waltz, a system "consists of a set of interacting units exhibiting behavioral regularities and having an identity over time."[11] States as units are all formally equal to each other (as independent states). What differentiates them are not the functions they perform within the system (as states they all perform the same function) but the power (or capabilities) they have.[12] This power differential is the organizing principle of the states within the system.

The North African system includes three major states—Egypt, Algeria, and Morocco; four minor states—Sudan, Libya, Tunisia, and Mauritania; and on the periphery—Chad and the Western Sahara. The states are differentiated in terms of their power or capabilities, Egypt being the most powerful and Morocco and Algeria being roughly equal in power. The peripheral states are not technically part of that system but are used as pawns in the political game played by the other nations in the region.

The North African system is also characterized by a strong sense of identity: Arab, African, and Islamic. All of the system's states are important members of the Arab League, the Organization of African Unity (OAU), and the Islamic Conference. They are contiguous and are separated from other regions by the Atlantic Ocean in the west, the Mediterranean in the north, the Sahara Desert in the south, and the Red Sea in the east.

The geographical contiguity and strong sense of identity of the North African states make for close intraregional relations. "This means," according to William Zartman, "that North Africans are thrown together and their foreign policies, above all, concern their relations with each other."[13] This orientation is especially true of Libya, Tunisia, Algeria, and Morocco. Egypt and Sudan are not generally included in that system because they also have close ties to other states in Africa and the eastern part of the Arab world (the Mashriq). Their inclusion in the North African system of states is nevertheless justified for three reasons: (1) they are located in North Africa, (2) like the Maghribi states they have the same Arab, African, and Islamic sense of identity, and (3) they interact regularly and frequently with all other states in North Africa, and their pattern of interaction is recurrent and predictable.

The construct described thus far presupposes that states generally behave in a purposeful way to achieve their goals and maximize their power and that governments have consistent interests, which they pursue through policies that can easily be understood by other actors on the international scene. Those policies will, however, not necessarily be similar under different administrations, although the goals of the policies may be the same; nor will the policies or those who make them be consistently rational or always able to achieve their objectives. Nevertheless, states have permanent interests that any ruler, whatever the ruler's ideological persuasion, will have to address. Thus, instead of approaching Libya's foreign policy from the point of view of Qadhdhafi's ostensibly irrational, erratic, and impulsive behavior, this book attempts to show that by and large and in his own way Qadhdhafi has tried to deal with the same problems faced by his predecessor and by many other small, weak, developing states.

Critics of neorealism believe this approach cannot successfully explain change because the balance-of-power construct focuses on the preservation of the system rather than on the transformation of the system.[14] This criticism implies that the balance of power is a somewhat static concept. This book views balance of power as a dynamic process, the function of which is not so much the preservation of the system as a whole as the protection of the territorial integrity and political sovereignty of each state within that system. The driving force behind this process is the fact that, as an early critic of the concept has noted, states in a system may not feel quite secure with situations over which they have little control: "There is no real security in being just as strong as a potential enemy; there is security only in being a little stronger. There is no possibility of action if one's strength is fully checked; there is a chance for a positive foreign policy only if there is a margin of force which can be freely used."[15]

Attempts by any state in the system to increase its power vis-à-vis the other states require those states to adopt measures constraining it from becoming too powerful and threatening their own regimes and territorial sovereignty. This ongoing process has its own recurring and predictable pattern.

Some analysts also believe that this approach does not pay enough attention to the role of ideas and values in determining foreign policy.[16] Realists of both the new and the old school recognize the significance of ideas and ideology in foreign policy but also emphasize their limitations. These analysts do not take ideologies at face value, preferring to view them functionally as means to political goals. On the other hand, these same analysts agree that no purely realist theory of international relations can exist. Edward Carr, in *The Twenty Years' Crisis*, puts the problem in a nutshell:

> We return therefore to the conclusion that any sound political thought must be based on elements of both utopia and reality. Where utopianism has become a hollow and intolerable sham, which serves merely as a disguise for the interests of the privileged, the realist performs an indispensable service in unmasking it. But pure realism can offer nothing but

a naked struggle for power which makes any kind of international society impossible.[17]

*Politics Among Nations,* by Hans Morgenthau, contains a chapter entitled "The Ideological Element in International Policies."[18] Morgenthau perceives the role of ideology in primarily functional terms: "Ideologies, like all ideas, are weapons that may raise the national morale, and with it the power of one nation and in the very act of doing so, may lower the morale of the opponent."[19]

This book accords an important place to the role of ideology in Qadhdhafi's foreign policy, which is viewed in functional terms. Ideology, it is argued here, has been used in Libya to explain events and policies, outline the final objective of those policies, justify the choice of friend and foe, and legitimize Qadhdhafi's domestic and regional authority.[20] The question of whether the Libyan leader does or does not believe what he says will, however, remain unanswered, as it belongs to the realm of the subjective and the conjectural.

Another criticism leveled against the rational model approaches, which include political realism and neorealism, is that they tend to ignore the role of domestic factors in determining foreign policy.[21] The domestic variables are identified as "(1) those related to the social order; (2) those related to the structures and processes of domestic political competition; (3) those related to the economic order."[22]

Power, one of the central concepts of neorealism, is defined in terms of a nation's domestic capabilities, including economic and military capabilities. To say therefore that this approach ignores domestic factors would be to rob it of its most significant contribution.

On the other hand, domestic institutions such as interest groups and ethnic and religious associations, which at times play an important role in the foreign policy of a nation, do not loom large in neorealism.[23] Under Qadhdhafi, social and political groups and organizations have not been permitted to hold or express views different from those of the Libyan leadership. The administrative bureaucracy that was set up under Qadhdhafi was an extension of the power of the state over its citizens. The Arab Socialist Union, the popular committees, the people's congresses, and later the revolutionary committees were primarily used to mobilize Libyans in support of the Qadhdhafi regime and its policies.[24] It would be fruitless therefore to try to incorporate them in the framework of this book. The only group that has expressed its views freely has been the Libyan opposition in exile. Its outspoken criticism of Libya's foreign and domestic policies, as well as its anti-Qadhdhafi activities, has affected the implementation of those policies. The Libyan opposition has therefore been included in this analysis for its role in affecting Libya's foreign policy in North Africa.

The impact of increasing oil revenues on Libya's foreign policy is also analyzed here. The use of this revenue to build a military infrastructure, to intervene militarily in other states, and to build alliances with neighbors is shown to be an important part of Libya's foreign policy in North Africa. Thus, both social and economic variables are incorporated in this analysis.

Finally, the neorealist school has been criticized for assuming that political actors on the international scene behave rationally. Governments do not always calculate the costs and benefits of alternative policies to maximize their usefulness. They do not always have sufficient information to make such calculations, and even when they do, they cannot always interpret that information to make rational decisions.[25]

These valid criticisms have been taken into consideration in this book. Libya's foreign policy behavior is perceived as rational (i.e., purposive) only inasmuch as it is directed toward the achievement of specific core objectives that are universally recognized as legitimate and rational—namely, the defense of the country's territorial integrity and the protection of its political regime—and only inasmuch as it is understood by other states within the system. Libya's foreign policy behavior is not necessarily rational in the absolute sense of calculating costs and benefits to maximize their utility.

Rather than speculate about how far from the rational ideal Qadhdhafi's foreign policy behavior in North Africa has strayed, this book identifies a pattern of foreign policy behavior that occurs when the Libyan leader perceives threats to the core interests of the Libyan state. This pattern of behavior is clearly recognizable; it is recurrent; it has clear, sometimes achievable objectives; and, it is understood by other states within the system whose foreign policy behavior is often similar although less ostentatious than that of Libya. The difference between their foreign policies has often been more one of style than of content.

## Ideological and Psychological
## Approaches to Libya's Foreign Policy

The approach adopted in this book is different from those of other academicians, journalists, and even policymakers who have written on Libya's foreign policy behavior under Qadhdhafi. Those analysts fall basically into two schools of thought. The first approaches Libya's foreign policy from the point of view of the psychological determinants of Qadhdhafi's personality and sees him as an irrational, bloodthirsty megalomaniac whose hegemonic ambitions are limitless and who lacks all sense of perspective and reality.[26] The second school of thought approaches the subject from the perspective of Qadhdhafi's ideological preferences and sees him as a more rational man dedicated to the pursuit of ideals of Arab nationalism, Islamic reformism, and some form of utopian socialism, which he has labeled his Third Universal Theory.[27]

The work produced by the first school lacks rigorous scientific analysis. The basic problem with such studies is that they emphasize only one aspect of Qadhdhafi's personality—namely, his presumed madness, or to put it more kindly, his irrationality or his unconventionality. Other aspects of the man are completely ignored. To explain the complexity of Libya's relations to other states in terms of Qadhdhafi's "madness" or "irrationality" is to miss the whole point of his foreign policy. In fact, if Qadhdhafi were so out of touch with reality, and if his perceptions and expectations were so irrational and distorted, it is very unlikely that he would have remained in power for so long or played such an active role in Arab and African affairs. As an expert on Libya points out, "To explain Libya by the temperament, eccentricity, even instability, of Gadafi is to make no meaningful explanation in terms of history and Libyan society."[28]

That so little is known about the personal life of Qadhdhafi makes a rigorous psychoanalysis of the man extremely difficult.[29] And yet if one were to use such an approach to the study of Libya's foreign policy, extensive material on his childhood, his relation to his parents, his early environment, and the various stages of his development would be essential to an understanding of what influenced him and molded his *Weltanshauung*.[30]

There is also the issue of interpretation. Two objectively similar events may be experienced quite differently by two different individuals. Yet the biographer or political analyst must interpret and evaluate different sorts of evidence "regarding motivations, drives, ambitions and other aspects of the inner life of his subject"[31] and then be able to relate those events to behavior occurring many years, even decades, later. The difficulty of such an endeavor cannot be overstated, especially when, as in the case of Qadhdhafi, the analysts know very little about the culture, the values, or even the language of the Libyan bedouin.[32] Nevertheless, some material does exist;[33] and perhaps someday a knowledgeable psychoanalyst will be able to delineate the various stages of Qadhdhafi's development and find a relationship to his role in Libya's history.

The second school of thought argues that however erratic Libya's foreign policy may appear to be, the goals are consistent with certain ideological principles held and propounded by Qadhdhafi. This argument is valid in many respects. Qadhdhafi has always claimed to be an Arab nationalist of the Nasirite brand, the natural heir to Jamal 'Abd al-Nasir. Qadhdhafi's pursuit of Arab unity, starting in the very early months after the 1969 coup, appears to be the natural outcome of such a goal.[34] Furthermore, he has considered himself a modern Islamic reformer whose task is to return Islam to its true essence,[35] and he has consistently supported Muslims and Muslim causes in Africa and Asia. He has also been a socialist at home and abroad,[36] supporting leftist governments and movements, although remaining critical of communism.

This approach leaves many questions unanswered, however. Although there is no doubt that during his early years in power Qadhdhafi was motivated by strong ideological considerations, beginning in the mid-1970s, and especially after his break with Egypt in 1974, his behavior seemed less ideologically motivated. How could an Arab nationalist justify his support for non-Arab countries when in conflict with Arab states, for instance? Yet after 1978, Libya supported Ethiopia against Sudan and Iran in its war against Iraq. How could an Islamic reformer support non-Muslims against Muslims? Yet Libya withdrew its support from Muslim Eritrea to support non-Muslim Haile Mengistu; it also supported Christians and animists in southern Sudan against the Muslim Arab northerners. How could a self-proclaimed revolutionary and socialist ally himself to a pro-Western traditional monarch? Yet in 1984, Libya and Morocco signed a treaty of unity.

A study carried out by William Zartman and A. G. Kluge on Libya's foreign policy sheds light on these dilemmas. Although the authors see ideology as playing a very important role in Libya's foreign policy behavior, they also recognize that Qadhdhafi is a pragmatic man: "It appears that Libyan foreign policy is a policy of opportunity, conducted on the basis of rather constant principles. . . . When opportunity presents itself, Libya acts. When opposition is too strong, Libya effects a strategic withdrawal, but not a change in goals."[37]

The dichotomy in Libya's foreign policy between the ideological and the pragmatic has led me to raise the fundamental question, when is Libya's foreign policy ideologically motivated, and when is it motivated by practical and purely political considerations?[38]

## A Pyramidal View of Foreign Policy

Qadhdhafi's foreign policy can be viewed as a pyramid made up of five overlapping levels. Each level includes a number of countries and certain policy orientations. As one moves from the top of the pyramid downward, a larger number of countries is included, and the content of Qadhdhafi's policy appears more diffuse and more ideological.[39]

At the very top of the pyramid stands North Africa: Egypt, Sudan, and Chad on Libya's eastern and southern borders and Tunisia, Algeria,

Morocco, and the Western Sahara on Libya's western border. Libya's foreign policy orientation toward these countries frequently involves Mauritania, Niger, Mali, Ethiopia, Uganda, and Somalia as well. Libya's policy at this level is determined primarily by national interests; ideological considerations, whether Arab, Islamic, or revolutionary, play only a secondary role.

The next level, which overlaps the first to some extent, includes the Arab world in general but focuses primarily on those states east of Egypt, in the Mashriq. At this level Arab nationalist ideology is a prime determinant of Libya's foreign policy. Rhetoric directed against Israel, support for the Palestinians, and support for Arab unity and Arab revolutions are the basic themes with respect to the region. The only exception here is Libya's support for Iran, a non-Arab, Shi'ite Muslim state, in its war against Iraq.

The third level of the pyramid comprises the Islamic world, which includes the countries in the preceding two levels as well as many states in Africa and Asia (such as Pakistan, Indonesia, and the Philippines) that are not Arab and to whose Islamic populations Libya has long been active in giving economic, military, and political support. At this level Islamic ideology does play a very important role in determining Libya's foreign policy.

The fourth level is made up of the Third World, which includes many of the states and groups at the previous levels as well as of others in Latin America, Africa, and Asia that are neither Arab nor Muslim. Qadhdhafi's "revolutionary socialism" partly determines his foreign policy toward these countries, from Nicaragua to New Caledonia to Zaire.

The fifth level is composed of the industrialized countries of both the Western and the Eastern blocs. Contrary to prevailing beliefs, Libya, especially in the early 1970s, had a similar orientation toward the two sides: a combination of pragmatism and ideological fervor. Libya traded with countries irrespective of ideology and was critical of both capitalism and communism. Qadhdhafi offered his Third Universal Theory, itself a brand of utopian socialism, as an alternative to capitalism and communism. But after the 1973 Arab-Israeli War and especially after the signing of the Egyptian-Israeli peace treaty, Libya moved closer to the Soviet Union because Libya perceived U.S. military aid to Egypt as a direct threat to Libyan security.

On the basis of this pyramidal model, two propositions can be made: (1) the farther a situation is from Libya's area of core interests (namely, North Africa), the more Libya's foreign policy becomes ideologically motivated; and (2) the closer a situation is to Libya's area of core interests, the more foreign policy is motivated by pragmatic, geopolitical considerations.

Nevertheless, this book focuses only on the top of the pyramid, where Libya's core interests are seen to be at stake. Although geopolitical considerations predominate in determining Libya's foreign policy in this area, ideology also plays a role.

### Foreign Policy and the Arab World

Because Libya is an Arab, an African, and a Third World country, its foreign policy must be viewed in these contexts. A survey conducted in the first half of the 1980s on the literature on Arab foreign policies in seven different languages (Arabic, English, French, German, Hebrew, Japanese, and Spanish) revealed, however, that there was only one book in English dealing with Egyptian foreign policy, none on Syrian foreign policy except as it related to Syria's intervention in Lebanon, only sections of larger works on Iraq, and only one on Israel's relation to three Arab states.[40] In terms of articles covering sixteen different Arab countries and the Palestinians (for the period 1965–1981), the authors of the survey identified 174 articles dealing with this subject, of which 52 were about Egypt and 32 about Saudi Arabia; Libya came in fourth with 21 articles.[41]

These figures make plain that until recently very little systematic work has been carried out on the foreign policies of Arab states. Since 1980, however, a spate of books, most of which were Ph.D. dissertations undertaken in France, have been published on the foreign policies of specific countries in the region. Of those, Nicole Grimaud's *La Politique Extérieure de L'Algérie* and Ghassan Salameh's work on Saudi Arabia's foreign policy are among the best.[42]

These two works have much to offer to a study of Libya's foreign policy. Both insist, for instance, on the importance of the geopolitical factor and on the location of a particular state within a regional context. Ghassan Salameh is also aware of the balance of power in the region (*mizan al-quwa al-iqlimi*); he analyzes the impact on Saudi foreign policy of the changes that have taken place since Iran entered so forcefully into the Arab political arena and Egypt withdrew from Arab affairs.

Nicole Grimaud shows that in the Maghrib there are two regional powers struggling for political supremacy: Morocco and Algeria. The alliances and the blocs that each creates with smaller nations in the region, such as Tunisia, Libya, or Mauritania, are aimed at increasing their power at the expense of the other.[43] The war in the Western Sahara is really no more than a power struggle between Algeria and Morocco. Grimaud sees any region, the Maghrib in this case, as having its own internal equilibrium, which is dynamic and perpetually changing and which is a major determinant of the foreign policy behavior of all states in the region.

In a similar vein, this book considers Libya as part of two regions: the Maghrib on the west and the Mashriq[44] on the east. Libya's foreign policy in the region is one of oscillation between the country's eastern and western neighbors. Many of Libya's major foreign policy decisions are determined by this uncomfortable position between the two regions. In contrast to Algeria or Saudi Arabia, which are regional powers, Libya is only a minor power whose policies cannot effect great changes in either of the two regions to which it belongs. Also unlike Algeria and Saudi Arabia, which are centrally located within one region (the Maghrib and the Arabian peninsula, respectively), Libya is peripheral to two regions. Thus, its foreign policy in the area requires a somewhat different analysis from that of Algeria and Saudi Arabia.

## Foreign Policy in Africa

"If the comparative study of foreign policy is underdeveloped in general, it is particularly so in the case of Africa. For despite the multiplicity of states on the continent, few rigorous comparative analyses have been attempted."[45] As in the case of foreign policy studies on Arab states, there is a dearth of analytical work published on Africa, although recently a number of good studies have come out.[46]

William Zartman's classic work, *International Relations of New Africa*,[47] is one of the earliest and most important studies in this field. He makes several important assumptions. First, North Africa and West Africa, which are usually kept distinct in comparative politics, can be treated as one for the purpose of analysis. Second, relations between the states of Western Africa are a meaningful subject for research. (This is a break from the more traditional approach of studying a Third World country's foreign policy in terms of its relations to the former colonial power or to one of the two superpowers.) Third, "the tools of diplomatic history can be applied to new nations as well as old."[48] And fourth, relations between the various states of western Africa were already developed in the preindependence period.

This book draws on and then extends Zartman's assumptions in four equally specific ways. First, this book assumes that the North African system extends beyond the traditional Maghrib to include Egypt, Chad, and the Sudan and that these states are significantly tied to Libya's core interests. Second, this analysis assumes that Libyan foreign policy in the region is intrinsically meaningful, therefore warrants attention, and can contribute to an understanding of the foreign policies of other small, strategically situated Third World states. Third, this discussion assumes that the same approach used to understand the foreign policies of old states can be applied to those of new states. The use of a universal model makes it possible to examine Libya's foreign policy on its terms, which is the way that the foreign policy of a developed state is viewed. Fourth, this work proceeds on the assumption that the roots of Libya's foreign policy in North Africa extend back beyond Libya's establishment as an independent state.

The significance of Zartman's work for this analysis does not end with the extension of his four assumptions. Of equal importance is his identification of some of the basic objectives of new and developing states in Africa.

> It would be tempting to hypothesize . . . that any state must conceive of its existence in terms of security and invent specific threats if no identifiable ones exist. It would also be intriguing to speculate that, in black Africa, the characteristic personal insecurity that accompanies the breakdown of tribal traditions and group identity creates an atmosphere responsive to leaders' cries of insecurity for the state. . . .
>
> [Zartman argues further that] it is not the country that is in danger of attack or conquest, but the government that is in danger of overthrow or collapse. Insecurity is thus endemic, inherent and political, rather than specific, external and military.[49]

In this statement Zartman identifies the core interests of the new and weak states that emerged in the postcolonial era. Libya is no different: Its main concerns are for security, both internal and external. Its foreign policy in the region revolves around two objectives: preserving its territorial integrity from external encroachments and protecting its regime from being overthrown. In fact, the danger in Libya may be primarily internal rather than external, political rather than military, but foreign policy is formulated and directed as if the principal threat were external.

The relevance of Zartman's work for this book goes even further. He identifies those foreign policy actions that are prevalent in Western Africa and demonstrates their limited range: "The worst possibilities are subversion, the breaking off of relations, and a flow of vile propaganda (military violence is usually excluded); the best possibility is close alliance and economic cooperation (loss of sovereignty through unification is usually excluded)."[50]

In fact, except for the military intervention in Chad, Libya's foreign policy actions fall within these parameters. Even those attempts at unity with countries on its eastern and western borders never really required Libya to give up its sovereignty (although that may be debatable in the case of the first attempt at unity with Egypt under Nasir in 1970).

Olajide Aluko, another major writer on the foreign policies of African states, discusses the factors that determine these foreign policies. He mentions domestic factors, such as the economic dilemma, faced by most African leaders, of trying to reduce "economic dependence on foreign powers and . . . raise the living conditions of their people."[51] But trying to achieve these goals involves two often mutually exclusive stances in foreign policy. On the one hand, reducing dependency on foreign powers would lead to a decrease in trading and a rejection of aid or foreign investment; on the other hand, improving the living conditions of the people would require the opposite relation to those powers. Libya was somewhat different because with its oil wealth it became a donor rather than a recipient of foreign aid. Nevertheless, the need to sell its oil and buy from abroad all its basic requirements—from foodstuffs to agricultural, industrial, and military products—has affected Libya's foreign policy behavior to a limited extent.

Aluko also points to internal political pressures from various interest groups as affecting the foreign policy actions of African states.[52] Again the situation may be somewhat different in the case of Libya because all political groups, interest groups, and other potential pressure groups have been prohibited from operating domestically. Foreign policy in Libya has remained very much the domain of the small group around Qadhdhafi, with Qadhdhafi himself being responsible for all major decisionmaking. Nevertheless, foreign policy successes do increase the regime's domestic legitimacy, and as a result foreign policy behavior may be indirectly affected by the leadership's need to maintain this legitimacy.

The colonial heritage is another determinant of a state's foreign policy in Africa, according to Aluko, especially when vis-à-vis that state's relationship to the former metropolitan power. Libya may be a weak example of this phenomenon: The Italian colonizer did not play a very significant role in terms of Libya's foreign relations, and although the colonial experience was brutal, it was also comparatively short. Thus, the Italian legacy in terms of foreign policy was very limited, and apart from "cordial" relations between the two states today and a number of labor and economic agreements, one cannot say that the colonial heritage has played an important role in the foreign policy of the Libyan Jamahiriya.

Finally, Aluko identifies two other determinants of foreign policy in Africa: ideology and geographical location. He sees both as having a significant impact on foreign policy decisionmaking. Those states, being new, lack the traditions and institutions that in older states provide a basis for continual relations between states. This is certainly the case in Libya, which has not built any major political institutions until now, least of all one that deals with foreign relations.

John Howell's study on the ideological underpinnings of Kenya's foreign policy and the impact of national interest considerations on this policy is an excellent illustration of the limitations of ideology in foreign policy.

> In foreign affairs, Kenya presents various faces to the international community. In global terms external policy has been markedly radical in nature and characterized by a strong sense of morality and idealism. . . . In East African affairs, however, Kenya's policy has often been governed by rather more conservative and legitimist thinking, notably where any radical departure from the *status quo* is contemplated. It would appear that where foreign policy issues touch directly on primary Kenyan interests—say national security, national development—the overt radicalism of Kenya's international policy is subject to considerable restraint.[53]

It is precisely this dichotomy that exists in Libya's foreign policy behavior. When core Libyan interests are at stake, Libya's foreign policy is dictated primarily by practical and political considerations, which might even be contrary to its ideological stands, without, for that matter, rendering that policy irrational or capricious.

Franklin B. Weinstein's work is also very important in drawing attention to the rationale behind the foreign policies of Third World nations, in this case Indonesia, and in steering away from the major trend that saw those policies as idiosyncratic and irrational. As Weinstein puts it:

> Scholars have shown a tendency to generalize about foreign policy in the less developed countries on the basis of the experience of those countries which have had flamboyant leaders and controversial policies. As a result, foreign policy analysis in the less developed countries frequently takes on the appearance of pathology—an effort to explain why leaders act in such apparently irrational ways.[54]

Weinstein believes that the foreign policy of Third World nations is determined by their "condition of weakness" and that although they want to be strong, independent, and self-sufficient, they are in reality weak, poor, and dependent. Because of this reality, and because the domestic political situation is generally so insecure, these nations tend to see the world as a hostile place where the "defense of the nation's independence against perceived threats" becomes a dominant concern.[55] In a noncompetitive situation, however, when domestic policies are oriented toward economic development, foreign policies become less oriented toward defense and more oriented toward the seeking of assistance from foreign donors to develop the nation economically.

Although, unlike most other Third World countries, Libya does not suffer from a lack of financial resources, it is plagued by very serious problems of underdevelopment (1) in the agricultural, industrial, and service sectors; (2) in the shortage of literate Libyans and of educational institutions at all levels; and (3) in the lack of viable political and social institutions. These problems have caused Libya to seek assistance from other nations. In fact, its relative underdevelopment in comparison to the neighboring states of Egypt, Tunisia, Algeria, and even Sudan has made Libya fear its neighbors, while at the same time depending on them for labor, professionals at all levels, and assistance in all major fields from health to education. Thus, the parallel with Indonesia is clear: Whereas Indonesia needed the Western powers' financial aid to help solve its economic problems but feared their encroachment on Indonesian political independence, Libya needs basic developmental assistance from its neighbors but fears their impact on the Libyan political system.

## Major Propositions of This Analysis

I contend that Libya's *core foreign policy objectives* in North Africa have been to protect the regime from external attempts to overthrow it and to defend Libyan territory from attacks and threats of invasion by neighboring states. Libya is, and always has been, a very weak state. By 1989 Libya had less than 4 million people, compared to Egypt's 54 million, Algeria's 25 million, and Sudan's estimated 25 million inhabitants. Libya's level of social and cultural development lags far behind that of most of the states in the system with the exception of Chad, the Western Sahara, and Mauritania. Economically, Libya is dependent on a very large foreign work force and on imports of most basic needs because the country has few natural resources. Of those, oil is the most important resource and has been used to increase Libya's military and political capabilities.

This oil wealth, however, has been perceived by the Libyan leadership as the main reason the nation and the regime are endangered. Time and again Libya has accused its neighbors and others of planning to take control of this oil wealth through invasion. The main contention of this book is that this perception of threat coupled with the knowledge of Libya's inherent weakness has been the main motivating factor behind Qadhdhafi's foreign policy in North Africa.

Those foreign policy goals in turn are achieved by means of *foreign policy actions*, which according to Kal J. Holsti are "the things governments do to others in order to effect certain orientations, fulfill roles, or achieve and defend objectives."[56] The foreign policy actions discussed here refer to six types of actions, which are either conciliatory or conflictual: (1) alliances and attempts at unity, (2) negotiations and peaceful settlement of conflicts, (3) trade and labor agreements, (4) military intervention, (5) subversive activities, and (6) arms buildup. The first three actions are conciliatory; the last three are directly or potentially conflictual.

Foreign policy actions do not take place in a vacuum. They have to be explained and justified within a broader context. This justification takes place by means of *ideology*—in this case the ideas and beliefs that are promulgated by Qadhdhafi in his speeches and in his writings and that are used to define Libya's relation to other Arab states and to the world in general. These ideas can be subsumed under three major, interrelated concepts: Arab nationalism, pan-Islamism, and revolutionary socialism.[57]

Qadhdhafi's conception of Arab nationalism is that of a nation extending from the Atlantic Ocean to the Persian Gulf linked by linguistic, cultural, ethnic, and historical ties and eventually uniting politically and militarily to form a powerful regional bloc on the international scene.

Qadhdhafi's pan-Islamism refers to the union of all Muslim nations and peoples; in this union the Arab world would play a central role in the revival of Islam.[58] This pan-Islamism is less politically oriented than Arab nationalism and is directed more toward spiritual union and religious reformism.

Qadhdhafi's revolutionary socialism, discussed at length in his *Green Book*,[59] was designed primarily for domestic purposes. In terms of Libya's external relations, however, revolutionary socialism means that Arab states that are not governed by their people but are headed by traditional potentates have to be "revolutionized" and, following Libya's example, transformed into socialist states governed by popular congresses and popular committees. Libya's role is to support all revolutionary movements intent on overthrowing traditional leaders and on taking over power.

The three variables in this book are therefore the *independent variable*, which is Libya's foreign policy objectives, including the protection of its regime and the defense of its territorial integrity; the *dependent variables*, which include Libya's foreign policy actions—namely, its attempts at unity, its subversive activities, its arms buildup, and so forth; and the *intervening variables*, which are Qadhdhafi's pan-Arab nationalism, pan-Islamism, and revolutionary ideology.

The following propositions are made based on these three variables:

1a.   When Libya perceives the regime or the country's territorial integrity to be threatened, it will generally resort to ideology as a means of enhancing its legitimacy domestically and regionally.

1b.   When Libya feels secure domestically and regionally, there is a decline in the use of ideology as a means of enhancing legitimacy.

2a.   When Libya perceives the regime or the country's territorial integrity to be threatened, it will seek the protection of at least one preponderant regional power.

2b.   If Libya fails to find a major regional ally, it will attempt to merge or unite with a minor regional power to strengthen itself against perceived external threats.

2c.   If Libya finds neither a major nor a minor regional ally, it may seek an ally external to the region for power protection.

2d.   When Libya feels secure regionally and domestically, it will generally not seek to unite or merge with major or minor regional powers. It may, however, retain previous alliances.

3a.   When Libya perceives the country's territorial integrity to be threatened, it will adopt a conflictual foreign policy involving arms buildup, subversion, and military intervention in the affairs of neighboring states.

3b.   When Libya perceives the regime to be theatened by external forces, it will adopt a conflictual foreign policy toward the state or states from which the threat comes.

3c.   When Libya perceives *both* the regime and the country's territorial integrity to be threatened simultaneously, it will generally adopt a conciliatory foreign policy behavior to diffuse the threats, including withdrawal of Libyan military forces from other states, resolution of pending conflicts, and negotiation of new trade and labor agreements with neighboring countries.

3d.   When Libya feels secure domestically and regionally, in most cases it will adopt a conciliatory foreign policy behavior toward neighboring states.

## Notes

1. Of the best known political realists in the field of international relations, Hans J. Morgenthau, Reinhold Niebuhr, and George Kennan are among those who have written most extensively on the subject. See, for example, Morgenthau's *Politics Among Nations*, Alfred A. Knopf, New York, 1973, 5th Edition; Niebuhr's *Christian Realism and Political Problems*, Charles Scribner's Sons, New York, 1953;

and Kennan's *Realities of American Foreign Policy*, W. W. Norton and Co., New York, 1966.

2. See Kenneth N. Waltz, *Theory of International Politics*, Addison-Wesley, Reading, Mass., 1979.

3. For a discussion of the assumptions of the school of thought of political realism in international affairs, see James E. Dougherty and Robert L. Pfaltzgraff, Jr., *Contending Theories of International Relations*, J. B. Lippincott Co., Philadelphia, 1971, pp. 65–101.

4. Morgenthau, p. 27.

5. See Robert C. Keohane, ed., *Neorealism and Its Critics*, Columbia University Press, New York, 1986, p. 11.

6. Waltz, p. 192.

7. Ibid., p. 191.

8. For the different usages of the concept of balance of power, see Iris L. Claude, Jr., *Power and International Relations*, Random House, New York, 1962, p. 25; and Ernst B. Haas, "The Balance of Power: Prescription, Concept or Propaganda," in *World Politics*, Vol. 5, July 1953, pp. 422–477.

9. See Kenneth B. Waltz, "Anarchic Orders and Balance of Power," in Keohane, p. 117.

10. See the discussion of the balance of power concept with Eugene V. Rostow in William Whitworth, *Naive Questions About War and Peace*, W. W. Norton and Co. Inc., New York, 1970, p. 18.

11. Keohane, p. 14; see also Waltz's discussion of the system in chapters 4–6 of *Theory of International Politics*.

12. Waltz, "Political Structures," in Keohane, p. 91.

13. See I. William Zartman, "Foreign Relations of North Africa," in *Annals*, *AAPSS*, No. 489, January 1987, p. 14.

14. See, for example, Robert W. Cox, "Social Forces, States and World Orders: Beyond International Relations Theory," in Keohane, p. 209.

15. Nicholas J. Spykman, *American Strategy and World Policies*, Harcourt, Brace and Co., New York, 1942, pp. 21–22.

16. See Keohane, p. 19; see also Cox's criticism and alternative framework described as "historical structures," which includes the role of ideas in foreign policy, in ibid., pp. 217–220.

17. Edward Hallet Carr, *The Twenty Years' Crisis 1919–1939: An Introduction to the Study of International Relations*, Harper and Row Publishers, New York, 1964, p. 93.

18. Morgenthau, pp. 88–100.

19. Ibid., p. 92.

20. Those functions of ideology are analyzed by I. William Zartman, "National Interest and Ideology," in Vernon McKay, *African Diplomacy: Studies in the Determinants of Foreign Policy*, SAIS and Praeger Publishers, New York, 1967, pp. 25–54.

21. See Bernard C. Cohen and Scott A. Harris, "Foreign Policy," in *Handbook of Political Science*, Vol. 6, edited by Fred I. Greenstein and Nelson W. Polsby, Addison-Wesley, Reading, Mass., 1975, p. 410.

22. Ibid., p. 411.

23. Ibid., p. 412.

24. See the work of Omar I. El-Fathaly and Monte Palmer, *Political Development and Social Change in Libya*, Lexington Books, Lexington, Mass., 1980.

25. Ibid., pp. 389–390; and Keohane, pp. 11–12, for instance.

26. See, for example, Edward Haley, *Qadhdhafi and the United States Since 1969*, Praeger Publishers, New York, 1984; and Charles Tripp, "La Libye et L'Afrique," *Politique Etrangere*, No. 2, Summer 1984, pp. 317–329.

27. See Ronald Bruce St. John, "The Ideology of Mu'ammar al-Qadhdhafi: Theory and Practice," in *International Journal of Middle East Studies*, Vol. 15, November 1983, pp. 471–490; idem., "The Determinants of Libyan Foreign Policy, 1969–1983," in *The Maghrib Review*, Vol. 8, Nos. 3–4, 1983, pp. 96–103; idem., "Libya's Foreign and Domestic Policies," in *Current History*, Vol. 80, No. 470, December 1981, pp. 426–429; Nathan Alexander (pseud.), "The Foreign Policy of Libya: Inflexibility Amid Change," in *Orbis*, Vol. 24, No. 4, Winter 1981, pp. 819–846; Rene Otayek, "La Libye revolutionnaire au Sud du Sahara," in *Maghreb-Machrek*, No. 94, October-December 1981, pp. 5–35; and Oye Ogunbadejo, "Qadhdhafi's North African Design," in *International Security*, Vol. 8, No. 1, Summer 1983, pp. 154–178.

28. Ruth First, *Libya the Elusive Revolution*, Penguin Books, Middlesex, England, 1974, p. 20.

29. There is almost nothing written about Qadhdhafi's relationship to his own father, for instance.

30. See, for example, the classic work of Erik Erikson on the relation between the psychology of an individual and his role in history, *Young Man Luther: A Study in Psychoanalysis and History*, W. W. Norton and Co. Inc., New York, 1958; see also two other more recent psychoanalytic studies on political leaders in the Middle East: P. J. Vatikiotis, *Nasser and His Generation*, Croom Helm, London, 1978; and Vamik D. Volkan and Norman Itzkowitz, *The Immortal Attaturk: A Psychobiography*, University of Chicago Press, Chicago, 1984.

31. John E. Mack, "T. E. Lawrence: Psychology in Biography," in L. Carl Brown and Norman Itzkowitz, eds., *Psychological Dimension of Near Eastern Studies*, Darwin Press, Princeton, New Jersey, 1977; see also Mack's excellent study, *A Prince of Our Disorder: The Life of T. E. Lawrence*, Little, Brown and Co., Boston, 1976.

32. Haley never once uses Arabic sources, and his previous writings have encompassed cultures as varied as those of Vietnam and Cambodia, Mexico and Lebanon. Although he deals primarily with U.S. foreign policy toward Libya, his explanation of Libya's behavior on the international scene is primarily psychological, or, rather, pathological.

33. See, for example, Frederick Muscat, *Ra'isi Ibni*, Adam Publishers, Valetta, Malta, n.d., which consists of interviews with Qadhdhafi's mother; and Mirella Bianco's interviews with Qadhdhafi, *Gadafi Voice from the Desert* (translated from the French), Longman, London, 1975.

34. Alexander, pp. 832–833.

35. See 'Ali 'Ali Mansur, *Khutwa Ra'ida Nahwa Tatbiq Ahkam al-Shari'a al-Islamiya fi al-Jumhuriya al-'Arabiya al-Libiya*, Dar al-Fatwa, Beirut, 1972, for the

changes in the legal system of Libya based on an Islamic code that Qadhdhafi was to introduce in the late 1970s.

36. Mu'ammar al-Qadhdhafi, *Al-Kitab al-Akhdar, al-Fasl al-Thany, Hal al-Mashkal al-Iqtisadi: al-Ishtirakiya,* Tripoli, al-Sharika al-'Amma lil-Nashr, wal-Tawzi', wal-I'lan, 1977.

37. I. William Zartman and A. G. Kluge, "Heroic Politics: The Foreign Policy of Libya," in Baghat Korany and 'Ali E. Hillal Dessouki, eds., *The Foreign Policy of Arab States,* Westview Press, Boulder, Colo., 1984; and idem., "Qaddafi's Foreign Policy," *American-Arab Affairs,* Fall 1983, No. 6, p. 183.

38. See also Lisa Anderson's article, "Qadhdhafi and the Kremlin," in *Problems of Communism,* September-October 1985, where she analyzes Libya's foreign policy towards the USSR; even though she speaks of "Qadhdhafi's idiosyncratic revolution," she shows how pragmatic and businesslike his relations with the Soviets really are.

39. The following section has appeared in a revised form in the *SAIS Review,* Vol. 6, No. 2, Summer-Fall 1986, pp. 151–162; and in Rene Lemarchand, ed., *The Green and the Black,* Indiana University Press, Bloomington, 1988.

40. Korany and Dessouki, p. 1.

41. Ibid., Table 1.1, p. 10.

42. See Nicole Grimaud, *La politique extérieure de l'Algérie,* Editions Karthala, Paris, 1984; and Ghassan Salameh, *Al-Siyasa al-Kharijiya al-Sa'udiya Mundh 'Am 1945: Dirasat fi al-'Ilaqat al-Dawliya,* Institute of Arab Development, Beirut, 1980.

43. Grimaud, p. 195.

44. The Maghrib primarily includes Morocco, Algeria, and Tunisia and secondarily includes Libya and Mauritania; the Mashriq primarily includes all the Arab countries east of Libya.

45. Timothy M. Shaw and Olajide Aluko, *The Political Economy of African Foreign Policy: Comparative Analysis,* St. Martin's Press, New York, 1983.

46. See, for example, ibid.; and also by Aluko, *Nigerian Foreign Policy, Alternative Perceptions and Projections,* St. Martin's Press, New York, 1983.

47. I. William Zartman, *International Relations in the New Africa,* Prentice-Hall, Englewood Cliffs, N.J., 1966.

48. Ibid., p. x.

49. Ibid., pp. 48, 49.

50. Ibid., p. 87.

51. See Olajide Aluko, "The Determinants of the Foreign Policies of African States," in *The Foreign Policies of African States.* Olajide Aluko, ed., Hodder and Stoughton, London, 1977, p. 5.

52. On classes and interest groups in foreign policy see Michael Schatzberg's article, "Zaire," in Shaw and Aluko, pp. 283–318.

53. See John Howell, "An Analysis of Kenyan Foreign Policy," *The Journal of Modern African Studies,* Vol. 6, No. 1, 1968, pp. 29–48, extract at p. 29.

54. See Franklin B. Weinstein, "The Uses of Foreign Policy in Indonesia: An Approach to the Analysis of Foreign Policy in the Less Developed Countries," *World Politics,* Vol. 24, April 1972, pp. 356–382; and idem., *Indonesian Foreign Policy and the Dilemma of Dependence: From Sukarno to Soeharto,* Cornell University, Ithaca, 1976, extract at p. 24.

55. Idem., "The Uses of Foreign Policy," p. 366.

56. K. J. Holsti, *International Politics, A Framework for Analysis*, 2nd Edition, Prentice-Hall Inc., Englewood Cliffs, N.J., 1972, p. 154.

57. For an analysis of those concepts see Marius K. Deeb, "Islam and Arab Nationalism in al-Qadhdhafi's Ideology," *Journal of South Asian and Middle Eastern Studies*, Vol. 2, No. 2, Winter 1978, pp. 12–26.

58. Mu'ammar al-Qadhdhafi, *Al-Sijil al-Qawmi, Bayanat wa Khutab wa Ahadith*, Vol. 8, 1971–1972, Tripoli, n.d., pp. 117–118.

59. Idem., *Al-Kitab al-Akhdar, al-Fasl al-Thani.*

# 2

---

# From Independence to Revolution: Libya's Foreign Policy During the Sanussi Monarchy, 1951–1969

When the Western powers decided in 1951 to give Libya independence, they felt the country was too poor to support itself and would need the aid of the international community to survive.[1] This newly independent status and a lack of resources were some of the basic determinants of Libya's foreign policy throughout the 1950s. Not only did Libya have to start building a new state out of three disparate provinces that regarded each other with suspicion; it had to find the resources to do so. Thus, in the first decade of independence Libya's core foreign policy objectives were to preserve the unity and integrity of the state, to obtain aid to help build up the state, and to ensure that no regional power took advantage of the country's weakness and tried to influence or control the internal or external policies of the Libyan state.[2]

## The Significance of Libya's Geographic Location

Libya was not a "prize" worth fighting for in the 1950s. Nevertheless, although it had no resources of any value, Libya remained important to the major Western powers, mainly because of its geographical location. In the aftermath of World War II, Libya had strategic value as a potential military base for the United States, Great Britain, and France in the Mediterranean; as a buffer state between French interests in the Maghrib and British interests in Egypt, the Sudan, and the Near East; and as a gateway to Africa in the south and to Egypt and the Suez Canal in the east.

Henry Villard, the first chief of the U.S. Mission to Libya, recognized this fact and wrote in 1956, "For the present, Libya's strategic location is, in a sense, its most important commodity. As long as the military requirements of the Western powers are important, the political and economic stability of Libya is of direct as well as indirect concern to them."[3]

The French were interested in Libya's strategic location because of its proximity to Tunisia, Algeria, and sub-Saharan Africa. France feared that an independent Libya would get involved with the Maghrib and would become a passageway for arms and military supplies from Egypt to the Algerian and Tunisian nationalists, who were fighting the French.[4] France tried to keep a foothold in the Fezzan until 1955, when after a treaty of friendship and good neighborliness it had to withdraw its forces from Libya.

Libya's geographic location also partly determined its relations with its neighbors. Libya was made up of three provinces that at times had been administered by different rulers and had different traditional links and loyalties to the countries on its borders.

## Cyrenaica

For centuries, Cyrenaica, the province in the east, had maintained close ties to Egypt. Oxford anthropologist E. E. Evans-Pritchard was posted as political officer to the British Military Administration of Cyrenaica in 1942. He conducted an in-depth study of that region and noted the extensive ties of the bedouins of Cyrenaica to Egypt.[5] He shows how the Cyrenaican bedouins who were defeated in tribal wars had gradually migrated to Egypt and eventually settled there as peasants. Others remained nomadic, keeping their way of life but moving to Egypt. Evans-Pritchard notes that in the 1940s, the most numerically significant bedouin element in Egypt consisted of Cyrenaican Arabs.[6] Members of the Harabi tribe alone accounted for 30,000 bedouins, most of whom resided in Fayyum in Egypt, while the Awlad 'Ali and their followers accounted for another 40,000.[7]

The Cyrenaican links to Egypt were not limited only to the movement of tribes. When Libya was under Italian colonial rule, Egypt provided Cyrenaicans with arms and supplies to assist them in their struggle for independence. The Italians eventually had to erect a fence of barbed wire along the Egyptian-Libyan border to prevent the passage of military supplies to the insurgents. In 1922 Sayyid Idris, the Cyrenaican Sanussi leader who was later to become king and the first leader of independent Libya, sought refuge in Egypt, where he spent almost thirty years until the liberation of his country. Émigrés from the Italian colony sought refuge in Egypt, where they were offered the right to acquire Egyptian citizenship.[8] Thus, the ties between Egypt and Cyrenaica were old and strong; they bore the stamp of tradition and consequently of legitimacy.

## Tripolitania

Tripolitania, the province in the west, had been drawn since antiquity toward Tunisia. "The desert comes down to the sea at the Gulf of Sirte and separates Cyrenaica from Tripolitania and these two countries [*sic*] have always gone each its own way. Cyrenaica was linked to Greco-Egypt, Tripolitania to Phoenician Carthage. Cyrenaica went with Byzantium, Tripolitania with Rome."[9]

Studies carried out in the 1950s and the 1960s on the rural and urban populations of Tunisia note the extensive Libyan migration to those areas. A study of the rural population of the Tunisian Sahel notes that the villages there seemed to emerge only in the eighteenth century.[10] The author shows that the populations of those villages originated from several regions within and outside of Tunisia and that a large number of them were Tripolitanians. Those villages appear to have been divided into distinct quarters in which those of similar origins lived together separately from the members of the village community. "The diversity of origin of those elements explains their distribution in ethnic quarters, long separated and distinctive as much on the human as on the material levels."[11] The Tripolitanians were identifiable by their names, and many were just identified as "Trabilsi" (from Tripolitania) or "Ahl Jdid," meaning new people or those who came recently.[12]

A national study based on the General Archives of Tunis traces the recent history of Tripolitanian migration to Tunisia. The author points to the difficulty in getting accurate figures for the Tripolitanians during the Italian colonial era because of the political implications of those figures. According to French estimates, 35,000 Tripolitanians had sought refuge in Tunisia by mid-1913, fleeing the Italian invader,[13] but many were to return home later. Again in the early 1930s, 6,000 to 8,000 Tripolitanian political refugees fled to southern Tunisia, where they were received by the local tribespeople.[14] By the mid-1930s there were 24,000 Tripolitanians in Tunisia, a number that remained constant for two decades and then declined gradually beginning in the mid-1950s.

Thus, the ties between Tunisia and Tripolitania have also been strong and old, like those of Cyrenaica and Egypt. A great many Tunisians are of Libyan descent, and the same families are often found on either side of the Libyan-Tunisian border. Habib Bourguiba, one of the major historical figures of modern Tunisian history, and Bahi Ladgham are both of Libyan descent.[15]

## The Fezzan

The third province, the Fezzan, located in the south, has been tied since ancient times to what Arabs used to call Bilad al-Sudan, that area that stretches from West Africa east to the Nilotic Sudan.[16] The links were commercial, political, and religious. The great trade routes from Central Africa to the Mediterranean passed through the Fezzan, and Murzuk, the capital of the Fezzan, became one of the major trading posts of the Saharan trade with the cities on the Mediterranean. Two major caravan routes—the Bornu-Kawar-Fezzan-Tripoli route and the Kano-Air-Ghat-Ghadames-Tripoli route—crossing the Fezzan operated until the mid-nineteenth century. A third—the Wadai-Kufra-Benghazi route—continued to function until the first decade of the twentieth century because it was used by the Sanussi members to propagate their faith.[17]

The ties of the Fezzan (and to some extent Cyrenaica as well) with the territories now constituting the Republic of Chad were strengthened in the late nineteenth century when Sayyid bin 'Ali al-Sanussi spread his revivalist Islamic movement to Chad, where he built a strong following. In Wadai, Sultan Muhammad Sharif and his successors, 'Ali and Yusuf, became Sanussi followers as well.[18] By 1899 the headquarters of the Sanussiya Order had moved to Gouro in Chad, where there were ten Sanussi lodges (there were fifteen in the Fezzan).[19]

In 1964 the Fezzan had only 79,326 inhabitants.[20] In the same year the Arabs in Chad constituted the second largest ethnic group, numbering 460,000, or 14 percent of the Chadian population.[21] Most of that population seemed to have been trickling through the Fezzan or the Sudan since the fourteenth century. Two of the three major tribes that make up the Arab population of Chad appear to have come from Libya either directly from the Fezzan or via the Fezzan from Tripolitania. Some of the tribes, such as Awlad Sulayman, are split between the Fezzan and Chad today and are living on both sides of the border.[22]

The Fezzan and southern Cyrenaica also had ties to the Sudan. A seventeenth-century manuscript on the Fezzan traces those relations to the end of the sixteenth century, when Fezzani tribes fleeing the Ottoman's punitive missions against those tribes that did not pay their taxes sought refuge in Sudan.[23] It appears that Sudanese men joined these tribes in their raids against Ottoman forces in the Fezzan.[24] Thus, the Fezzan's ties to the Sudan, Chad, and northern parts of Mali and Niger are as old as those of Cyrenaica to Egypt and Tripolitania to Tunisia.

### The Influence of Traditional Alliances

Libya's ties to Egypt, the Sudan, Chad, and Tunisia were so strong that it would have been impossible during the early years of the monarchy to have a foreign policy that did not take into account those states. In fact, those traditional alliances were at the very heart of King Idris's dilemma: the necessity of steering a course of action that was independent and served the interests of a unified Libya without upsetting the Libyans' traditional relations to outside powers. King Idris knew that if those traditional alliances were not respected, his regime would be in trouble. He and his government therefore had to formulate a policy that fostered a sense of loyalty to the new Libyan state and superseded traditional ties without either antagonizing neighboring countries or compromising Libya's national interests.

The king was never able to resolve that dilemma successfully. Traditional alliances and loyalties that were revived and maintained by Nasir's active propaganda machine proved to be more important to Libya than the cautious yet rational policies based on self-interest advocated by the monarchy. A U.S. vice-consul in Tripoli, Marion J. Rice, commenting on Egyptian-Libyan relations on the eve of independence, notes, "The fortuitous disagreement of Cyrenaican leaders with Egypt as a result of political differences . . . created in Cyrenaica (and Libya) an official pro-Western dressing which will not last as it does not reflect the real sentiments of the people."[25]

## Religion and Foreign Policy Under Idris I

Libya's strategic geopolitical location was not the only determinant of its foreign policy. The principles of the Sanussiya Order were very important to King Idris, who was both the temporal ruler of Libya as well as the religious leader of the Sanussiya Order. Sanussi principles and ideology were also a major determinant of Libya's foreign policy during the 1950s and the 1960s.

Ideologically the Sanussi movement was a reformist one. It started in the Hijaz in 1837 and a few years later moved to Bayda' in Cyrenaica where the Grand Sanussi set up his headquarters and those of his order. The theological beliefs of the Sanussiya, in which many of Qadhdhafi's ideas on Islam are rooted, are not of interest to us here. Suffice it to say that the Sanussiya emerged in part as a reaction to what the Grand Sanussi perceived, from his travels to the Hijaz, Egypt, and elsewhere in the region, as a declining Muslim world.[26] He was critical of Egypt and the Muhammad 'Ali dynasty, which he saw as more concerned with politics than with religion. He was also suspicious of the Ottomans' intentions in North Africa and feared that they were acting in "connivance with the powers against the interests of the Muslims."[27] From his travels and experiences in Tripolitania, Algeria, and Tunisia, his suspicions of Turkish intentions concerning the region increased. The Grand Sanussi remained aloof from the conflicts that were taking place in neighboring states and did not appear to have been involved in the struggle of the

Algerians against the French, despite what the latter claimed.[28] He also left Tunisia and returned to Cyrenaica when the Tunisian authorities did not allow him to move freely in that country.[29]

Thus, the Sanussiya of the nineteenth century was primarily a missionary movement whose function was to spread the call and mediate conflicts, not get involved in them. The Grand Sanussi, and later his son Mahdi, mediated tribal conflicts throughout the region. In the last half of the nineteenth century they were able to bring an end to a large number of intertribal wars.

Nevertheless, the Grand Sanussi and his successor feared foreign encroachments on the regions under their control and urged their followers to arm themselves and be prepared to retaliate if they were attacked. The Sanussi lodges consequently became not only centers of learning but also centers of defense.[30] Thus, when the Italians attacked them in the first decades of the twentieth century, they were prepared to respond with force.

These Sanussi tenets were of vital importance to the foreign policy of King Idris. He remained wary of the intentions of the major regional powers—Egypt, Turkey, and Algeria. Like his forebears, he shunned direct military involvement and conflict, especially those between Arab states, preferring to act as the mediator. Although peace loving, King Idris was also very much aware of his state's weakness and vulnerability and like his forebears planned to protect and defend Libya's interests and security.

### The Politics of Underdevelopment

Libya's foreign policy during the 1950s was also determined by Libya's capabilities, or lack of them. In 1951, the United Nations created a commission of seven experts to make an assessment of the condition of Libya's economy. *The General Economic Appraisal of Libya* issued by the commission gives a fair view of the situation in Libya in the early 1950s.[31] The report confirms that Libya was extremely poor, with an annual per capita income of $35. Libya had a large and chronic balance-of-payments deficit, and exports did not cover one-half the cost of imports. The country survived in the 1940s on foreign aid grants from the administering powers and on military expenditures by the foreign powers with troops in Libya.

Agriculture was the mainstay of Libya's economy, with cereals as the most important element in the local diet and livestock the most significant source of income. Productivity, however, was low, and a severe drought in the late 1940s brought hardship and famine to the country.[32]

In terms of industrial development, the U.N. experts agreed that it would be hampered by a lack of fuel and raw materials as well as by a shortage of skilled labor.[33] Furthermore, what little industry had existed prior to World War II had been destroyed by the heavy bombing of Cyrenaica during the war.

In 1951 a United Nations Education, Scientific, and Cultural Organization (UNESCO) commission came to Libya. The commission's subsequent report stated that Libya's educational system had improved somewhat by the end of the British Military Administration but was still very weak.[34] Ninety percent of the population was illiterate, there were no secondary schools for girls (apart from a teachers' training center), only fourteen Libyans had received university degrees (mostly from Egypt), and there remained an urgent need for teachers and for schools at all levels of education. (This figure did not include those who studied at Islamic institutes of higher education.)

By 1961 Libya began to export oil. Per capita income rose from $35 at the beginning of independence to $6,000 two decades later. The characteristics of this period were that of a typical oil economy during the early stages of its development: little growth in the agricultural and industrial sectors and tremendous growth in the service sector. Oil wealth was a boon for this poverty-stricken country, but it also created tremendous problems for the political system and for the regional foreign policy of the Idris regime. The paucity of resources during the 1950s made Libya completely dependent on Western powers for economic and financial aid, in exchange for which it offered them military facilities on its territory. During the 1960s, however, oil wealth created many new domestic demands, among which was a demand for the withdrawal of all Western forces and bases from Libya because the country no longer needed foreign subsidies for its development. The political implications of this changed state of affairs were far-reaching.

### The Monarchy's Regional and International Alliances

On December 24, 1951, Libya became the first country to attain its independence through the United Nations.

Simultaneously, the Sanussi leader took the title of King Idris I. The representatives of Britain and France transferred their last remaining powers to the Libyan state, which became the only legitimate power responsible for the conduct of foreign and domestic policies.[35]

On the following day in Benghazi the first government of independent Libya was formed, headed by Mahmud Bey Muntasir as prime minister. Muntasir's first foreign policy statement announced that Libya would apply for membership in the United Nations as well as in three of its agencies: the Food and Agriculture Organization, the World Health Organization, and UNESCO. This was to be expected because the United Nations had helped create the independent state of Libya.

What was not expected was the Soviet Union's veto of Libya's membership in the United Nations. Although the USSR had supported the 1949 U.N. resolution granting Libya independence, it had become dissatisfied with the turn of events. As Villard wrote at the time, "The prospect of Libyan orientation toward the West and the utilization of Libyan bases for the defense of the free world conjured up a spectacle highly displeasing to Moscow."[36] Thus, Libya's first independent foreign policy action encountered opposition. It was not until December 1955 that Libya was finally permitted to join the United Nations as a member, after a "package" deal had been reached between the Soviet Union and the Western power to admit Libya and sixteen other nations.[37]

In March 1953 Libya became a member of the Arab League.[38] The decision to join the Arab League so soon after independence and before treaties with the major Western powers had been negotiated was a response to Arab, primarily Egyptian, pressure.[39] Egypt hoped that through the Arab League it could play a more significant role in influencing Libya's foreign and domestic policies. The Libyan prime minister was opposed to Libya's joining the Arab League before making agreements with the Western powers because he feared Egypt's influence. The U.S. Legation in Tripoli reported in September 1953 that

> he [Muntasir] had always advocated a policy of first negotiating treaties with the three Western powers before Libya should join the Arab League. The U.S., U.K., and France were the three friends on whom Libya had to depend, and only when relations were cemented with them could Libya become embroiled in the ramifications of Arab League politics. . . . [Nevertheless] Libya had joined the Arab League first, before concluding the Western agreements, and was now exposed to an Egyptian attempt not only to exert direct influence on Libyan officials and members of Parliament but to put Libya completely in the Egyptian pocket politically.[40]

### The Anglo-Libyan Treaty

Libya's new government, however, quickly concluded the twenty-year Treaty of Friendship and Alliance with Great Britain in July 1953. The treaty gave each nation what it wanted: Libya received a pledge of significant financial assistance during a twenty-year period as well as £5,000,000 for economic development and £2,750,000 in budgetary aid for the first five years.[41] At the end of each five-year period a reassessment would take place in order to decide how much aid would be needed and in what fields it should be spent.

In turn Britain obtained military facilities and a military base in Libya. These consisted of airstrips at the airport near Tripoli and at al-Adham in Cyrenaica, both locations "on the strategic air corridors to places of continuing British interest in Africa, the Indian Ocean and the Far East."[42] These facilities allowed British troops to train and to study some of the major battles that had taken place there during World War II between 1940 and 1942.

The treaty was also important to Libya because the passage and movement of British land and air forces in Libya and the supply of equipment and arms to the Libyan army would ensure the protection of Libya's territory from foreign aggression. This would permit the Libyan state, or so it was hoped, to pursue its foreign and domestic policies unfettered by constraints imposed by outside powers, particularly Egypt.[43]

The Anglo-Libyan treaty created an uproar. In Egypt the treaty was called an act of "treason."[44] The Arab league said it would "obstruct the passage" of the treaty, and offered Libya an annual grant of £4,000,000 to reject or amend it.[45] In Tripoli police had to suppress demonstrations against the treaty. It was too important to Libya to be jeopardized by external or domestic pressures. After the Libyan Defense and Foreign Relations Committee studied the treaty, it issued a report stating that "the treaty fortifies Libya's independence . . . and maintains it against external aggression."[46] That the defense aspect of the treaty, rather than the economic component, was the most important element was demonstrated by Libya's refusal of the generous offer of the Arab League.

Two of Libya's core foreign policy objectives at this early stage were to ensure independence and protect the country's borders. Libya achieved these objectives by becoming a member of the Arab League, which supported Libya's status as an independent Arab state, and by entering into an alliance with Great Britain that ensured Libya's protection from military aggression, especially from Egypt, which was having its own problems with Great Britain.

### The U.S.-Libyan Treaty

The Treaty of Friendship with Great Britain was followed by a treaty with the United States in September 1954.[47] This treaty helped Libya achieve its second major foreign policy objective: to obtain aid in building the state. The United States was seen primarily as a source of economic aid for Libya and only secondarily as a deterrent to aggression against that state. On the other hand, for the United States, Libya was of strategic importance as a base for the air defense of North Africa and the

Mediterranean against Soviet encroachment, as a transit stop for U.S. armed forces en route east, and as an important training base for North Atlantic Treaty Organization (NATO) forces in an area that had witnessed some major battles between Allied and Axis forces during World War II.[48] According to the treaty provisions, the United States could continue to keep the Wheelus base near Tripoli as well as U.S. troops (which were already stationed in Libya), and the United States could construct communications outside the areas in which U.S. military equipment was operated.[49]

The U.S. assistance to Libya was substantial and was increased even further in 1955 and again in 1959. During the fiscal year 1955–1956, U.S. aid to Libya amounted to $9 million in development aid and included 25,000 tons of wheat in famine relief. The next year the amount increased to $11 million, 5,000 tons of wheat sent to help Libyans still affected by the drought conditions, and enough military equipment to expand the Libyan army to 1,000 troops.[50]

### The French-Libyan Treaty

France had hoped to have a treaty with Libya similar to those obtained by Britain and the United States. But the Libyan government refused to make a treaty before French forces were evacuated from the Fezzan. When the new Libyan prime minister, Mustafa Bin Halim, was asked why he objected to the 450 French troops in the Fezzan when there were 20,000 British and U.S. forces on Libyan soil,[51] he is reported to have replied "that the military alliance with Britain was sufficient to protect the country, whilst the U.S.A. was financing the greater part of Libya's economic development. Libya did not therefore need a French alliance."[52]

On August 10, 1955, the Franco-Libyan treaty was signed, and France agreed to withdraw its forces by November 1956. France retained certain military prerogatives, however, and both sides agreed to maintain economic and cultural relations.

The major foreign policy actions taken by the Libyan government in the first five years of independence were aimed at achieving Libya's core foreign policy goals of protecting its borders and ensuring its survival. But Libya's strategic location proved a double-edged sword. It made Libya so attractive to Western powers that they were willing to defend and support that state. But it was also Libya's geographic proximity to Egypt and the ties that bound the two nations that would ultimately draw Libya away from its self-chosen pro-Western path and into the arena of Nasirist politics.

## Libya and Egypt: An Uneasy Relationship

Egypt's interest in Libya during the 1940s and until independence was based on many factors. Because of the geographic proximity and traditional ties between the two countries, Egypt felt that it should have a say in the final disposition of that Italian colony. In September 1945 Egypt submitted a memorandum to the Four Powers, which were meeting in London to discuss a peace treaty with Italy, suggesting that Egypt should be consulted on the fate of Libya. Egypt also suggested that a plebiscite determine whether Libyans wanted to be independent or whether they preferred to be united with Egypt.[53] This proposal, made under a monarchy in Egypt, was not based on the ideals of Arab nationalism and Arab unity propounded a few years later by Nasir; rather, the proposal assumed that traditional ties and geographical propinquity made unification the "natural" thing to do.

The Libyans, however, chose almost unanimously to become completely independent. Consequently, realizing that Libya would not accept unification and the Western powers would not grant Egypt the trusteeship of Libya, Egypt submitted a second memorandum in August 1946. This memorandum asked that the Egyptian-Libyan border be modified to include the Jaghbub oasis, the plateau of Sallum, as well as other minor border areas ostensibly taken from Egypt by the Italian colonial rulers in Libya.[54] The memorandum described these as vital to Egyptian national security.[55] This issue continued to be brought up at irregular intervals with Libya and remained a source of strain in Libyan-Egyptian relations for many years.

Despite small frictions and mutual suspicions, however, Libya's ties to Egypt were very strong. Marion J. Rice, the U.S. vice-consul in Benghazi, reported as early as September 1951 that although Libya's official attitude was critical of Egypt (for the reasons stated here), Egypt's influence on Libya should not be underestimated. Apart from common ethnic, religious, and linguistic bonds, most newspapers and magazines in Libya came from Egypt, and Libyan schools were staffed primarily by Egyptian teachers.[56]

He went on to describe how the Libyan population identified with Egypt's struggle against British colonialism and how difficult the Egyptian influence was to assess because it "[is] not measured so much in only political organizations, parties, or government activity as it is in the thought pattern of the people in the general cultural and political sphere."[57]

Libyan-Egyptian relations took a new turn in the early 1950s. Libya had become independent and pro-Western and was therefore entering into treaty agreements with the major Western powers, against which

Egypt under Nasir was fighting over the issue of the Suez Canal. Egypt, which considered this turn of events extremely threatening, was trying to prevent Libya from allying itself to those powers, particularly Great Britain.[58]

Throughout 1953 Egypt tried to dissuade Libya from granting military facilities to Britain. At first Egypt attempted to influence the Libyan prime minister, who was in control of the Libyan Parliament, but when that failed, Egypt focused its attention on the king. An Egyptian legation was established in Benghazi rather than in Tripoli so that legation officials could be in closer contact with the king, whom they asked to start negotiations for a treaty with Egypt before entering into a treaty with Great Britain or any of the other Western powers. When the king refused, Egypt offered publicly to supply Libya with all its financial requirements in order to obviate the necessity of granting military facilities to Great Britain or the United States. As this offer was made in *Al-Ahram*, the Egyptian daily, it created an uproar in Libya, with demands for the immediate acceptance of the Egyptian offer and the cessation of negotiations with the British.[59]

All of Egypt's efforts failed to change the course of events, and the Anglo-Libyan treaty was signed. As a consequence, Egypt began a press campaign against Libya and against Prime Minister Muntasir, whom the Egyptian press accused of being "a tool in the hands of imperialists."[60] Using its powerful press, Egypt was trying to influence Libyan public opinion directly and bypass those politicians whom it could not influence.

During those early years, Libya was in a difficult position because on the one hand it needed the economic and political benefits accruing from a relationship to the West and on the other the geographical proximity to Egypt made it imperative that Libya take that country's wishes seriously.[61]

To pacify Egypt, King Idris took a conciliatory step. When the issue of the Libyan succession was brought up, the king, who had no direct heir, agreed to take another wife to ensure the Sanussi succession to the throne of Libya. After an initial hesitation, the king married an Egyptian in 1955 (a marriage that was dissolved in 1958 when it did not produce an heir). The choice of a wife, especially by a tribal leader, is generally a political decision aimed at cementing an alliance. Thus, King Idris was making a public commitment to close ties with Egypt.

By the time of the Suez Canal crisis in 1956, Libyan-Egyptian relations had reached a critical level. During the previous two years, Mustafa Bin Halim had tried to allay Egypt's fears concerning the British bases in Libya, even going so far as to refuse to join the Baghdad Pact in order to placate Egypt.[62] When on July 26, 1956, Nasir declared that the Suez Canal Company had been nationalized, Libya immediately supported the action although that meant antagonizing the British. Furthermore, several highly placed Libyan government officials, in the absence of Bin Halim, who was in Turkey, began declaring that Libya would not allow any foreign state to launch an attack on Egyptian territory from Libya's ports or from the foreign bases on its soil.

When Egypt was finally attacked by Israel in October 1956, Bin Halim realized the gravity of Libya's situation. If the British were to join in the attack, they could use Libyan bases to do so. Such an action would have severe repercussions on Libya's relationship to Egypt and on the domestic front. So Bin Halim asked for an absolute guarantee that Britian would not attack Egypt from Libyan bases. Some assurances were given, but they did not satisfy local nationalist demands. Demonstrations broke out in Tripoli in support of Egypt. The demonstrators condemned the British and French operations against Egypt, demanding the breaking off of relations with those countries and threatening to attack British forces.[63]

Despite the British guarantees to the Libyan authorities concerning the use of the bases, Egypt again intervened directly in Libyan politics. An Egyptian military attaché, Ismail Sadiq, began encouraging the disturbances in Libya in support of Egypt and distributed arms as well as promoted attacks on British and U.S. installations. Sadiq was eventually expelled after strong British protests.[64] This action, however, cost Bin Halim his popularity in Egypt, and like his predecessor, he, too, was accused by the Egyptian press of being a tool of Western imperialism.

The 1956 crisis passed with no further major incident. Libya had been able to weather the storm without breaking its diplomatic relations with any of the Western powers and without severing its traditional ties to Egypt. But the Suez Canal predicament was the harbinger of more serious events—the 1964 and 1967 crises—that would undermine the legitimacy of the Sanussi monarchy and eventually pave the way for Qadhdhafi's military takeover.

The 1956 events also demonstrated the extent to which Egypt was ready to get involved in Libyan affairs to further its own ends. Egypt influenced the Libyan political scene by using the powerful Egyptian radio and press to reach the public and bypass those politicians whom it could not pressure, by encouraging demonstrations, and by arming extremist groups. Libya was continually obliged to take into consideration the Egyptian viewpoint on every major foreign policy decision, and although under the circumstances Libya maintained a remarkably independent stand on foreign policy issues, it did have to make a number of concessions. One was refusing to join the Baghdad Pact; another was remaining neutral on all major intra-Arab conflicts in the region.[65] In 1958, when a coup took place in Iraq in which the royal family of the

Hashemite House was murdered, King Idris could not bring himself to condone such an action or to recognize the government that had perpetrated it. Consequently, the Egyptian radio, Sawt al-'Arab, began an anti-Libyan propaganda campaign, spreading the word throughout the Arab world that Libya and Israel were the only two countries in the region that did not recognize the new government of Iraq. Libya was subsequently obliged to formally recognize the new Iraqi regime on August 4, 1958.

The 1960s heralded a new era in Libyan-Egyptian relations. The changes that took place were primarily the result of the tremendous increase in the kingdom's revenues after 1961 when it began exporting oil and the cumulative impact of ten years of Egyptian ideological propaganda on Libyan youth. Nasir had become their hero, the most admired non-Libyan statesman, and his picture was seen everywhere in Libya, displayed almost as widely as that of the king.[66]

The Libyan role in Arab politics throughout the 1950s had been cautious, dull, consciously uninfluential, and most annoying to the young Libyans who wanted to participate more actively in regional affairs. The oil wealth that began entering the Libyan economy in the early 1960s increased the disparity in the viewpoints of young Libyans and the state. Whereas the former saw the oil wealth as a means to rid Libya of its foreign military bases and troops and permit Libyans to participate more fully in Arab politics, the state hoped the wealth would consolidate its domestic power, strengthen its alliance with the West, and be used to placate Egypt and keep it out of Libyan affairs.

Between 1961 and 1964, the state began using its wealth to unify the country and consolidate the power of the monarchy. Major development projects were undertaken to distribute the benefits of the oil wealth among the largest number of Libyans. Libya was declared a unitary state in 1963,[67] after having been a federated state for more than a decade, so that the oil wealth that was primarily generated in Cyrenaica could be more fairly spent throughout the country.

Nothing changed, however, on the foreign policy scene until January 1964, when a major demonstration of students broke out in Benghazi to protest an Israeli proposal to divert the waters of the Jordan River. The demonstration was also in support of Cairo's summit meeting of Arab states convened to discuss countermeasures against the proposal. The Cyrenaica Defense Force was sent to control the demonstrators but instead shot an undisclosed number of students. This led to more demonstrations throughout the country and to the resignation of Prime Minister Muhiy al-Din al-Fikini.[68] Although the situation eventually returned to normal, it revealed the strong Arab nationalist feelings of

Libyan youths and their opposition to the neutral stands of the Sanussi regime in foreign policy matters regarding the Arab world.

The situation was exacerbated by President Nasir, who was bent on exploiting the incident to push for the removal of the British and U.S. bases from Libya. On February 22, 1964, Nasir made a speech calling for the closure of the military bases in Libya and Cyprus. "What guarantees," he asked, "are there that the American and British bases in Libya will not be used against the Arabs in the event of a clash with Israel?"[69]

The new prime minister had no choice, especially in the wake of the January 1964 student clashes, but to assert publicly on February 23 that Libya had no intention of renewing or extending its military agreements with the United States and Great Britain. The Libyan prime minister also declared that the bases would under no circumstances be used for aggressive purposes against any Arab country and that the safety of the Arab homeland took priority over the safety of any one particular Arab state.[70]

On March 16, 1964, the prime minister declared in Parliament that he had asked the United States and Britain to enter into negotiation "for the termination of the treaties, the liquidation of their bases, and the fixing of an evacuation date."[71] The Chamber of Deputies unanimously approved a resolution in those very terms, as well as one that affirmed that if the negotiations were unsuccessful, Parliament would pass legislation to abrogate unilaterally those treaties and to close the bases.[72]

A few days later it was announced that King Idris had decided to abdicate the Libyan throne on grounds of ill-health. That announcement led to a strong show of support for the ailing monarch. Libyans crowded in front of the royal residence in Tobruk and demanded that he remain on the throne. He subsequently retracted his abdication and the crisis passed. But his abdication was interpreted by Western diplomats in Libya at the time as a protest and countermove against Eygptian, and to a lesser extent Algerian, pressure on Libya to change its foreign policy vis-à-vis the West and the Arab world.[73] The strong show of support for the king demonstrated to him that he still had the loyalty of his people.

Why did Libya, which had up to that time managed to maintain a relatively independent foreign policy, cave in so easily under Egyptian pressure? And why was Egypt still so interested not only in maintaining its political influence in Libya but in increasing it, now that the Suez Canal crisis had been resolved in its favor and the British were no longer a real threat?

Oil was the apparent reason for Egypt's interest. Libya's revenues had increased by leaps and bounds since 1961, when those revenues totaled

$3 million; they rose to $40 million in 1962 and to $211 million in 1964.[74] Libya could no longer legitimately claim that it needed the foreign bases to subsidize development. As a member of the Arab League, Libya could not maintain to its people that it needed protection from aggression by a neighboring Arab state. Libya was thus obliged to pay lip service to nationalist demands for an end to the military facilities given to Britain and the United States; in practice, however, the government did not do much about the situation.

Britain, which by then had decided that the bases were no longer of much strategic importance, withdrew most of its forces by 1966; a limited number remained in Cyrenaica. The United States entered negotiations with Libya over the evacuation of its base, but nothing much happened, and U.S. troops continued to remain in Libya. The Libyan government could thus claim truthfully that it was negotiating for the termination of the military agreements with Britain and the United States and had succeeded in evacuating the British forces. Meanwhile, Libya retained the U.S. Wheelus base, which provided the deterrent to external aggression that the Libyan state sought.

Despite Libya's success in reducing the U.S. and British presence, Egypt's interest in Libya continued because of its oil wealth.[75] All the oil discoveries up to that time (and later as well) pointed to the fact that Cyrenaica was Libya's main oil-bearing region. Lying so close to Egypt, those oil fields rendered Libya "a property of immense financial value."[76] Egypt, whose economic problems were increasing rapidly, as was its population, wanted to be in control of a region so close and so wealthy. The economic and political potentials of Cyrenaica opened new vistas for the Egyptian government, which had no intention of allowing external forces to control the area and/or to use it as a base for launching attacks against Egypt.

The measures taken by the Libyan government to meet the popular demands for the closure of the U.S. and British bases did not satisfy Libyan students.[77] Student unrest came to a head during the June 1967 Arab-Israeli War. Very serious anti-American and anti-British riots broke out in Tripoli and Benghazi, and the government declared a state of emergency. By then, students were not the only protestors; "mobs" and "crowds" attacked the British Embassy in Benghazi as well as U.S. and British armored trucks and cars. Port workers boycotted British ships, and oil workers led by Sulaiman Maghrabi (who would later become prime minister in Qadhdhafi's government) refused to return to their jobs and ignored government appeals to do so. A ban on oil exports to the United States and Great Britain was imposed.

The Libyan government found itself again in the position of requesting the liquidation of the U.S. military base and the withdrawal of U.S.

troops from Libya "as soon as possible."[78] The Libyan government was losing its ability to decide the country's relations to the Western world because Libya was being pulled irrevocably into the political sphere of influence of Nasir's Egypt. The government did stall, however, and refuse to sever diplomatic ties with Britain and the United States, even at the height of the confrontation.

The government of Prime Minister Hussain Maziq, however, no longer had control of the situation and as a result resigned in July 1967. Maziq was replaced temporarily by 'Abd al-Qadir Badri, but in late October 1967 'Abd al-Hamid Bakkush (who would later become one of Qadhdhafi's main opponents) was asked to form a new government. During the next several months, a new course of action was pursued in foreign policy. The two pillars of that policy were financial aid to Arab states and a major military buildup for Libya. By 1968, it had become apparent to all concerned parties that the Western bases had ceased to be a deterrent force to external aggression. In fact, they had become the focus of Arab anti-Libyan propaganda, which had in turn fueled domestic crises and upheavals and undermined the legitimacy of the state. That the bases and foreign troops had to go was only a matter of time. But how then was Libya to be protected from external aggression? Oil again provided the means for a solution to the problem.

Because Libya's great wealth had made it an attractive prey to neighboring countries with hegemonic ambitions, the Libyan government set out to placate them with large grants and loans. By 1965 Libya, in response to Egyptian pressure, had begun supporting the United Arab Military Command with a $42 million contribution.[79] By the end of August 1967, Libya had become a major aid donor, rather than an aid recipient, as in the 1950s. It pledged at the Khartoum Summit of Arab States held that month to give Egypt and Jordan $84 million per annum for an unspecified number of years. This resolution took place in conjunction with another, which was to lift the oil embargo against Western nations.[80]

In the short term this tactic of placating neighboring states with large sums of money worked. "Although it was tacitly assumed that the kingdom was defending itself [before 1967] against Nasserist Egypt, the fact remained that since the 1967 war, defeated Egypt had ceased to appear a menacing neighbor and had instead become a grateful recipient of Libyan financial aid."[81] Libya had found a way to resume and maintain good relations with Egypt and decrease the danger of aggression against itself.

Temporary pacification could not be a lasting solution to Libya's security problem, however, once the British had evacuated the bases and withdrawn most of their troops and the United States was prepared to do the same. Libya had to upgrade its own army and security forces and build a security system that would ensure the protection of the state. As early as October 1967, Prime Minister Bakkush announced the increase of the Libyan military forces from 7,000 to 10,000 troops. The navy, which was equipped and trained by Britain, and the air force, which was trained and equipped by the United States, were still in a formative stage and were not ready to assume the difficult task of defending Libya.

The primary means devised to protect Libyan borders consisted of the acquisition of an ultramodern defense system, produced by the British Aircraft Corporation, the cost of which eventually rose to $1.4 billion. This system included short-range guided defense missiles, Thunderbird long-range and medium-range defense missiles, three-dimensional radar, and all the necessary installations and communications.[82] The system required very highly trained personnel, who would be British because Libya did not have such personnel of its own. Some have alleged that this was a way for Britain to maintain a military presence in Libya without being the target of nationalist ire. It also made good sense economically to the British to be there and to be paid for their work rather than maintain bases that they no longer needed and for which they had to pay. In April 1969, five months before the military coup, another agreement was signed between Libya and Great Britain to provide the former advanced tanks, artillery, and antiaircraft guns.[83] The Soviet Union had also begun giving military assistance to Libya after the 1967 Arab-Israeli War, although sizable shipments of Soviet weapons were not delivered to Tripoli until after Qadhdhafi came to power.[84]

### Libyan-Maghribi Relations, 1951–1969

When Libya obtained its independence the Maghrib countries were still under colonial occupation, and there was little that Libya could do vis-à-vis its western neighbors but maintain friendly relations. Libya was, however, very supportive of Algeria's anticolonial struggle against the French. In November 1954 when Libya's prime minister, Mustafa Bin Halim, visited Egypt, he was asked to allow the passage of arms from Egypt to the Algerian forces. Although this action could have compromised Libya's relations with France, King Idris gave his permission for the secret transfer of Egyptian weapons through Libya.[85] When the transfer was discovered, the Libyans claimed that they had been trying to contain the arms traffic to Algeria, an explanation that was apparently accepted by the French.[86]

In September 1958 when the "Free Algerian" government in exile was formed, headed by Farhat 'Abbas in Cairo, most of the countries of the Arab world recognized it within three days. Despite the French warning that recognition of the rebel government would be considered an unfriendly act by France, Libya also recognized the Algerian government in exile.[87]

After Algeria's independence, Libyan-Algerian economic and political relations expanded. The Libyan government, however, became concerned with internal developments in Algeria, which was becoming a socialist state, as well as with its external policies, which were similar to those of Egypt.[88] When the Comite Permanent Consultatif du Maghreb was formed in late 1964, however, Libya sent its minister of the economy to the meetings, which were also attended by representatives of Algeria, Tunisia, and Morocco.[89] The primary aim of that committee was "to harmonize economic development plans in general" in the Maghrib.[90] Its work was also perceived as a step in the direction of unity of the Greater Maghrib. Libya, however, did not play an important role and gradually faded from the committee without making a lasting impact.

Libya's relations with Morocco during the Sanussi period were relatively low key. True to the Sanussi principle of remaining uninvolved, Libya sent only an observer to the Tangier Conference for the Unification of the Arab Maghrib in 1958.[91] As in the case of Algeria, however, and throughout the early 1950s, Libya allowed the Armée de Liberation Marocaine to use Libyan territory. Thus, Libya's traditional links to the Maghrib were maintained in a fashion that did not compromise Libya's relations to the major Western powers on which it relied.

As the years passed and Libya became more independent from those powers as a result of new oil revenues, it also became more vocal about its belief in Maghribi unity. By 1967 a permanent consultative committee for Maghribi affairs had been established in Tripoli, the aims of which were primarily economic.

King Idris's government seems to have been active only with respect to Tunisia. On January 16, 1957, a few months after Tunisia's independence, the Treaty of Brotherhood and Good Neighborliness was signed between Libya and Tunisia. Unlike the written and unwritten agreements with Algeria and Morocco that had been either economic or cultural, the treaty with Tunisia was primarily political. Of its most important clauses, one on mutual defense established the principle that the two countries would consider themselves directly affected by any threat from a major foreign power against either one of them.[92] A second clause described one purpose of the treaty as "harmonizing their policies towards neighboring sister countries and toward Western and Eastern states."[93]

The political implications of this treaty for the region were not lost on Egypt. That treaty more than any previous foreign policy action institutionalized Libya's position as part of the Maghrib. Only Tripolitania, and the Fezzan at times, had been previously regarded as part of the Grand Maghrib; the rest of Libya had been perceived in terms of the Arab Mashriq. Consequently, this inclusion of Libya in the Maghrib was understood in the region to be at the expense of Libya's ties to the Mashriq and more specifically to Egypt.

Furthermore, this treaty, which had been initiated by Libya, was seen in Egypt as a means by which Prime Minister Bin Halim hoped to distance Libya from Egyptian political influence and strengthen Libya's pro-Western position in the region by allying it to another state that was pro-Western. In fact, Bourguiba, Tunisia's new head of state, had been quick to respond to Libya's offer because, as Majid Khadduri shrewdly points out, he had "himself been trying to lead a Northwest African Bloc counteracting Nasir's East Arab bloc."[94] The Libyan-Tunisian treaty and the attempt at bloc formation set a precedent in the region: the practice of bloc formation and counterbloc formation that has characterized North Africa's intraregional politics in the last three decades.[95]

As was to be expected, Egypt took umbrage to the treaty, which it perceived quite rightly as an attempt at bloc formation on its western borders.[96] In fact, Egyptian-Tunisian relations began to deteriorate rapidly. A year later, on November 24, 1958, the High Court of Tunisia brought Salah Bin Yusuf (in absentia) and fifty-four of his supporters to trial on charges of conspiracy to overthrow the Bourguiba regime. They were accused of having smuggled arms to Tunisia and having planned to create an opposition party. The Tunisian leader accused Egypt, where Salah Bin Yusuf was residing, not only of fomenting those subversive activities but also of having actively participated in the foiled coup attempt. Several Egyptian officers were arrested and brought to trial, but Egypt denied any participation.[97] Bourguiba and Nasir remained at loggerheads throughout the Nasir era, and Libya found itself in a very difficult position between its two feuding neighbors.

Grimaud succinctly analyzes Libya's relation toward the Maghrib during the Sanussi monarchy: "The fear of having to take sides with either Bourguiba or Nasser, a distancing from Algeria in the throes of socialism, a reluctance to share its wealth with less fortunate neighbors, and a wider vision of Arab unity, inspired the Senoussie monarchy with caution."[98]

## Chad and the Sanussiya

In the nineteenth and twentieth centuries, the main links between Libya and Chad were those established by the Sanussiya Order. As head of the order, King Idris had a strong interest in Chad. In 1954 he attempted to occupy the Aouzou strip in northern Chad by sending

Libyan motorized units there, which were repulsed by the French forces in the region.[99] Throughout the 1950s and until 1960 when Chad became independent from French colonial rule, he continued to provide Chadian insurgents with arms, food, and bases in the Fezzan.[100]

When the rebellion against the Tombalbaye regime broke out in Chad in October 1965, Libyan soldiers of Chadian origin, as well as students from the university of Beida in Cyrenaica, joined the rebellion. One of the major Chadian tribes that played a crucial role in the rebellion used the Fezzan as a base for its activities and as a haven for those fleeing Chad's dictatorship.[101]

## King Idris's Legacy

In less than two decades King Idris achieved certain major successes. With no significant domestic strife he was able to preserve the unity and integrity of the Libyan state. With political alliances and diplomacy he protected his very weak country from external aggression and intervention. He obtained the assistance Libya needed to feed the population as well as to build schools and hospitals at a time when Libya was one of the poorest countries in the world.

The discovery of oil transformed the Libyan political scene, as did the rise of Nasir as a major charismatic figure in the Arab world. Perhaps a younger, more aggressive leader could have been more effective in adapting Libyan politics to the changing times. Idris I was old and sick and had lost interest in the day-to-day running of the affairs of his country. But it may not have been possible for any leader to change the situation without jeopardizing Libya's ties to the West or provoking a serious domestic confrontation between the state and the Libyan population. The foreign policy goals of the Idris monarchy remained those of his successor, and his policies formed the basis upon which Libya's foreign policy evolved in the following two decades.

## Notes

1. On November 21, 1949, the U.N. General Assembly voted to adopt the resolution that Libya was to be granted its independence, which it received on December 24, 1951. See the study by Adrian Pelt, the U.N. assistant secretary general, who was appointed U.N. commissioner in Libya. He discusses the process of granting Libya independence and how the major Western powers could not agree on a formula and so decided that the issue should be put to the U.N. General Assembly. Adrian Pelt, *Libyan Independence and the United Nations: A Case of Planned Decolonization*, Yale University Press, New Haven, 1970.

2. See Majid Khadduri's discussion of those issues in *Modern Libya: A Study in Political Development*, The Johns Hopkins University Press, Baltimore, 1963, pp. 264–286.

3. Henry S. Villard, *Libya: The New Arab Kingdom of North Africa*, Cornell University Press, Ithaca, N.Y., 1956, p. 147.

4. John Wright, *Libya: A Modern History*, Johns Hopkins University Press, Baltimore, 1982, pp. 84–85.

5. E. E. Evans-Pritchard, *The Sanusi of Cyrenaica*, Clarendon Press, Oxford, 1949, p. 47.

6. Ibid., p. 48.

7. Ibid., p. 51.

8. Khadduri, pp. 25–27.

9. Evans-Pritchard, p. 47.

10. Ben Adjmia, "Structure des villages et origine de leur population dans le Sahel Septentrional," *Cahiers de Tunisie*, Vol. XII, 1964, p. 101.

11. Ibid., p. 106. My translation.

12. Ibid.

13. John I. Clarke, "Some Observations on Libyans in Tunisia," *Cahiers de Tunisie*, Vol. VI, 1958, p. 91.

14. Ibid.

15. Interview with Prime Minister Bahi Ladgham, Carthage, Tunisia, June 1986.

16. Ahmed Said Fituri, "Tripolitania, Cyrenaica and Bilad As-Sudan: Trade Relations During the Second Half of the Nineteenth Century," unpublished Ph.D. dissertation, The University of Michigan, 1982, p. 8.

17. Ibid., pp. 64–67.

18. See John Wright, "Chad and Libya: Some Historical Connections," *The Maghreb Review*, Vol. 8, Nos, 3–4, 1983, p. 93.

19. Ibid., p. 94.

20. Richard Nyrop et al., *Area Handbook for Libya*, U.S. Government Printing Office, Washington, D.C., 1973, p. 60.

21. Harold D. Nelson, *Area Handbook for Chad*, U.S. Government Printing Office, Washington, D.C., 1972, p. 44; see also for a discussion of the demographic aspect of Libyan-Chadian relations, Sa'id 'Abd al-Rahman al-Hundiri, *Al-'Ilaqat al-Libiya al-Tchadiya 1843–1975*, Markaz Jihad al-Libiyin, Vol. XX, Tripoli, 1983, pp. 35–41.

22. Nelson, p. 49.

23. *Mustafa Khawjat, Tarikh Fazzan*, edited eighteenth-century manuscript, Markaz Jihad al-Libiyin, Tripoli, 1979, pp. 13–14.

24. Ibid.

25. U.S. National Archives, Despatch from Marion J. Rice, Benghazi to Department of State, Washington, D.C. 673. 74/9 551. "Egyptian Influence in Cyrenaica," September 5, 1951.

26. Nicola A. Ziadeh, *Sanusiyah: A Study of a Revivalist Movement in Islam*, E. J. Brill, Leiden, 1968, pp. 85–86.

27. Ibid., p. 86.

28. Abdulmola S. El-Horeir, "Social and Economic Transformations in the Libyan Hinterland During the Second Half of the Nineteenth Century: The Role of Ahmad Al-Sharif Al-Sanusi," unpublished Ph.D. dissertation, University of California, Los Angeles, 1981, pp. 113–114.

29. Ibid., p. 114.

30. Ziadeh, p. 115. *Zawiya* is the Arabic term for "lodge."

31. John Lindberg, *A General Economic Appraisal of Libya*, United Nations Publications, Sales No. 1952.11.H.2 (ST/TAA/K/LIBYA/1, 22 September 1952), summarized in Pelt, pp. 674–679.

32. See Shukri Ghanem, "The Libyan Economy Before Independence," in E.G.H. Joffe and K. S. McLachlan, eds., *Social and Economic Development of Libya*, Middle East and North African Studies Press Ltd., Cambridgeshire, 1982, p. 152.

33. Pelt, p. 675.

34. R. L. Le Tourneau, "Libyan Education and Its Development," in UNESCO, *Report of the Mission to Libya*, Johannes Weisbecker, Frankfurt, 1952.

35. *Keesing's Contemporary Archives* (hereafter KCA), Vol. 8, July 1950–June 1952, p. 11917.

36. Villard, p. 151.

37. Khadduri, p. 262.

38. U.S. National Archives, Despatch from Henry Villard in Tripoli to the Department of State, Washington, D.C., 673.74/6-1853 XR 741.56373. "Possible Egyptian Intentions in Cyrenaica," June 18, 1953, p. 2.

39. Robert W. MacDonald, *The League of Arab States: A Study in the Dynamics of Regional Organization*, Princeton University Press, Princeton, N.J., 1965; see Appendix G, Session 18-1 of Arab League members, approving of Libya's membership application to the Arab League, in Cairo, March 1953, p. 356.

40. U.S. National Archives, Despatch from Henry Villard in Tripoli to the Department of State, Washington, D.C., 673.74/9-1253 XR 641.73. "Prime Minister's Comment on Egyptian Influence in Libya," September 12, 1953, p. 1.

41. KCA, Vol. 9, July 1952–December 1954, p. 13046.

42. Wright, *Libya: A Modern History*, p. 83.

43. See Chapter 1.

44. *Al-Nida'*, Cairo, August 11, 1953, quoted in Wright, *Libya: A Modern History*, p. 229.

45. KCA, Vol. 9, July 1952–December 1954, p. 13183.

46. Quoted in Khadduri, p. 230.

47. U.S. Department of State, *United States Treaties and Other International Agreements*, Vol. 5, Part 3, 1954, U.S. Government Printing Office, Washington, D.C., 1956, pp. 2451–2472, 2492–2493.

48. See Khadduri, p. 255.

49. See U.S. Department of State, pp. 2492–2493.

50. KCA, Vol. 10, January 1955–December 1956, p. 14988.

51. Ibid., p. 15273.

52. Ibid., p. 14047.

53. Muhammad Fu'ad Shukri, *Milad Dawlat Libya al-Haditha: Watha'iq Tahririha wa Istaqlaliha,* Matba'at al-I'timad, Cairo, 1957, p. 32. The term used was *indimam,* which implies a merger where a weaker state merges into a stronger one, rather than the term *wihda* used later by Qadhdhafi, which implies the unity of two more or less equal partners.

54. This referred to an agreement between the Italians and Sayyid Idris (later King Idris) on October 25, 1920, under which he was given the hereditary title of Amir over Cyrenaica, which according to the Italians included the areas later claimed by Egypt.

55. U.S. National Archives, Despatch from Jefferson Caffery in Cairo to the Department of State, Washington, D.C., 673.7431/9-1450 XR320. "Egyptian-Libyan Border Question at General Assembly," September 14, 1950.

56. U.S. National Archives, Despatch from Marion Rice in Benghazi to the Department of State, Washington, D.C., 673.74/9-551. "Egyptian Influence in Cyrenaica," September 5, 1951, p. 1.

57. Ibid., p. 2.

58. U.S. National Archives, 673.74/6-1853, p. 1.

59. Ibid., p. 2.

60. Khadduri, p. 229.

61. U.S. National Archives, Despatch from Peter R. Chase in Benghazi to the Department of State, Washington, D.C., 673.82/7-2254 XR773.13, "Libya's Relations with Turkey," July 22, 1954, p. 2.

62. See Khadduri, p. 269.

63. Ibid., pp. 267–274.

64. Ibid., pp. 273–274.

65. See also Macdonald, pp. 78–79.

66. Wright, *Libya: A Modern History,* p. 94.

67. KCA, Vol. 14, January 1963–December 1964, p. 19340.

68. Wright, *Libya: A Modern History,* p. 98.

69. KCA, Vol. 14, January 1963–December 1964, p. 19986.

70. Ibid.

71. Ibid.

72. Ibid.

73. Ibid.

74. "OPEC Oil Report," *Petroleum Economist,* London, 1977, Table V, p. 38.

75. Wright, *Libya: A Modern History,* p. 96.

76. Ibid.

77. First, p. 84.

78. KCA, Vol. 16, January 1967–December 1968, p. 22135.

79. This United Military Command headed by the Egyptian 'Ali 'Ali Maher was in theory supposed to be an Arab defense force made up of troops from the various Arab countries.

80. KCA, Vol. 16, January 1967–December 1968, pp. 22275–22276.

81. Wright, *Libya: A Modern History,* p. 106.

82. KCA, Vol. 16, January 1967–December 1968, p. 22710.

83. For a discussion of the various military contracts between Libya and Britain, see First, pp. 89–96.

84. See I. William Zartman, "Arms Imports—The Libya Experience," in *World Military Expenditures and Arms Transfers 1971–1980*, U.S. Arms Control and Disarmament Agency, Washington, D.C., 1983, p. 15.

85. Khadduri, p. 269.

86. See the statement made by Daniel Moyer at the French National Assembly, KCA, Vol. 10, January 1955–December 1956, p. 15273.

87. KCA, Vol. 11, January 1957–December 1958, p. 16410.

88. See Grimaud, p. 218.

89. Habib Slim, "Le Comite Permanent Consultatif du Maghreb Entre le Passé, le Present at L'Avenir," *Revue Tunisienne de Droit*, 1980, pp. 241–252. See also J.C. Santucci, "L'Unification Maghrebine: Realisations institutionelles et obstacles politiques," in Roger Le Tourneau et al., *L'Unite Maghrebine Dimensions et Perspectives*, CNRS, Paris, 1972, p. 144.

90. KCA, Vol. 15, January 1965–December 1966, p. 20507.

91. Wright, *Libya: A Modern History*, p. 95.

92. KCA, Vol. 11, January 1957–December 1958, p. 15376.

93. Quoted in Khadduri, p. 279.

94. Ibid.

95. See Grimaud's discussion of the practice in the region, p. 195.

96. *Al-Ahram*, Cairo, October 10, 1957.

97. KCA, Vol. 12, January 1959–December 1960, p. 16637.

98. Grimaud, p. 218. My translation.

99. Benyamin Neuberger, *Involvement, Invasion and Withdrawal: Qadhdhafi's Libya and Chad 1969–1981*, Occasional Papers, No. 83, Tel Aviv University, Tel Aviv, 1982, p. 23.

100. Y. Berri and S. Kebzabo, "Que Fait Khaddafi au Tchad?" *Jeune Afrique*, 768, 26 September 1975, p. 19.

101. Neuberger, p. 23.

# 3

## The Libyan Coup of 1969: The First Year Reconsidered

On September 1, 1969, a coup overthrew the eighteen-year-old Libyan monarchy. For the next fifteen days there was a general news blackout, except for radio reports from Cairo and Cyrenaica. The earliest reports from Cairo announced that army units had moved into Tripoli and Benghazi to certain appointed locations—the royal palace, the public security forces' headquarters, the army command headquarters, and the broadcasting station in Benghazi—and had taken them over without resistance.[1] The reports also announced that the Revolutionary Command Council (RCC) did not wish to disclose the names of its members, except for that of Colonel Sa'd al-Din Abu Shuwayrib, who had been appointed chief of staff,[2] and for those officers who called themselves Al-Dhubbat al-Ahrar al-Wahdawiyyin, or the Unionist Free Officers.

On September 4, 1969, Abu Shuwayrib began making statements that were broadcast in Libya and reported by the Middle East News Agency in Cairo. He described the aims of the Unionist Free Officers as the achievement of "the people's hopes for a free and dignified life dominated by social justice, socialism and unity."[3] This statement was the first mention of the principles of the revolution that would soon become its slogan.[4]

With regard to the Western powers, Abu Shuwayrib affirmed that Libya only wanted "mutual respect [and] reciprocal treatment," and he asked them not to interfere in Libya's domestic affairs.[5] He added that Libya's foreign policy was Arab and Islamic and that the issue of Palestine was the major foreign policy issue for all Arab countries.

The members of the RCC appeared apprehensive of the British reaction and threatened force if the British intervened. By September 4, 1969, however, the Bayda Domestic Service was reporting that Britain had rejected King Idris's request to land British troops in Benghazi and Tripoli and was prepared to maintain good relations with the new Libyan leaders.[6]

It was in this way that the world first learned about the military coup in Libya and about the objectives and policies of the coupmakers. Their identities, however, remained shrouded in mystery a few days longer.

### The New Libyan Government:
### Moderates and Radicals

On September 8 the veil of secrecy began to lift. The RCC announced the formation of its new cabinet: the prime minister was Dr. Mahmud Sulayman al-Maghribi, the leader of the oil workers strike against British and U.S. tankers in 1967; the unity and foreign affairs minister was Salih Buwaysir; the defense minister was Lieutenant Colonel Musa Ahmad; petroleum, labor, and social affairs minister was engineer Anis Ahmad Shutaywi; economy, planning, and industry minister was 'Ali 'Umaysh; education and national guidance minister was Muhammad al-Shatwi; minister of justice was Muhammad 'Ali al-Jadi; and minister of health, public works, and communications was Dr. Muftah al-Usta 'Umar.[7] This new cabinet took certain stands on foreign and domestic policy issues that were changed and then revoked when Qadhdhafi entered into the limelight in the last quarter of 1969.

On September 13, 1969, Prime Minister Maghribi addressed the Libyan people on issues of domestic and foreign policy. He expressed his support and that of his cabinet for all Arab causes, especially the Palestinian cause; their respect for all international agreements, in particular the oil agreements; and state protection for the property of non-Libyans working in Libya.[8] In an interview with *Agence France Presse* on September 16, Maghribi elaborated those policies. He stated that the new government would consider international commitments in light of the changed circumstances. He affirmed that no change in the status of the U.S. and British bases would take place until the treaties expired, at which point they would not be renewed.

Maghribi also promised to continue providing Egypt with the financial aid promised in Khartoum in 1967 after the Arab-Israeli War. When questioned on the issue of unity with Egypt, however, Maghribi replied, "There will be no union with Egypt in a matter of weeks or months. But at a later date, the union is the dream of all the Arabs,"[9] meaning the union of the whole Arab world.

Concerning the oil sector, Maghribi assured the reporter that there would be no major change in Libya's oil policy as long as the interests of Libyans were taken into consideration. He believed this could be achieved by an improved control of the oil industry's activities and the development of the Libyan National Company.

When asked what Libya's choices on domestic policy were, Maghribi was general. He spoke of socialism in terms of social justice, adding that Libya would not imitate any foreign system and that because Libya did not have any major industry, discussion of nationalization was meaningless.[10]

Two days later, Maghribi reiterated Libya's foreign policy objectives in a meeting with the chief editors of Libyan newspapers. He asserted that the treaties with the United States and Britain pertaining to the bases in Libya would not be renewed once they expired but that they would be considered terminated only "when the legal period ends."[11]

These early statements indicated that the group in power during the first three weeks after the revolution comprised moderate civilians and military officers who wished to reform the system domestically because of the high degree of corruption that had existed during the years of the monarchy. Although strongly nationalistic, this group was not antagonistic to the Western powers and was prepared to develop good relations with them after the evacuation of the bases. Regionally, the group was more Arab oriented than the previous regime and spoke more openly of Arab causes, Arab unity, and the Palestinians. In regard to Egypt, however, the group was cautious and seemed wary of Libya's powerful neighbor, offering to continue providing it with financial aid but unwilling to consider unity.

With regard to oil, this moderate group of Libyan leaders wanted better terms for their principal export but were unwilling to introduce any drastic change in their agreements with the major U.S., British, and other oil companies. The foreigners who lived in Libya (presumably the Italians) were to be allowed to keep their property, and although socialism and social justice were discussed, the first Libyan Cabinet did not plan to nationalize any sector of the economy.

These policies, however, were never implemented. As Qadhdhafi began rising to power within the RCC, the official statements changed in tone and content, gradually at first and then more forcefully, and deeds soon followed words and sometimes even preceded them.

On September 16, 1969, Qadhdhafi gave a speech of which there are two versions. The first was broadcast on the Bayda Domestic Radio Service,[12] and the second was reported by the official Directorate of Information and National Guidance.[13] In the first version, a live address to workers and student representatives, Qadhdhafi's radical rhetoric stood in clear contrast to the low-key speeches of moderate Prime Minister Maghribi. Qadhdhafi spoke of world imperialism for the first time and of "revolution every day in every area." The second version, which appears less likely to have been delivered that day because it was not reported by the Bayda Domestic Service, was much more restrained in tone and in content and did not mention either world imperialism or revolution, only freedom, socialism, and Arab unity (the slogan of the revolution).

Two days later, in one of his earliest interviews with a French journalist, Qadhdhafi's tone was again cautious and restrained. He spoke of his wish to develop close ties with France, citing that country's arms embargo to Israel as proof of its friendship toward the Arabs.[14] This may have been a way of keeping links to the West—especially access to the latest and most sophisticated weapons in Europe's arsenal—while simultaneously playing the anti-British and anti-U.S. role to enhance his own revolutionary stance.

Beginning on September 21, Maghribi's statements were already being revoked by the new government: Foreigners were informed that they could no longer engage in any commercial agency activity; a number of foreign companies were banned from operating in Libya; British, German, Spanish, and Norwegian ships were blacklisted;[15] and the work contracts of many foreign workers were ended. Three days later, the moderate members of the Cabinet began resigning in protest, as their policies were not being implemented and Qadhdhafi was pursuing his own goals, unconcerned with their opinions.[16]

By mid-October, Qadhdhafi started discussing his interpretation of socialism, which included nationalization as a means of redistributing the national wealth. The implementation of this policy began as early as November, with the nationalization of foreign banks followed by the nationalization of some of the oil industries and the small privately owned factories and commercial enterprises.

With respect to foreign relations, Qadhdhafi defined Libya's foreign policy as one of "neutrality, non-alignment and support for all causes of liberation and freedom in the whole world."[17] He also made an issue of the U.S. and British bases, referring to their evacuation as "a main condition for our freedom."[18] He pursued this issue throughout this first year, building it into a heroic confrontation between Libya and the Western superpowers, trying perhaps in that way to emulate Egypt's confrontation over the Suez Canal. The two bases were eventually evacuated in 1970, before their leases expired.

Finally, Qadhdhafi presented a seven-point program to achieve a transitional stage before reaching complete Arab unity. This program included establishing an Arab capital fund, unifying trade between Arab countries, unifying the Arab information media, creating an Arab information market, exploiting the resources of the Arab world, establishing an Arab scientific and technological research organization, and carrying out regular studies of the economy and trade of Arab states.[19]

Unlike the first postcoup government, Qadhdhafi advocated radical change on both the domestic and the foreign policy levels. He fully endorsed Nasirism as a doctrine and went about implementing policies that were at loggerheads with those of his colleagues in the new Libyan Cabinet. Years later he would write to Anwar Sadat about that period, "After the 1 September Revolution the Libyan people accepted the Egyptian revolution from A to Z. They accepted the Egyptian anthem— Allahu Akbar—then they accepted the Egyptian flag, the Arab Socialist Union, its charter and its statutes. They also accepted the slogan 'freedom, socialism and unity,' as well as the eagle emblem."[20]

By adopting the Nasirite ideology, Qadhdhafi secured the support of Egyptian authorities, who were interested in having a strong influence over both their neighbors, Sudan and Libya. In contrast to the other members of the new Libyan government, Qadhdhafi was willing to toe the line behind Egypt, evacuate the foreigners from Libya, and invite Egyptian forces in to replace them. He thus distinguished himself from his colleagues by means of his ideological adherence to Nasirism and his willingness to do Egypt's bidding. In return, Egypt supported him and made sure that he was not toppled before implementing his policies.[21]

Ideology served a dual function in that first year. Qadhdhafi used ideology to achieve his core objectives of securing Egypt's support for his leadership and protecting Libya's borders; he also used ideology to enhance his own legitimacy domestically and regionally. By imitating Nasir, the most charismatic of Arab leaders and playing the revolutionary, Qadhdhafi very quickly outshone his more sedate colleagues in the Cabinet and the RCC.

## The Military Buildup

Although the military buildup that began in 1969 was a means to achieve Libya's core objectives, it was closely linked and subordinate to the process of consolidating Libyan ties to Egypt. For in order to survive during that first year in power, Qadhdhafi needed Egypt's support and protection. The military buildup was therefore a means of cementing those ties by satisfying some of Egypt's security needs as well as those of Libya.

The buildup of Libya's military forces and the expansion of its arsenal of weapons had already started during the last year of the monarchy. Qadhdhafi speeded up the process. Because the foreign bases were being evacuated, there was no power that could be entrusted with the defense of Libya's borders. Therefore, the new Libyan regime had to build its own forces to undertake this task. Qadhdhafi believed that the army could also be used for more lofty purposes and that it could "make positive contributions to the common Arab struggle"[22] in case of a war with Israel. The Libyan army, however, would have to become "a force of defensive and offensive potential" before it could join other Arab armies.[23]

In October 1969, an Egyptian agent, Fathi al-Dib, initiated an arms transaction with France on behalf of Libya, and a month later a Libyan delegation arrived in France to begin negotiations. In that delegation, there allegedly were a number of Egyptian officers with Libyan passports. French defense minister Michel Debré, who was involved in the negotiations, as well as some of his top aides were supposed to have been aware of that.[24] The arms deal was exceptionally important. It included 100 Mirage jet fighter planes, 50 Mirage 5, 30 Mirage III-E for interception, and around 20 Mirage III-B for training and reconnaissance.[25] They were to be delivered during a period of four years, from 1971 to 1974.

Egypt had much to gain from this deal. France had imposed an arms embargo on sales of weapons to all the major belligerents in the Arab-Israeli War (Libya was therefore not included), and Egypt had to find an alternative source of armaments (although it still obtained most of its arms from the Soviet Union). Libya was the ideal alternative source to negotiate a deal with France to procure weapons for Egypt.[26] Ruth First claims that Nasir advised the RCC "not to antagonize the United States; not to rush ahead with oil nationalization; to shop for arms in France."[27]

Israel and the United States strongly criticized France for the sale of the Mirages to Libya. Debré responded that if France had not made the sale, the United States or the USSR would have sold their own fighter planes.[28] Tunisia, which had kept a low profile during the storm that erupted on the international scene over the sale of the Mirages, concurred with France. On January 24, 1970, Tunisia argued that Libya would have bought Soviet MiGs if it could not have obtained the French Mirages. In terms of regional security, therefore, Libyan cooperation with France was preferable.[29] But despite French assertions about preempting sales from the USSR, Libya began receiving Soviet-made weapons during the summer of 1970, including 75 field and antiaircraft weapons, 200 tanks, 36 amphibious vehicles, and supporting equipment,[30] all of which had been contracted under the previous regime.

There was another consideration involved in the French arms deal. In exchange for the Mirages, Libya had agreed to end its support for the insurgents working against the Tombalbaye regime in Chad,[31] which was backed by France and French troops. This was to set a precedent in Libya's foreign policy vis-à-vis France and to a lesser extent the United States. Withdrawal of troops from Chad and an end to support for insurgents, rebels, or Muslim northerners would be used again and again by Libya as a bargaining chip in its negotiations with the Western powers.

France had other interests in the arms deal as well. It wished to replace Britain and the United States in Libya and thus have sole influence over a large part of the North African coast. There was even some talk about France taking over the Wheelus, al-Adham, and Tobruk bases after U.S. and British troops left.[32] And the economic benefits that France would reap from such a sale would amount by some estimates to $400 million,[33] the largest single French aeronautic arms deal with one foreign client ever concluded.[34]

The 1968 arms contract between the Idris administration and Great Britain to set up a complete missile air defense system in Libya was revoked by the RCC in early November 1969. Defense Minister Adam al-Hawwaz stated that the missile system served the purpose of the imperialist powers in the region,[35] and was not really defensive. The Libyan government, however, insisted on retaining the £150 million arms deal with Britain for the Chieftain tanks ordered under the previous government. Libya even threatened to withdraw all its hard currency assets from Britain if the British refused to sell the tanks.[36] At this stage the British air defense missile system had been ordered to protect Libya from external intervention—namely, by Egypt. With the improved relations between Libya and Egypt, such a system was perceived as no longer necessary by the new regime. The tanks, however, could easily be moved to Egypt if needed in its ongoing war of attrition with Israel.

The Libyan armed forces were also revamped. After the coup, military cadets were sent to the Egyptian Military Academy to be trained for a year and then brought back to Benghazi for a second year of study. In this way Egypt ensured its control over the Libyan military from the outset.[37]

Ruth First writes that steps were taken during the early months of the coup to secure the loyalty of the army. Officers ranking above major were either posted abroad, pensioned off, or even arrested; lower ranks were promoted, their salaries were doubled, and some were decorated for bravery.[38]

The Libyan military buildup during the first year after the coup had a number of consequences. First, the role of the armed forces shifted: once a symbol of independence under King Idris, they became the most powerful institution in the country. Second, the arms acquisitions cemented Libya's ties to Egypt because the arms were understood to be for Egypt. Third, Egypt's control over Libya tightened when the former began to train and supervise the latter's army. Finally, negotiating an arms deal with the Western powers involved a new political and regional dimension. A trade-off on Chad had taken place in the Libyan-French negotiations, for instance. Libya was beginning to use political leverage in the region to obtain international concessions.

Thus, Libya's arms buildup became a means to achieve some of its core objectives. The military was a defensive force protecting Libya's borders, especially since the Western bases had been evacuated; it was a means to increase Libya's prestige regionally and internationally and to extend Libyan influence beyond the country's borders. The army also became a base of political power for Qadhdhafi and ensured the protection of his regime.

## Unity with Egypt: A Libyan Predicament

The coup had taken Egyptian officials by surprise. There were several plots being hatched to overthrow the regime at that time, and this was not the one they believed would take place.[39] According to Ruth First, upon learning of the coup, Nasir immediately sent Muhammad Hassanein Heikal, one of his closest confidants and the editor of *Al-Ahram*, the Egyptian daily, on a reconnaissance mission to Libya. The Egyptian delegation was followed on the same day by a Sudanese delegation headed by Major General Ja'far al-Numayri, chair of the Sudanese Revolutionary Council, and Brigadier General 'Abd al-Hamid, a special adviser to the Sudanese armed forces.[40] Both Egypt and Sudan were among the first states, along with Iraq, to recognize the new Libyan regime on September 2, 1969. They were also the ones that were to have the greatest influence on Libya's foreign policy in the region.

Qadhdhafi's need for a major regional ally to achieve his core objectives was there from the earliest days of the coup. Throughout this first year he sought to strengthen his alliance with Egypt while at the same time retaining some independence from that country. Although this alliance was crucial in keeping him in power and in protecting Libya from external intervention, too close a relationship to Egypt might have undermined his credibility and his domestic legitimacy.

There were two divergent views on Libya's relationship to Egypt among its new leaders in the immediate aftermath of the coup. The more ideologically moderate leaders wished to maintain good relations with the West, were not interested in radical changes domestically such as nationalization or Libyanization of industries or trade, and did not want too close ties to Egypt. This group was probably best represented by the original members of the first postcoup Cabinet.

Those who opted for closer ties to Egypt and Sudan were the military members of the second Cabinet of January 1970, headed by Qadhdhafi as prime minister and minister of defense; Major 'Abd al-Salam Jallud, vice-prime minister and minister of the interior and local administration;

Major Bashir Hawwadi, minister of education and national guidance; Captain 'Umar al-Muhaishi, minister of economy and industry; and Captain Muhammad Abu Bakr al-Muqarif, minister of housing and municipalities.[41] (The civilian members of the Cabinet were not to play a significant role in Libya's history in the years to come.)

This ambivalence toward Egypt among the new leaders reflected the ambivalence that existed among the Libyan people. Perhaps the only authentic document that we have concerning the way Libyans really felt about domestic and foreign policy issues in those early days after the coup are the proceedings of the Libyan Intellectual Seminar of May 1970, which were broadcast throughout the country. Only the military members of the January 1970 Cabinet attended, and all discussed relatively openly a broad spectrum of political issues. When it came to unity with Egypt, Minister Muhaishi was best able to express the fears and doubts of those attending by saying, "We are small in number and afraid of vanishing when united with other Arab countries."[42]

Qadhdhafi addressed the problem in the manner of a politician trying to sell an idea not easily acceptable to his constituents. He asserted that although he was "more Libyan than any other Libyan,"[43] he did not believe that Libyans would lose their identity if they were united with other countries. If that were the case, he added, "the personality of the Egyptians would also vanish."[44]

Addressing the concern that Libyan oil wealth would be taken by the Egyptians, Qadhdhafi argued that Egypt had no need for Libyan oil because it was a rich country. He assured his listeners that Egypt did not benefit in any way from unity between the two countries and was receiving less aid from Libya than it had under the Sanussi monarchy.[45]

He then told his audience that they had to choose between the U.S. side and seek its protection as the previous regime had done or the side of the Arab progressive forces that had stood by the revolution.[46] He spoke in pragmatic, nonideological terms (although certainly not in truthful terms) and tried to convince his listeners that it was in their own best interest to unite with Egypt and that they had nothing to lose and everything to gain. Egypt was presented as the donor, not the recipient, the protector against external threats, not the major external danger. Egypt was described as the power that could metaphorically make Libyans more Arab without undermining their Libyan sense of identity.

In the first year of the coup, the issue of unity with Egypt was not a popular one, nor could it be taken lightly. Libyans were divided on that issue. Twenty years earlier when the Libyans had been asked to choose by referendum between being integrated into Egypt and becoming independent, they had opted almost unanimously for independence. Even in the most exalted days of pro-Nasirism, Libyans had never voiced a desire to unite with Egypt—only to join a greater Arab union in the name of Arab nationalism.

## Power Struggle in Tripoli

Although dissonant voices in the Cabinet and the RCC were already being heard during the third week of September, the showdown between the two groups did not take place until early December 1969. On December 10, a coup attempt against the regime was announced with a great deal of fanfare (never to be repeated for any of the subsequent attempts at overthrowing the regime). Qadhdhafi accused Defense Minister al-Hawwaz and Interior Minister Ahmad of being the major conspirators in the coup and absolved all civilians from any connection with the plot. He charged them with obstructing his reforms by attempting to prevent the nationalization of banks and the evacuation of the foreign bases and insinuated that they had received U.S. assistance.[47] The next day a constitutional proclamation was issued giving all powers to the Revolutionary Command Council and proclaiming it the supreme authority in the land.[48] On December 13, the Libyan-British evacuation agreement was signed in Tripoli, and from then on Qadhdhafi and the RCC became the sole leaders of the Libyan Arab Republic.

Whether a coup had really taken place or whether Qadhdhafi had simply rid himself of his troublesome colleagues and a large number of high-level army officers by fabricating the story is debatable.[49] The fact remains that Egypt took Qadhdhafi's side in the showdown to ensure his success.[50] According to diplomatic sources in Libya, 8,000 Egyptian troops were sent to Libya at Qadhdhafi's request at the time of the alleged coup. At the Arab summit in Rabat in late December 1969, King Hasan of Morocco reportedly asked Nasir about those troops, and Nasir admitted that there were some Egyptian military experts in Libya who were training the army but that they did not number 8,000. The Algerian and Tunisian delegations, however, verified the report on the number of troops as correct.[51]

To consolidate his own power and that of the RCC at the expense of his more moderate colleagues, Qadhdhafi needed Egyptian assistance.[52] Sadat, when reminiscing about the early days of the Libyan revolution, said in an interview that the first thing Qadhdhafi had asked Nasir was that he send Egyptian troops to protect Qadhdhafi and his revolution. Nasir obliged by sending special commando and parachute forces as well as trainers for the Libyan military.[53] In January 1970, diplomats reported that there were "up to 2,000 uniformed Egyptian soldiers in garrisons in Tripoli and Benghazi."[54]

## The Tripoli Charter

This timely assistance was necessary to help consolidate the power of the more radical wing of the new Libyan leadership. In return Qadhdhafi had to sign the Tripartite Agreement of December 1969, which was sought by Egypt (and Sudan), not by Libya as has generally been believed. According to Sadat:

> It was natural that, despite the presence of Egyptian forces in Libya at Egypt's expense in order to protect the Libyan regime, we should proceed to discuss unity prior to completing it. A series of meetings was held among Egypt, Libya and Sudan. These meetings continued and completed the Tripoli Charter, which 'Abd an-Nasir proclaimed.[55]

After the 1967 war, Egypt tried to rebuild its army and reconstruct its alliances on a new level. Egypt needed strategic depth for a possible second round of fighting with Israel. Consequently, Egypt had to have some control over the two adjacent countries on its borders, Sudan and Libya, so that Egyptian troops and military equipment could be moved more easily. In early 1970, after the Tripartite Agreement was signed, Egypt relocated its military staff colleges to Sudan and Libya, moved air cadets to the Wheelus air base, and moved military cadets to Jabal Awliya' in Sudan.[56]

Qadhdhafi resisted entering into this agreement until the eve of the Arab summit in late December 1969. At that time he was interviewed by the Lebanese daily *Al-Nahar* on whether Libya would join in a tripartite agreement with Egypt and Sudan, and he denied it, saying, "We believe in comprehensive Arab unity only. . . . We will not join little blocs."[57] Even during the Arab summit conference on December 23, 1969, Qadhdhafi reportedly was unwilling to give in to Egyptian demands. The conference began falling apart when Nasir, Yasir 'Arafat, and 'Abd al-Khaliq Hassuna (the secretary-general of the Arab League) walked out of the meetings in response to the refusal of some of the major oil-producing countries to increase substantially their financial aid to Egypt and Jordan beyond the levels decided upon in the Khartoum conference in 1967. Among the most reluctant was Libya, which was willing to increase its share by only £10 million.[58] Two days later, however, after further consultations with Nasir, Qadhdhafi offered £20 million for special arms contracts and promised to give equipment and weapons to the confrontation states (meaning Egypt and Jordan).[59]

Numayri, Nasir, and Qadhdhafi then flew to Tripoli on December 25, 1969, and two days later announced the signing of the Tripoli Charter. This was an agreement among Egypt, Libya, and Sudan to create a series of ministerial commissions to coordinate activities in a number of fields, including foreign policy, military strategy, communications, education, transport, industry, and agriculture.[60] There was, however, no mention of unity of any kind among the three countries.

When Nasir visited Sudan on January 1, 1970, Sudan's Day of Independence, he made a long speech in which he spoke of unity: "Brothers, the unity of the Sudanese, Libyan and the Egyptian revolutions, and the agreement concluded in Tripoli, are only a step along the path of joint struggle and joint action."[61]

But Ja'far al-Numayri in his speech on that occasion talked only of coordinating the capabilities of the three countries after "harmonizing their political intentions," and concluded by assuring Nasir that the Sudanese military and civilians would stand by Egypt in the Arab struggle.[62] By January 13, Numayri was beginning to sound like Nasir and was referring to the Tripoli Charter as the beginning of the "amalgamation process of forming one organized state to serve as a model for comprehensive Arab unity."[63]

Qadhdhafi did not mention the issue of the Tripoli Charter in any of his speeches during that period.[64] A perusal of the Arab press in those early months after the coup reveals that Egypt was advocating unity and cooperation among the three countries while Libya appeared less than enthusiastic.

The Tripoli Charter permitted Egypt to tighten its hold over Libya. The Egyptian Ministry of Agriculture and Agrarian Reform sent technicians to advise and train Libyans on how to implement the Agrarian Reform Law; aviation agreements were signed with Egypt and Sudan to set up a unified Arab aviation;[65] the Egyptian minister of public works and communications sent experts to Libya. and an agreement was reached to train Libyans in Egypt in the field of communications; Egyptian technicians started to run the radio and the television; and there were Egyptian security police officers in Tripoli and Benghazi.[66] Libyans felt overwhelmed by Egyptians, and in January 1970, posters began to appear on the walls of Tripoli carrying the slogan "Welcome Egyptian Conquerors."[67]

The process was temporarily halted, however, on April 7, 1970, by a French warning that directly threatened Egypt's interests in Libya. Foreign Minister Maurice Schumann said that France would stop delivery of the Mirages if Libya and Egypt merged into one state or if they "set up a unified military command."[68]

After the French warning, Egypt shifted gears to show that the Tripoli Charter was primarily an economic agreement. On April 20, 1970, the three countries announced in Cairo the conclusion of an alliance to integrate their economies and permit freedom of transit and transport among the three countries; freedom of entry, work, and residence for each other's citizens; and the end of import custom fees.[69] When Nasir, Qadhdhafi, and Numayri attended the tripartite summit in Khartoum a month later to celebrate the first anniversary of the Sudanese "revolution," Nasir was cautious about discussing any form of unity with Sudan and Libya. He evaded the issue by saying that the three leaders "had agreed not to take any step before having it discussed among the people in each of the three countries."[70]

Finally, on the first anniversary of the Libyan coup, Qadhdhafi made a speech in which he spoke of Arab unity in general, rejected the old methods of making treaties and agreements, and again made no specific mention of Egypt and Sudan.[71] On September 4 in Benghazi, he appeared to answer critics by saying that Libya was giving only limited financial aid to a number of countries including Sudan, but he gave no figures for Egypt.[72] A year after the coup, Qadhdhafi was still being cautious about discussing Libya's relation to Egypt and was still very much on the defensive concerning financial assistance to Egypt.

The second half of 1970 was marked by domestic turmoil in Libya, the battle with the oil companies, nationalizations and Libyanization of foreign companies and the property of Italian residents, another coup attempt against Qadhdhafi, and his first major tour of the Arab east to sell a plan to form a unified front against Israel. Relations among Egypt, Libya, and Sudan cooled, as each dealt with major domestic and foreign crises and paid less attention to its relations to the others. With the death of Nasir on September 28, 1970, a new era in Libya's relations with Egypt began.

### Libya's Relations to the Maghrib and Chad

The Libyan coup changed the political scene in the Maghrib. The close ties Libya developed with Sudan and Egypt alarmed the leaders of Algeria, Morocco, and Tunisia. Algeria took ten days to recognize the new regime across its border,[73] even though on September 2, 1969, it had issued a statement that the change in government would "not affect the age-long links that unite Libya and Algeria, brother countries and neighbors."[74] Tunisia also responded cautiously, noting on September 2 the change in government and issuing a statement that Tunisia "believes that recent events are of a domestic nature and do not affect diplomatic relations, fraternal cooperation . . . between the two countries."[75] Tunisia waited until September 6, 1969, when it was officially notified of the military takeover, to recognize the new regime. There were no congratulations. Morocco was also reserved toward the Libyan coup, which had overthrown the only other monarchy in North Africa.

### Bloc Formation in the Maghrib

The fear of an Egyptian-dominated bloc on the eastern flank of the Maghrib was perceived as a grave threat to the three North African nations. Their first step was to close ranks and form a bloc themselves. This was demonstrated by the dramatic improvement in relations among Algeria, Morocco, Tunisia, and Mauritania that took place the first year after the coup. Until 1969, Morocco had refused to recognize Mauritania as a sovereign and independent state (although the latter had become independent from France as early as 1960). As a result of the active diplomacy of the Algerians and the Tunisians, however, Morocco recognized Mauritania at the Islamic summit in Rabat at the end of September 1969.[76] A treaty of fraternity, friendship, and good neighborliness was signed on June 8, 1970, in Rabat by King Hasan of Morocco and President Mokhtar Ould Daddah of Mauritania.

A twenty-year treaty of good neighborliness, brotherhood, and cooperation was signed between Algeria and Tunisia on January 6, 1970, as was an agreement and protocol on the Tunisian-Algerian borders, which had been a source of conflict between the two nations for a number of years.[77] It was the Libyan coup in September 1969 that finally convinced Bourguiba of the necessity of concluding a treaty with Algeria.[78]

Although a Moroccan-Algerian treaty of solidarity and cooperation had already been signed in January 1969 at Ifrane, another, more important agreement to put an end to border disputes between these two countries was announced in Tlemcen on May 27, 1970.[79] Both states also agreed to set up a joint Moroccan-Algerian company to mine the iron ore 100 miles southeast of the contested area of Tindouf.[80]

The second step in the Maghribi strategy vis-à-vis Libya was to woo it away from Egypt and back into the Maghribi fold. This step started with an announcement that a Maghrib economic conference would be held in March 1970 to discuss the coordination of the Maghribi economies with the aim of eventually creating Maghribi unity.[81] Libya appeared hesitant to attend the conference, and in response the Tunisian foreign minister, Habib Bourguiba Jr., challenged Libya in a February 1970 speech delivered in Muntasir, Tunisia, accusing Libya of having reservations about joining the Maghrib; "The Libyan Government has not yet declared itself in favor of unity, without reservation, of the great Arab Maghrib."[82] It was the first time that such an accusation was made publicly, although Tunisians were already aware of the reservations Libya had "always manifested regarding the building of a Maghribian whole."[83]

Eventually, the members of the sixth conference of the ministers of economic affairs of Tunisia, Algeria, and Morocco met in Rabat on March 9, 1970. Although Libya had agreed to participate in the meeting,[84] its minister of economic affairs failed to show up. A last minute excuse was given that for "technical reasons" Libya would not be able to attend the meeting.

The reaction of the three countries was one of disappointment but not of surprise. Bourguiba Jr. said that Tunisia had been trying to convince the Libyans "of the similar destiny that unites the four Maghrib countries"[85] but to no avail. Eventually, the decision was made to postpone the meeting until Libya was able to attend. This decision was taken under Algerian pressure, even though the Tunisians and Moroccans wanted to proceed with the meeting despite Libya's absence.[86]

Although not much evidence substantiates the assertion that Egyptian pressure prompted Libya to change its mind about attending the meeting in Rabat, this remains a plausible explanation. Egypt certainly had no intention of allowing Libya to join the Maghribi bloc. In fact, on the very day that Libya agreed to attend the Maghribi economic conference, an Egyptian and a Sudanese delegation arrived in Tripoli headed by some of the highest military officers in those two countries' respective governments, including Egypt's war minister, Lieutenant General Muhammad Fawzi, and Sudan's defense minister, Major General Khalid Hasan 'Abbas.[87] The Rabat press immediately connected Libya's subsequent withdrawal from the Maghribi conference to the arrival of those two delegations.[88]

By the end of April 1970, it was becoming apparent that Libya, despite common interests with Algeria, was not going to join any form of greater Maghrib union.[89] The official Tunis daily, *L'Action*, wrote that Libya was obviously not prepared to recognize a Maghrib, or for that matter a Mashriq, and that Tunisia, Algeria, and Morocco had waited long enough and should now "go ahead and sign a treaty setting up a Maghreb economic community."[90] Clearly, this round in the tug-of-war between Egypt and the three Maghribi countries over Libya had been won by the Egyptian-Sudanese bloc, and Libya was not at liberty to join any Maghribi plan without Egypt's approval.

## Development of Bilateral Relations with Maghribi States

Another strategy the countries of the Maghrib took was to develop bilateral relations with Libya to ensure some control over the policies of that country toward them. Because of Algeria's common borders with Libya, it was more interested than Morocco in developing bilateral ties to counteract Egypt's influence in the region.

In early December 1969, the Algerian foreign minister, 'Abd al-'Aziz Bouteflika, visited Libya. During that visit, a number of bilateral cooperation agreements were signed between the two nations covering agricultural research, technology, administration, tourism, and information; the formation of a joint commission for economic, technical, cultural, and scientific cooperation;[91] and the setting up of a joint oil company that would prospect, produce, market, and transport oil.[92] Plans were made to create a joint commission to study the possibility of Algerian-Libyan cooperation in trade, air transport and communications, and postal service.[93]

Libya had its own reasons for signing these bilateral agreements. The country needed an alternative to the all-powerful and all-encompassing Egyptian influence on every sector of the Libyan political, military, economic, and cultural systems. Libya also needed Algeria as an ally in its battle against the large U.S. and European oil companies in the country.

Starting in April 1970, serious negotiations began with the major oil companies over a reduction in production, an increase in prices, and control of the companies' operations in Libya.[94] With expert advice, the Libyans managed to call the oil companies' bluffs and to threaten them with nationalization if they did not agree to Libya's terms. To pursue those negotiations Libya needed the support of other oil-producing countries, and Algeria, which was engaged in similar negotiations with the oil companies, was the most natural ally. On April 9, 1970, both countries announced the establishment of a joint oil organization "which will present a united front in the face of foreign trusts and monopolies." Both states also sought the support of Organization of Petroleum Exporting Countries (OPEC) members, but only Iraq joined them.[95] This closing of ranks proved successful and started the process of raising oil prices in the region that was to culminate in the mid-1970s with tremendous profits not only for Algeria and Libya but for all the other OPEC countries as well.

Tunisia also began to develop bilateral ties with Libya, but rather more cautiously than Algeria. Libya's ties to Egypt, and to a lesser degree to Algeria, isolated Tunisia politically. Consequently, it sought greater French protection as well as a more unified Maghrib in which Morocco could counterbalance Libya's and Algeria's influence in the region.

Relations between Libya and Tunisia were cool after the coup. On his return from France on June 8, 1970, after a long illness, Bourguiba spoke of a "feeling of hostility"[96] between the two countries. But by mid-June, relations between the two countries had improved to the point where they had decided to set up a joint committee "to settle certain outstanding questions, look in the question of entry visas and exchange cultural programmes."[97]

A delegation headed by Tunisia's foreign minister, Muhammad Masmudi, arrived in Libya on August 11, 1970, for a six-day visit. At the end of it, Masmudi and his Libyan counterpart, Salih Buwaysir, signed an agreement on economic, technical, and cultural cooperation.[98] The two sides also agreed to revive and reactivate other bilateral agreements that had been reached under the previous Libyan regime.

Morocco kept a distance from the Libyan revolution. It hosted the Islamic summit in September 1969, the Arab summit in December 1969, and the Maghribi economic conference in March 1970 and invited Libya to participate in all of them. But there were no other major attempts at developing bilateral relations between the two countries. In June 1970, Morocco's foreign minister, 'Abd al-Hadi Boutalib, visited Libya on the occasion of Libya's Evacuation Day celebrations and made a general statement to the Libyan daily *Al-Thawra* that Morocco believed "in Maghreb unity 'but in stages,' " thus presumably leaving the door open for Libya to join in Maghribi affairs at a later date.[99]

Thus, during the first year after the coup, Qadhdhafi had turned down offers to unite with other states in North Africa. Libya's alliance with Egypt and Sudan was sufficient to meet its security needs and to achieve its core objectives. Feeling secure regionally, Libya did not actively seek to merge or unite with its neighbors.

### The Chadian Equation

Libya's relationship to Chad was more complex. The French had made the withdrawal of Libya's support for the Chadian insurgents a condition for the sale of the Mirages. The first Libyan public reaction to this condition came in December 1969, when Libya denied assisting the Muslim rebels in Chad. But the Libyan government admitted that Chadian refugees fleeing from the zones of conflict in that country were entering the southern part of Fezzan. Salih Buwaysir, the Libyan minister for unity and foreign affairs, added that Libya had tried to mediate between the warring factions in Chad.[100] A month later, however, Libya changed its tone and was demanding the ouster of Israeli experts working in Chad as a condition for "improving their relations with the neighboring state of Chad,"[101] presumably meaning it would stop supporting the Chadian rebels.

Libyan policy toward Chad, despite France's assertion of a deal with Qadhdhafi, remained ambiguous for months. This ambiguity consisted "in tolerating within certain limits the activities of the people of the FROLINAT [Front pour la Liberation Nationale du Tchad] while being aware that France tolerates this tolerance."[102] In fact, Libyan support for the rebels was very limited in 1969–1970, as the French themselves admitted.[103] Enough French pressure, however, must have been exerted for an alleged 2,000 Chadians to be expelled from Libya in early July 1970, with no reason given.[104]

France thus inadvertently introduced the Chadian issue in Libyan-Western relations by making arms sales conditional on the withdrawal of the very limited Libyan support for Chadian rebels. Qadhdhafi realized that Chad was important to the West and subsequently used the Chad issue to bargain with the West.

## Notes

1. Cairo, Middle East News Agency (MENA), 2 September 1969, in Foreign Broadcast Information Service Daily Report: Middle East and Africa, Washington, D.C. (hereafter FBIS-MEA), 3 September 69, T5.

2. Ibid., T1. MENA reported that Col. Sa'ad al-Din Abu Shuwayrib was the chairman of the Revolutionary Command Council. Cairo, MENA, 4 September 1969, in FBIS-MEA, 4 September 69, T1. This statement was denied a few hours later with the correction that he was only chief of staff of the Libyan Army, not the chairman of the RCC. Ibid., T2.

3. Ibid., T1.

4. Ruth First claims that "Colonel Abu Shweirib was no longer in the army and had not even been in Libya when his name was announced. Who chose him as the straw man of the coup? . . . For a few brief days he was cast in the role of Libya's Neguib, until its Nasser came forward and announced himself" (p. 112). Although she is not the only one to ask questions about Abu Shuwayrib, it is unlikely that he was cast in any role at all. He probably belonged to the more moderate group of leaders in the postcoup period. On 5 November Abu Shuwayrib was reported to have been appointed ambassador to Cairo. Tripoli, Libyan News Agency (LNA), 5 November 1969, in FBIS-MEA, 6 November 69, T2.

5. Cairo, MENA, 4 September 1969, in FBIS-MEA, 4 September 69, T1.

6. Ibid., T3.

7. Al-Tali'a, Cairo, 9 September 1969; see also *The Libyan Revolution: A Sourcebook of Legal and Historical Documents: Vol. 1 September 1969–30 August 1970*, Meredith O. Ansell and Ibrahim Massaud al-Arif, eds. Oleander Press, Harrow, England, 1972, p. 62.

8. Cairo, MENA, 13 September 1969, in FBIS-MEA, 15 September 69, T2.

9. Ibid., T3.

10. Ibid.

11. Cairo, MENA, 18 September 1969, in FBIS-MEA, 19 September 69, T2.

12. Bayda Domestic Service, 16 September 1969, in FBIS-MEA, 17 September 69, T1.

13. Ansell and Arif, pp. 63–69.

14. Paris, AFP, 18 September 1969, in FBIS-MEA, 19 September 69, T5.

15. Bayda Domestic Service, 21 September 1969, in FBIS-MEA, 22 September 69, T5.

16. Bayda Domestic Service, 24 September 1969, in FBIS-MEA, 24 September 69, T1.

17. Cairo, MENA, 11 October 1969, in FBIS-MEA, 13 October 69, T3, T4.

18. Bayda Domestic Service, 16 October 1969, in FBIS-MEA, 17 October 69, T2.

19. Cairo, MENA, 29 November 1969, in FBIS-MEA, 2 December 69, T3.

20. Message from Qadhdhafi quoted in Sadat's memoirs, *October*, Cairo, 5 June 77, pp. 14–17, in FBIS-MEA, 10 June 77, D5.

21. Sadat in his memoirs talks of the Egyptian forces that were sent to Libya to protect the regime at that time; twenty-third installment of Sadat's memoirs published in *October*, 17 April 77, pp. 9–11, in FBIS-MEA, 27 April 77, D7.

22. Cairo, MENA, 11 October 1969, in FBIS-MEA, 13 October 69, T4.

23. *Arab Report and Record*, No. 3, 1–14 February 1970, p. 93.

24. *New York Times*, 23 January 1970; see also *Facts on File*, Vol. 30, 1970, p. 31.

25. *Le Monde*, Paris, 23 January 1970, p. 1.

26. Wright, *Libya: A Modern History*, quotes Heikal delivering a message to Qadhdhafi about the importance of the Mirages for the Arabs, p. 145.

27. First, fn. 9, p. 265.

28. *Le Monde*, Paris, 23 January 1970, p. 4.

29. *Le Monde*, Paris, 24 January 1970, p. 2.

30. I. William Zartman, "Arms Imports—The Libyan Experience," *World Military Expenditures and Arms Transfers 1971–1980*, Washington, D.C., U.S. Arms Control and Disarmament Agency, 1983, p. 15.

31. *Le Monde*, Paris, 23 January 1970, p. 4. This support antedated Qadhdhafi— King Idris also backed the insurgents.

32. *New York Times*, 19 December 1969, p. 5.

33. Ibid.

34. *Le Monde*, Paris, 23 January 1970, p. 1; see also Wright, *Libya: A Modern History*, for France's interests in the arms deal, p. 145.

35. Cairo, MENA, 7 November 1969, in FBIS-MEA, 7 November 69, T2.

36. *Al-Thawra*, 4 November 1969, in FBIS-MEA, 4 November 69, T3.

37. First, fn. 6, p. 265.

38. Ibid., p. 115.

39. See, for instance, Ruth First's description of the various plots, p. 106.

40. Bayda Domestic Service, 3 September 1969, FBIS-MEA, 4 September 69, T4.

41. The civilian members of the January 1970 Cabinet were Salih Buwaysir, minister of unity and foreign affairs; Muhammad al-Jadi, minister of justice; and Dr. Muftah Usta 'Umar, minister of health; all three stayed on from the

first cabinet of September 1969. The new civilian members were Dr. 'Umar al-Hadi Ramadan, minister of communications and public works; Dr. Jum'a Shariha, minister of agriculture; 'Izz al-Din al-Mabruk, minister of petroleum and minerals; 'Abd al-'Ati al-'Ubaidi, minister of labor and social affairs; and Muhammad Hilal Rabi', minister of the treasury. *The Official Gazette,* Tripoli, 16 January 1970.

42. Proceedings of the 8 May 1970, session of the Libyan Intellectual Seminar, in Ansell and Arif, p. 279.

43. Proceedings of the 10 May 1970, Session of the Libyan Intellectual Seminar, in ibid., p. 288.

44. Ibid.

45. Ibid., pp. 288–289.

46. Ibid.

47. Bayda Domestic Service, 10 December 1969, in FBIS-MEA, 11 December 69, T1–T3.

48. Bayda Domestic Service, 11 December 1969, in FBIS-MEA, 12 December 69, T1–T4.

49. Many of the accusations that were made against these two men by Qadhdhafi were palpably false. For instance, he said that Musa Ahmad did not participate in the coup of September 1969, Cairo, MENA, 13 December 1969, in FBIS-MEA, n.d., T1. Yet Ruth First writes about Musa Ahmad, "For it was Musa Ahmad who immobilized the headquarters of the Cyrenaica Defence Force—the first ring of defense round the King and his regime—and without this action the coup had absolutely no hope of success" (p. 108). Qadhdhafi himself admitted on 9 September 1969, that he had cooperated with Musa Ahmad "in seizing the armoured cars of the public security forces in the eastern provinces," Cairo, MENA, 9 September 1969, in FBIS-MEA, 9 September 69, T6.

50. Egyptian journalist Abu al-Majd in his reminiscences of the early days of the Libyan coup says that many Libyans complained that Egypt had taken Qadhdhafi's side against Ahmad al-Hawwaz. Sabri Abu al-Majd, *Bayn Misr wa Libya, Da'iman 'Ilaqat Qawiya Azliya Muzdahara,* n.p., n.d., p. 72.

51. *Al-Hayat,* Beirut, 15 January 1970, in FBIS-MEA, 20 January 70, T4.

52. Abu al-Majd, p. 74.

53. Ibid.

54. *Arab Report and Record,* No. 2, 16–31 January 1970, p. 66.

55. Sadat's memoirs, twenty-third installment, in *October,* D7.

56. See Peter K. Bechtold's chronology in "New Attempts at Arab Cooperation: The Federation of Arab Republics, 1971–?" in *Middle East Journal,* Vol. 27, No. 2, Spring 1973, p. 154.

57. 'Alya al-Solh, "Al-Qadhdhafi Lacks 'Faith' in Western Powers," *Al-Nahar,* Beirut, 19 December 1969, in FBIS-MEA, 23 December 69, T2.

58. Paris, AFP, 23 December 1969, in FBIS-MEA, 24 December 69, A2.

59. Cairo, MENA, 25 December 1969, in FBIS-MEA, 29 December 69, A9.

60. KCA, Vol. 17, 31 January–7 February 1970, p. 23808; *Facts on File,* Vol. 29, No. 1522, 25–31 December 1969, p. 833.

61. Nasir's speech in Khartoum, 1 January 1970, in *Al-Watha'iq al-'Arabiya*, American University of Beirut, Beirut, n.d., p. 6.

62. Numayri's speech in Khartoum, 1 January 1969, in ibid., pp. 11–12.

63. Cairo, MENA, 13 January 1970, in FBIS-MEA, 14 January 70, T3.

64. Abu al-Majd, p. 73.

65. *Arab Report and Record*, No. 4, 15–28 February 1970, p. 121.

66. *Arab Report and Record*, No. 2, 16–31 January 1970, p. 66.

67. Ibid.

68. *Arab Report and Record*, No. 7, 1–15 April 1970, p. 210.

69. *Facts on File*, May 1–14, 1970, Vol. 30, 1970, p. 305.

70. *Arab Report and Record*, No. 10, 16–31 May 1970, p. 304.

71. *Arab Report and Record*, No. 17, 1–15 September 1970, p. 497.

72. Ibid.

73. Bayda Domestic Service, 10 September 1969, in FBIS-MEA, 10 September 69, T1.

74. Paris, AFP, 2 September 1969, in FBIS-MEA, 4 September 69, T6.

75. Tunisia, TAP, 2 September 1969, in FBIS-MEA, 4 September 69, T9. Parts of this section on Libyan-Maghribi relations have appeared in Mary-Jane Deeb, "Inter-Maghribi Relations Since 1969: A Study of the Modalities of Unions and Mergers," *Middle East Journal*, Winter 1989, Vol. 43, No. 1, pp. 23–24.

76. Grimaud, p. 206; see also John Damis's discussion of Moroccan-Mauritanian relations in *Conflict in Northwest Africa: The Western Sahara Dispute*, Hoover Institution Press, Stanford, 1983, p. 29–34; and idem., "Mauritania and the Sahara," *Middle East International*, No. 71, May 1977, pp. 17–19.

77. See the study on the Algerian-Tunisian border issue by Ahmed Ben Salem, "L'Affaire de la Borne 233 et le Droit International Public," unpublished dissertation for the Diplome d'Etudes Superieures en Droit Public, School of Law, Political Science and Economics, University of Tunis, Tunisia, 1971–1972.

78. Grimaud, p. 202.

79. *Arab Report and Record*, No. 10, 16–31 May 1970, p. 289.

80. Ibid.

81. Paris, AFP, 5 March 1970, in FBIS-MEA, 6 March 70, T3.

82. Paris, AFP, 22 February 1970, in FBIS-MEA, 25 February 70, T6.

83. Ibid.

84. Paris, AFP, 9 March 1970, in FBIS-MEA, 10 March 70, T4.

85. Ibid.

86. Rabat, *Al-'Alam*, 11 March 1970, in FBIS-MEA, 12 March 70, S2.

87. Paris, AFP, 5 March 1970, in FBIS-MEA, 6 March 70, T3.

88. *Arab Report and Record*, No. 5, 1–15 March 1970, pp. 149–150.

89. In an interview with Bahi Ladgham, who was prime minister that year, he said that at one of the early congresses in Morocco, he had approached Qadhdhafi on the subject of Maghribi unity. The Libyan leader had rejected the idea outright, calling it "Anglo-Saxon politics—the idea of the Fertile Crescent." Interview with Bahi Ladgham, Carthage, 20 June 1986.

90. *L'Action*, Tunis, 25 April 1970, in *Arab Report and Record*, No. 8, 16–30 April 1970, p. 250.

91. Bayda Domestic Service, 9 December 1969, in FBIS-MEA, 10 December 69, T1.

92. *Arab Report and Record*, No. 23, 1–15 December 1969, p. 505.

93. Ibid.

94. *Arab Report and Record*, No. 8, 16–30 April 1970, p. 243.

95. Wright, *Libya: A Modern History*, pp. 235–240.

96. *Arab Report and Record*, No. 15, 1–15 August 1970, p. 4452.

97. *Arab Report and Record*, No. 12, 16–30 June 1970, p. 359.

98. *Arab Report and Record*, No. 16, 16–31 August 1970, p. 474.

99. *Arab Report and Record*, No. 12, 16–30 June 1970, p. 360.

100. Tripoli, LNA, 16 December 1969, in FBIS-MEA, 17 December 69, T4.

101. Jerusalem Domestic Service, 11 January 1970, in FBIS-MEA, 13 January 70, T2.

102. *L'Express*, Paris, 16–22 March 1970, pp. 22–24, in FBIS-MEA, 30 March 70, V1.

103. *Le Monde*, 23 January 1969, p. 1.

104. Fort Lamy Radio, 7 July 1970, *Arab Report and Record*, No. 13, 1–15 July 1970, p. 387.

# 4

# Unions, Federations, and
# Mergers, 1970–1973

When a new regime in a small Third World nation takes power by means of a coup, it faces certain major challenges. To guard against countercoups, the regime must establish legitimacy and credibility on a basis other than the mere monopoly of force; and to deter external intervention, the regime must gain swift recognition by the regional system of states to which it belongs.

A radical regime may attempt to establish legitimacy at the start by adopting a vociferously nationalist domestic policy, which is then translated into antiforeign actions involving the nationalization of foreign property and the expulsion of nonnationals. These actions, in turn, may weaken the new regime by depriving its administration and the country's economy of skilled personnel and the state of the protection of one or more foreign powers.

Once Qadhdhafi had begun to nationalize the property of non-Libyans, evacuate the U.S. and British bases, and take over a greater share of the oil profits of the Western companies, he brought upon himself and his regime the ire of Libya's erstwhile protectors. He therefore had to secure and retain the protection of Egypt during this period, as well as the recognition and support of the other North African states.

### Alliances and Bloc Formation:
### The Federation of Arab Republics

Between the death of Nasir in September 1970 and the Arab-Israeli War of October 1973, a number of attempts at unions and mergers took place. Those attempts, however, did not all originate with Libya and must be understood in their regional context.

Between 1969 and early 1972, it was Egypt that pursued the idea of setting up unions and federations with Libya. Qadhdhafi, although intent on retaining Egypt's support and protection, was ambivalent about such unions as they threatened to undermine his domestic legitimacy.

By 1972, however, the situation had been reversed. Sadat began losing interest in Libya when he found alternative sources of military and financial aid in the Arab Gulf states, while Qadhdhafi, fearing the loss of Egypt's protection, actively sought a merger with Egypt. Domestic discontent had become less threatening to the Libyan regime than regional isolation, given that Qadhdhafi had effectively consolidated his power by 1972.

After Nasir's death the leaders of the Tripoli Charter member states (Libya, Egypt, and Sudan) met in Cairo between November 4 and 8, 1970, to confirm their alliance and to assure the Arab world that the Egyptian-Libyan-Sudanese bloc was still powerful, despite the death of its leader. They issued a communiqué announcing the formation of a unified national security council, a higher planning committee, and a number of subcommittees on economic, political, and cultural affairs.[1] Libya was assigned the task of coordinating the domestic and foreign policies of the three states, Egypt was entrusted with coordinating their economic policies, and Sudan was left in charge of the information sector.

In November 1970 a coup d'état took place in Syria, led by Hafiz al-Asad, who immediately declared his intention to join the Tripoli Charter states. The inclusion of Syria infused new blood in that Arab bloc, strengthening it well beyond the formation of committees and commissions. From January to March 1971 the Tripoli Charter members reached a number of economic agreements concerning free trade among them, exemption from customs for exchanged commodities, and assistance in projects including land reclamation, road building, housing, and development of port facilities.[2]

Each state had different reasons for joining this bloc. President Sadat needed a strong supportive bloc in the Arab world to face Israel and to demonstrate Egypt's power despite its defeat and the loss of Nasir. Asad needed the legitimacy that joining such a bloc would give him. Qadhdhafi continued to need Egypt's protection for possible countercoup attempts and/or potential external interference. Numayri, however, had no such reasons. In fact, there was little domestic support for Sudan's continued inclusion in the charter. And so on April 14, 1971, he announced that Sudan would no longer be an active member of the Tripoli Charter. Three days later, at a tripartite summit meeting in Benghazi, Qadhdhafi, Sadat, and Asad announced the establishment of the Federation of Arab Republics (FAR).[3]

Unlike the Tripoli Charter, the FAR established a political union at the outset. The federation's constitution stated that the union of the

Arab republics had one flag, one capital, and one socialist, democratic political system[4] (the constitution also raised the issue of a single nationality for the citizens of the three states). The constitution no longer spoke of coordinating foreign policies but of unifying them and entrusted the process of decisionmaking on such issues as waging war, making peace, or signing treaties and accords with foreign states and international organizations solely to the federation.[5]

## Determinants of Regional Alliances

Most writers on Libya have not understood that country's involvement in the Tripoli Charter and the FAR. The reason for this lack may be that most writers analyzing the early years of the Qadhdhafi regime have relied heavily on two major sources of information: the Egyptian press, particularly articles by Heikal, the editor in chief of the semiofficial daily *Al-Ahram*, and Ruth First's work *Libya: The Elusive Revolution*. Excerpts of Heikal's articles appeared in the Western press, such as *Le Monde*, and were then used as primary sources. But Heikal was Nasir's spokesperson. A politically motivated and ambitious man, he may have been the main architect of the Sudanese-Egyptian-Libyan axis (the Tripoli Charter),[6] and he "discovered" Qadhdhafi. Heikal was an image builder and more than anyone else was responsible for the early image of Qadhdhafi as the young, heroic, idealistic revolutionary leader following in Nasir's footsteps and pursuing single-mindedly the goal of Arab unity.[7] To take his statements at face value would therefore be misleading.

When Ruth First in her otherwise excellent work on the Libyan coup explained the Tripoli Charter and the FAR as attempts at unity initiated by Qadhdhafi for ideological reasons, other writers followed unquestioningly in her footsteps. She thus became the second major source of this misinterpretation. For example, she writes that "shortly after the Tripoli Charter was signed, the Libyan army leaders began to press for full constitutional unity of the three states. Nasir still bruised by the collapse of the Egyptian-Syrian union made clear his reservations."[8] In fact, the opposite was true. Nasir wanted nothing better than to reestablish the Egyptian-Syrian union. He needed those alliances more than ever after his defeat in 1967. Sadat writes about Nasir's attitude toward Syria in the aftermath of the signing of the Tripoli Charter:

> He had a weak spot for Syria. After the break between Syria and Egypt (1961) 'Abd an-Nasir's heart and pride both were wounded. Therefore when he saw signs of new unity between Egypt and Syria [December 1969] he was happy—'Abd an-Nasir told me when he returned to Egypt

that he had prepared a telegram to this effect and that he had decided to go from Libya to Damascus in order to declare unity from there.[9]

In fact, Heikal himself, who claimed that Qadhdhafi had wanted union with Egypt since the early days of 1969,[10] admitted that both the Tripoli Charter and the FAR were Nasir's ideas:

> President Nimeiry came to Libya with Nasser, and the three Presidents signed what was called the "Tripoli Pact" [the Tripoli Charter of December 1969]. . . . This represented one half of the military equation which Nasser had been trying to work out for the past two years: how to weigh up the rival advantages of an active second front and of greater depth. Libya and Sudan offered Egypt depth; a federation would consolidate this.[11]

This concept remained an integral part of Egyptian foreign policy throughout Sadat's first year in power. After Nasir's death, Sadat and his powerful foreign minister, Isma'il Fahmi, pursued this policy. In his memoirs of the period, Fahmi explains Egypt's foreign policy during the pre-1973 war period: "We had to create a cohesive Arab military alliance based on Egypt east up to the Gulf, south deep into the Sudan, west into Libya and perhaps further. For this reason, we needed close military cooperation with our neighbors, and we had to play the leading role in these relationships."[12]

Thus, after the Libyan military coup Nasir had begun to implement his strategy with the Tripoli Charter, and Sadat had taken it a stage further to the Federation of Arab Republics, which represented the second half of the military equation of Nasir's strategy. With the FAR Sadat was combining the advantages of both: a second active front with the inclusion of Syria in the federation and greater depth with Libya. In fact, Sadat viewed the establishment of the FAR as another stage in the realization of the objectives of the Tripoli Charter and a continuation of Nasir's policies in the region: "The unity plan was prepared by Jamal 'Abd an-Nasir: he himself drafted it. . . . The basis of the plan provided for the establishment of the United Arab Republics."[13]

Despite all his Arab nationalist rhetoric, Qadhdhafi was very ambivalent about the federation at the outset, although he did support it strongly at a later date. Sadat appeared to doubt Qadhdhafi's unionist intentions. He described him as trying "to appear as though he was an extreme unionist."[14] According to Sadat, his vice-president, 'Ali Sabri, told him before the Benghazi meeting of April 1971 (where FAR was declared) that Qadhdhafi had not wanted unity but had been pressured by Sadat into accepting it.[15]

Furthermore, Qadhdhafi was not too pleased with the inclusion of Syria in the federation. He wanted a strategic alliance in which Egypt was primarily dependent on Libya for strategic depth, as well as military and economic aid, in return for which Egypt protected Libya's new regime and territorial integrity. Qadhdhafi saw Syria as a competitor that drew Egypt's attention away from Libya because of Syria's strategic importance in Egypt's confrontation with Israel.

Sadat's description of the negotiations among Egypt, Syria, Sudan, and Libya to set up the FAR captures these tensions:

> The need for unity between Egypt and Syria has been determined because it is a national and vital cause and necessary for the battle which was undoubtedly coming. President Numayri declared that he would support the battle with all he had and that Sudan represented a depth for the united countries or the Confederation of Arab Republics. At this point Qadhdhafi resorted to the policy of destroying everything and went on to attack unity between Egypt and Syria.[16]

For Qadhdhafi, therefore, the FAR did not represent a first step in the direction of greater Arab unity, as Ruth First and others have maintained. Had Arab unity been the primary consideration for Qadhdhafi, he would have welcomed the inclusion of Syria in the federation. Instead, he tried to keep Syria out, and when that failed, he began to pursue the idea of a merger with Egypt that would have excluded all other states. In other words, what was important to Qadhdhafi was a close alliance to Egypt, not a larger union of Arab states in which Libya would play an insignificant role.

Qadhdhafi, with no other major ally in the region and no Western protector, did not have much choice but to accept any type of alliance proposed by Nasir or Sadat. To antagonize Egypt at that point, when the regime was still weak, would have been political suicide. On the positive side, unity with Egypt gave Libya a formidable ally in the region and boosted the legitimacy of Qadhdhafi's regime on the international scene. Qadhdhafi made a point of this in a speech delivered the day after the FAR was announced. "It is a great honor for the Libyan Arab people that the unity charter was signed on their soil, that the agreement proclaiming the union of Arab republics and the referendum date of September 1 was reached on their soil. This strengthens the Libyan people."[17]

In fact, one of the major reasons Libya, Sudan, and later Syria entered into these alliances with Egypt and with each other in the first place was to strengthen their regimes domestically. In mid-July 1971 when an attempted coup against Numayri of Sudan took place, Libya and Egypt reacted immediately and came to his assistance. On July 22, 1971, Libya intercepted a British plane from London to Khartoum and forced it to land in Benghazi. The Sudanese coup leaders on board, Colonel 'Uthman Abu Bakr al-Nur and Major Faruq 'Uthman Hamdallah,[18] were eventually turned over to Numayri. This pivotal action robbed the Sudanese coup of its top leaders. Egypt also intervened militarily on the side of Numayri by using Egyptian officers posted in the military colleges in Jabal al-Awliya' in Sudan, where they had been sent the previous year as part of the Tripoli Charter agreements. It was reported that in assisting Numayri they drove the tanks and armored cars and were joined by pro-Numayri Sudanese officers, who eventually returned Numayri to power.[19]

President Sadat justified such external interference in the domestic affairs of Sudan by referring to the Tripoli Charter. Qadhdhafi was even more explicit about the role of the FAR in defending the national interest of each member state. At a public rally in August 1971, Qadhdhafi explained the Libyan role in defending Numayri: "Should an aggression be launched against Libya some day, Egypt and Syria would fight with you."[20] He added, "If there are domestic disturbances threatening the revolutionary regime in Egypt, Syria, Libya or Sudan, all states forming the Federation will participate in the defense of the revolutionary regime in any of these countries."[21] These words clearly indicated that the Tripoli Charter and the FAR had been understood by all concerned parties as ensuring the protection of their regimes and borders against external threats and domestic opposition.

Consequently, I disagree with those writers on Libya, who, like Ruth First, claim that "the Federation between the three had produced little more than a liaison of the superstructures of their governments, and a conscientious exchange of minutiae between their legal and administrative staffs."[22] These unionist agreements gave legitimacy to the new regimes of Libya, Sudan, and Syria after their coups; they prevented a countercoup attempt in Sudan from succeeding; they led to the establishment of mutually beneficial economic relations, especially between Libya and Egypt; they ensured the transfer of major financial aid and military hardware from Libya to Egypt; and they created a bloc that strengthened all concerned states on the regional level.

## The Demise of the FAR

Toward the end of 1971 the regional situation began to change as Sadat prepared Egypt for war with Israel. Having obtained what he needed from Libya, he now turned to the Arab east, primarily to the conservative states of Saudi Arabia and Kuwait. During the early months of 1972, Sadat sent envoys, including Lieutenant General Sa'ad al-Din al-Shadhili, the Egyptian chief of staff, to the Arab world to assess what resources could be mobilized on Egypt's behalf.[23] Even Iraq was tapped for assistance, and despite problems with the Kurds in the north and Iran in the south, Iraq managed to send a squadron of Hawker Hunters to Egypt.[24] Sadat's successful campaign for arms and funds in the Arab world made Egypt less dependent on Libya and consequently less interested in the federation with Libya.

The same situation was occurring on other fronts as well. After the 1971 military coup attempt in Sudan against Numayri, which had been spearheaded by leftist officers, Numayri began to purge the country of its communist party members as well as of those suspected of communist sympathies. Concomitantly, he began shifting his sympathies toward the United States and the conservative states of Saudi Arabia and Kuwait and away from socialism and, to some degree, from Libya.[25]

On the Maghribi side, new developments were taking place that did not involve Libya. Muhammad Masmudi, Tunisia's foreign minister, would claim in 1974 that when President Houari Boumediene of Algeria first visited Tunisia, he proposed that the two countries unite, but Tunisia refused.[26] That first visit occurred in April 1972, and the speeches given then by Boumediene and Bourguiba of Tunisia indicated that the offer had been made at that time.[27] Boumediene's speech, although general enough, did disclose Algeria's intentions:

> When the world is currently witnessing economic groupings and regional amalgamation, the sincere brotherhood which has united our two countries since the depths of history, and the bonds of blood, language, culture, religion and of common struggle which exist between our two peoples, beyond the links of kindred and alliance, the shared sacrifices and memories, have given an unusual importance to this meeting between two brothers whom everything unites and nothing divides.[28]

Boumediene also added, "We are only seeking to clear a new stage which could reinforce similar initiatives taken in the Arab east,"[29] probably referring to the FAR and the impending merger between Libya and Egypt.

Bourguiba's speech on that occasion was clearly a polite refusal of the proposal:

> Our good neighborliness and the rehabilitation of our relations which consolidate the fraternity of the Algerian and Tunisian peoples require us to establish cooperation leading to the economic progress and development of the two countries, while waiting until it is possible for us to embark

on the construction of the Great Maghreb, that is the progressive building
of an economic, cultural and maybe even political ensemble.

But we must also envisage this enterprise with clarity and patience.
Haste or utopia would doom our efforts to failure.[30]


During that period Algerian-Moroccan ties were also reinforced.
President Boumediene visited King Hasan of Morocco in the spring of
1972,[31] and both agreed to sign what became known as the Rabat
agreements, which settled the border issues between their two countries.
The agreements were signed at an OAU summit meeting on June 15,
1972.[32]

Between 1972 and 1974, Mauritania's links to the Maghrib were
strengthened further. Mauritania moved closer to Algeria and realigned
its foreign policy, withdrawing from defense treaties with France and
joining the Arab League.[33]

All these events isolated Libya from the rest of the Arab and the
North African worlds. Libya was no longer indispensable to Egypt,
which was finding other sources of arms and funds, and the Maghrib
was closing ranks and thinking of forming unions of its own. Even
Sudan, which Libya had assisted at a crucial time, was turning from
Libya for domestic reasons of its own.

Qadhdhafi perceived Libya's growing isolation as a threat because it
weakened the regime domestically and allowed opposition voices in exile
to point out that no Arab country was taking Libya's leaders seriously.
Isolated, Libya also became weaker regionally and internationally. It
lacked a protector, and consequently foreign powers could intervene
militarily or otherwise in Libya and perhaps even topple the regime.
Libya became weaker even in terms of its bargaining position vis-à-vis
the oil companies.

Qadhdhafi's foreign policy behavior in the face of the threat of isolation
during this phase would recur predictably throughout his tenure in
power. He sought to retain the protection of his major regional ally to
safeguard his regime and defend Libya's borders. Failing to do so, he
began searching for a minor regional ally to strengthen Libya's position
regionally and enhance his legitimacy domestically.


### New Attempts at Unity Between Egypt and Libya

Qadhdhafi pursued a relentless policy of greater rapprochement with
Egypt and called for a merger between the two states. In his memoirs
Sadat recalls how Qadhdhafi started a vast media campaign in the
summer of 1972 to mobilize the Libyan masses in support of a merger

with Egypt.[34] This time the idea of the merger was incontestably Qadhdhafi's, and he pushed it forth vigorously and impatiently.

The offer of a merger with Egypt had in fact been made as early as February 1972.[35] Egypt, however, had not responded favorably then for fear of a French embargo on the Mirages that had been promised Libya.[36] France had warned Libya that if it entered into any form of union with Egypt, the Mirages planes would not be sent.

When the offer of a merger with Egypt was made again on the twentieth anniversary of the Egyptian revolution, Sadat took it more seriously and flew to Benghazi to discuss it with Qadhdhafi.[37] The temporary change in Sadat's attitude may be attributed to one major event that took place in Egypt: the expulsion of the 15,000 Soviet military advisers and experts on July 17, 1972.[38]

The reasons for the expulsion are complex and not directly relevant to this analysis. The immediate consequences, however, are significant. After the expulsion of Soviet personnel, the major source of weapons for Egypt became uncertain. Consequently, Sadat had to make sure that he had as many channels open for arms procurement as possible. Libya therefore loomed large again on the Egyptian horizon, and if the price was a merger, Sadat was willing to give it serious consideration.

The French embargo on the Mirages in case of a union between Libya and Egypt was no longer deemed an obstacle. Sadat probably calculated that if Soviets were being expelled from Egypt, France would no longer object to the merger. As Sadat shrewdly guessed, "I knew that the entire world (including Egypt) had interpreted my expulsion of the Soviet military experts as an indication that I wasn't going to fight."[39] And in fact the French did continue to send the Mirages to Libya despite the proposed merger between the two countries.

On September 18, 1972, Sadat and Qadhdhafi signed a document on the decision to unify the two countries, which followed the August 2, 1972, Tobruk-Benghazi declaration. Some of the major decisions were that Cairo would be the capital of the new United Arab Republic;[40] that it would have a "consultative, democratic, republican system of government;"[41] that it would have a single political organization and judicial authority; that other Arab states could join in provided they accepted the objectives of the new state; and that the merger should take place in stages.[42]

By the end of 1972, however, hopes for the union with Egypt began to fade again. According to Heikal, the reason was red tape and bureaucratic hair splitting in Cairo.[43] The real reason was that the Soviets had been alarmed by Sadat's action and had decided to resume major arms shipments to Egypt rather than lose Egypt to the West. According to Sadat, the biggest arms deal ever concluded between Egypt and the

Soviet Union took place in early 1973.[44] Sadat's strategy had paid off. A union with Libya was therefore no longer of vital importance, and Sadat turned his attention once more to other foreign policy issues, leaving union discussions to the committees and subcommittees that had been appointed to draw up a constitution and set up the institutional framework for the union.

The change in attitude was not lost on Qadhdhafi, who, fearing that Libya was going to be isolated again, tried to retain the protection of his major regional ally.[45] This time he used Libya's economic and military resources to effect an improvement in Libyan-Egyptian relations. Qadhdhafi began transferring his whole Mirage fighter force to Egypt in April 1973. The process may have started at an earlier date, but it was only then that the major transfer took place. The London *Daily Express* reported that fifty cargo planes as well as computers, radars, and jamming devices (the ground control equipment of the Mirages) had been sent to Egypt in early April.[46] The other planes were to follow as soon as the equipment was set up. This transfer of planes was interpreted by the British press as an attempt "to show the world—and the Arab countries in particular—that the political union between Egypt's President as-Sadat and Libya's Colonel al-Qadhdhafi is meaningful and not just a paper deal.[47] The transfer did more than that: It strengthened Egypt's ties to Libya and enhanced Libya's prestige in the region as it became the major Arab source of weapons to Egypt.

Qadhdhafi also transferred a large part of Libya's gross national product to Egypt. Heikal admitted that Libya gave $1 billion in aid to Egypt,[48] a figure mentioned by others as well. An independent Lebanese newspaper discussing Libya's foreign aid to states and revolutionary movements mentioned that Libya had given $1.5 billion in foreign aid in 1972 alone, of which Egypt had received $1 billion.[49]

Qadhdhafi used yet another means to push forward the union with Egypt. In July 1973 thousands of Libyans were organized to march 1,500 miles from Ra's Jabir in Libya to Cairo to meet with Sadat and ask him for a complete Libyan-Egyptian merger.[50] This dramatic action was aimed at mobilizing public opinion in Libya and Egypt in support of Qadhdhafi's aims and at pressuring the Egyptian leader and his government to accede to Qadhdhafi's wishes. His strategy worked. Although the marchers were stopped in 'Alamayn, Sadat did meet with a small Libyan delegation and promised them a union with Egypt.

On July 20, 1973, Sadat formed a high ministerial committee to draw up a plan for the merger of Libya and Egypt. By mid-August a formula had been devised by the Egyptians, and a referendum on the union's constitution was to take place three months hence.[51] Nevertheless, Qadhdhafi was reluctant to accept the Egyptian proposal because of its stress on unity by stages.[52] But as observers pointed out, Libya either had to accept Egypt's formula or else have no merger at all—in which case Libya would have lost its most important ally while Egypt turned to the Gulf states and Saudi Arabia for more financial and military aid.[53]

The principle of unity was proclaimed on September 1, 1973, but became a dead letter once the Arab-Israeli War of October 1973 broke out. Qadhdhafi was left out of the battle for which he had been waiting so impatiently.

## The Search for Allies

As early as February 1972 Qadhdhafi attempted to revitalize the Federation of Arab Republics and to consolidate Libya's ties to Egypt and Sudan. He paid a brief visit to Sudan and invited that country to join the federation,[54] but Numayri was either unwilling or unable to respond to that offer, and it came to nothing.

In May 1972 on the third anniversary of the Sudanese coup, Qadhdhafi paid another visit to Sudan. There he made a speech in which he reminded Numayri of Libyan assistance the previous year and promised to stand by him whenever the need arose. Qadhdhafi emphasized the significance of Sudan's membership in the Tripoli Charter and pointed to the importance of Libya's, Egypt's, and Sudan's strategic locations: "Egypt, Libya and Sudan constitute a geographical unity in the Arab world . . . a strategic area overlooking the Red Sea. . . . This geographical unity between Egypt, Libya and Sudan is the greatest natural factor for unity. . . . It constitutes a nucleus of Arab unity."[55]

He thus appealed to a common loyalty to the Arab nation; to the importance of allies in times of need; to Sudan's strategic concerns, presumably to draw Sudan closer to Libya; and to Egypt as well, with which tension was mounting. But Qadhdhafi's appeal was again to no avail. Numayri answered, "We employ our foreign policy to solve our domestic issues,"[56] and a policy of unity with Libya or Egypt would have only exacerbated the domestic problems Numayri was already facing.

Furthermore, after the attempted leftist coup of July 1971, Sudan had moved politically toward the West and the conservative Arab states. Sudan received aid and support from the United States and significant financial and economic assistance from Saudi Arabia. Numayri had no intention of jeopardizing those relations by being too closely associated with Qadhdhafi.

In September 1972 a crisis over the transport of troops and arms from Libya to Uganda through Sudanese airspace led to a complete deterioration of Libyan-Sudanese relations. An abortive invasion of

Uganda had taken place by supporters of former Ugandan president Obote, who came from Tanzania. Libya supported Idi Amin, while Sudan supported Milton Obote. Consequently, Sudan, on the pretext that it had not been notified about those flights, forced the Libyan planes to land in Khartoum, impounded the arms and equipment, and sent the Libyan troops to the barracks of the Sudanese People's Armed Forces.[57] The crisis lasted several weeks with Libyan newspapers calling for the downfall of Numayri.[58] The relations between the two countries were never again to become as cordial as they had been in the first year after their respective coups, although relations did improve on several occasions.

Finding both Egypt and Sudan reluctant to move toward greater unity, Qadhdhafi turned toward the Maghrib. In December 1972 he paid a visit to Tunisia and made a speech at a public rally urging Tunisians to unite with Libyans.[59] Bourguiba was not at the rally but was following the speech on the radio. When he realized the portent of Qadhdhafi's words, Bourguiba rushed to join Qadhdhafi on the platform and gave an impromptu speech of his own, explaining why Tunisia could not unite with Libya.[60] "What does unity mean? It means that we would be stronger. . . . What strength can we get by adding up 1.5 million Libyans to 5 million Tunisians?"[61]

Although the attempt at unity failed, the relations between Tunisia and Libya improved markedly. A number of agreements were signed between the two countries, especially regarding labor exchanges. Furthermore, Bourguiba became involved in an attempt to bring about a reconciliation between Morocco and Libya. He sent a private emissary, Habib al-Shatti, at the end of December 1972 to see King Hasan of Morocco about Moroccan-Libyan relations. The king's response was conciliatory.[62] Libyan-Algerian relations continued to be good. Libya supported Algeria in its difficult oil negotiations with France as well as in its discussions with the United States on gas exports.[63]

## Conflict in Chad and Uganda

A pattern of conflictual foreign policy behavior emerged about a year after the coup. The pattern would recur whenever Qadhdhafi perceived his regime or Libya's borders to be threatened, when he felt isolated, or when his offers of unity were rejected. At these times, he initiated foreign policy actions that included sabotage, military interventions, and support for opposition groups against the states he felt threatened by.

### Libyan-Chadian Relations

Between 1970 and 1973 this type of conflictual foreign policy behavior was most apparent in Libya's relation to Chad. Qadhdhafi had reached some kind of informal agreement with France in 1970 to curtail Libya's support for FROLINAT, the organization of Muslim northerners who were rebeling against the southern-dominated government.[64] Qadhdhafi agreed to this change in policy because he did not want to endanger the Mirages deal with France.[65] On August 27, 1971, however, there was a coup attempt against the Chadian president, Francois Tombalbaye, who accused Qadhdhafi of having backed it.[66] Chad broke diplomatic relations with Libya, and Chadian-Libyan relations became very tense.

In an interview with *Le Figaro*, Tombalbaye charged that Qadhdhafi's aim was to annex northern Chad and take its minerals.[67] Libya denied any involvement in the matter. Some experts on Chad, however, believe that Libya was involved in the attempted coup against Tombalbaye and explain the timing of the coup as related to an attempt by Tombalbaye to reconcile Muslim northerners with his regime and the southerners.[68] That, in turn, would have meant that Libyan involvement would no longer have been needed or welcomed in northern Chad. France's role south of Libya's territory would have been strengthened, which Qadhdhafi would probably have considered a threat to Libya's territorial integrity.

There may have been another reason as well. Qadhdhafi had been warned that Libyan opposition leader 'Umar 'Shalhi, who was in Europe, was masterminding a countercoup in Libya. As in the case of the previous year's coup attempt by Prince 'Abdallah al-Sanussi, the Black Prince,[69] one of the groups involved in the countercoup was to have entered Libya by way of Chad during the summer or fall of 1971.[70] By toppling the Tombalbaye regime, Qadhdhafi could have created a situation in Chad that would have kept any coup attempt against the Libyan regime from originating on Libya's southern borders.

In early 1972 Libya began to mend its fences with Chad and on April 17, 1972, the two countries resumed diplomatic relations. In a conciliatory gesture, Qadhdhafi promised to reduce Libya's support for FROLINAT, in return for which Chad broke off relations with Israel in November 1972.[71] A month later the two countries signed a treaty of friendship, and Fort Lamy Domestic Service announced that Libya was making a loan to Chad of 23 bilion CFA francs to help it finance development projects in the country.[72] This change in foreign policy seemed to be related to an agreement that was reached between Tombalbaye and Qadhdhafi over the Aouzou strip in northern Chad.[73]

In January 1973 Libyan military vehicles entered the oasis of Aouzou and distributed food and inoculated the inhabitants. Sometime between March and June 1973 Libyan forces established a military post in the Aouzou oasis and were followed by civilians who also settled there. Food was again distributed to the inhabitants, as were Libyan identity cards.[74] Finally the Aouzou strip was incorporated administratively into the municipality of Kufra of the Khalij province of Libya.[75]

Tombalbaye, who was fully aware of the events taking place on Chad's northern borders, never raised his voice in protest. That led to the rumor that there had been a secret agreement between him and Qadhdhafi in 1972 to give up the Aouzou strip to Libya in return for substantial economic aid and a halt of Libyan support for the FROLINAT insurgents.

Bernard Lanne, an expert on Chad, argues that it is very unlikely that such an agreement was ever signed between the two parties concerned. He contends that legally such an agreement would have been invalid because a Chadian president cannot make territorial concessions to another state without prior ratification of a law permitting this to take place.[76] Furthermore, Lanne argues, if such an agreement had existed, Qadhdhafi would have produced it after Tombalbaye's death in 1975, when Qadhdhafi was so harshly criticized by the OAU in 1977 for his actions in Chad.

According to Lanne, after Tombalbaye signed a friendship treaty with Libya, he expected a decline in support for the FROLINAT insurgents and substantial economic aid for Chad. He therefore closed his eyes to what the Libyans were doing in northern Chad in order not to undermine the agreement between the two states. He reserved, however, the option to object to the Libyan presence in Aouzou if that state did not keep its promises to Chad.

Whatever the explanation, Qadhdhafi was able to move into northern Chad unchallenged. His strategy of threatening the Chadian government with a coup and with support for FROLINAT had paid off, and he was able to control a zone that he perceived as vital to Libya's security.

### Libyan-Ugandian Relations

Libya became directly involved during that period in another conflict on the periphery of North Africa—namely, in Uganda. Qadhdhafi backed Idi Amin in September 1972 against the supporters of Obote, who in turn were getting assistance from Numayri. Qadhdhafi supported Idi Amin for a number of reasons, one of which was geopolitical. Qadhdhafi was always very much aware of the strategic location of states. After the September 1972 events, when Sudan forced Libyan planes carrying troops and weapons to Uganda to return to Libya, Qadhdhafi explained his support for Idi Amin's regime by referring to the protection of Sudanese interests: "The rebels who had risen against the Sudanese Government in the south had Uganda as their base in Obote's era; because Uganda has common borders with Sudan. In other words, Uganda was Sudan's lower base. Hence all the acts of rebellion and disobedience against the Sudanese Government came from Ugandan territory."[77]

In other words, Qadhdhafi was claiming that by supporting Idi Amin he was helping the Numayri regime against those who were giving assistance to the rebels in southern Sudan. Because Numayri was supporting Obote against Amin, this argument seems far-fetched. It does, however, shed light on the way Qadhdhafi viewed the importance of Uganda's geographical location vis-à-vis Sudan. As in the case of the Western Sahara's location at the base of Morocco, Uganda's common border with southern Sudan was perceived by Qadhdhafi as strategic. Uganda could become a base for anti-Numayri activists, who would be permitted to operate there by a regime that was basically antagonistic to Numayri's. By supporting Amin, Qadhdhafi was acquiring new leverage over the Ugandan regime and consequently over its relation to Sudan. Numayri was forced to take this Libyan-Ugandan alliance seriously and could no longer turn his back on Libya and isolate it on the regional level.

In return for Qadhdhafi's support, Idi Amin broke his relations with Israel and began to profess very strong pro-Arab sentiments.[78] This in turn legitimized Qadhdhafi's claims that he had intervened in the Ugandan conflict to defend not only Sudan's interests but also those of the Arab world as a whole.

## Ideology and Libyan-Moroccan Relations

Throughout his tenure in power, Qadhdhafi has used ideology to enhance his legitimacy. He has used ideology to explain and justify his policies and to build the public image of a revolutionary leader in order to win popular support the way Nasir had done two decades earlier. In the early years this image was created to contrast with that of the "corrupt" monarchs of the Arab world. Qadhdhafi could play the reformer, the leader of the masses, the man of the people. At a later stage, this public persona would challenge an even greater evil—namely, an Egyptian president who had "betrayed" the Arabs by making peace with Israel. And, finally, in the 1980s Qadhdhafi would undertake his greatest confrontation yet with the most "powerful nation on earth"—the United States.

Early on, however, he focused on Arab monarchs and traditional rulers and openly criticized the Moroccan, Jordanian, and Saudi kings. At the Islamic summit in Rabat in December 1969, he took a firm stand and addressed all the kings assembled there as brothers, a breach of protocol that even Nasir had refrained from doing, preferring to address them as "Brother King Hasan" or "Brother King Faisal."[79]

Qadhdhafi described monarchies as corrupt and immoral and in collusion with the West and with Israel.[80] When an attempted military coup took place in July 1971 against King Hasan, Qadhdhafi was jubilant. Bayda Domestic Service broadcast speeches and editorials in support of the Moroccan "masses," who had acted "against the extravagance and immorality of the luxurious palaces."[81] Qadhdhafi also placed Libya's armed forces in a state of full alert in case foreign powers intervened in Morocco on the side of the king.[82]

The reaction of the Moroccan monarch and the press was anger and dismay at Libya's hasty support for the insurgents. When the king was asked about Libya's involvement in the coup, he answered that the coup was "in Libyan style, full of imperfections and holes."[83] But he would not completely commit himself on Libya's role: "All I can say is that the Libyan Government is continually broadcasting appeals to the Moroccan people to support the mutineers."[84] Significantly, it was not Morocco, the offended party, that broke relations with Libya, but Libya, the offender,[85] that broke relations with Morocco.

When a second attempt was made to overthrow Hasan II in August 1972, the king and the Moroccan press accused Libya, unequivocally this time, of arming and financing the Moroccan insurgents.[86] Although it is difficult to assess the extent of Libya's involvement in the attempted coup, a qualitative change in Libyan-Moroccan relations had taken place between 1971 and 1972. During his first two years in power, Qadhdhafi had merely criticized the Moroccan king on radio broadcasts, but by 1972 Qadhdhafi may have begun financing and actively supporting Moroccan opposition leaders. His shift from words to actions occurred at the time when he felt isolated and realized that Egypt *and* the Maghrib were ignoring Libya and forming coalitions and blocs in which Libya had no role to play.

Qadhdhafi objected not only to King Hasan's domestic policies but to his foreign policy as well. The reformer became the freedom fighter as Qadhdhafi took up the issue of the Spanish Sahara. In a June 1972 speech broadcast on Tripoli Domestic Service, he claimed that Morocco was "trying to conspire to sell the freedom of an Arab land," namely, the region of Saqiya al-Hamra', the northern part of the Spanish Sahara. He continued:

The freedom of the Arab territory of Saquia el-Hamra is part of the freedom of Libyan territory. Therefore, we have told all parties concerned that unless a final solution is reached regarding this issue by the end of 1972, we will shoulder our historic and national responsibility by kindling a popular war for liberation in that sacred land.[87]

That threat may have been aimed as much at Morocco as at Spain, the ostensible target of the speech. Qadhdhafi's support for Saqiya al-Hamra' was meant to demonstrate his support for Arab freedom against Western imperialism as opposed to the king's pro-Western stands in the region. Furthermore, the "kindling of a popular war" on Morocco's borders was a direct challenge to King Hasan. Qadhdhafi was indicating that he could support and finance an opposition to the monarch not only within his own territory but outside it as well. Qadhdhafi was, according to this strategy, to be taken seriously by the Moroccan king and not ignored or left out of regional alliances and bloc formations.

## Notes

1. Bechtold, p. 154.
2. Ibid., pp. 155–156.
3. See the official declaration in "Documents: Federations des Republiques Arabes," in *Annuaire de l'Afrique du Nord,* Vol. 10, 1971, CNRS, Paris, 1972, pp. 842–854.
4. See ibid., the articles of the Constitution of the Federation of Arab Republics, of 20 August 1971, proclaimed in Damascus, pp. 847–854.
5. See Article 14 of the 1971 Constitution of the Federation of Arab Republics in ibid.
6. Heikal writes in *Road to Ramadan,* "For my part I have always been a believer in a union between Egypt and Libya. I still believe in it. I thought then that both countries had a unique and historic opportunity to pool their resources, to combine their lands, peoples and economies into one country which in ten years or so would become a single strong country, a major power placed at the strategic center of North Africa and on the bridge between Africa and Asia," Muhammad Heikal, *The Road to Ramadan,* Quadrangle, The New York Book Co., New York, 1975, pp. 189–190.
7. See, for instance, Heikal's article on Qadhdhafi in *Al-Ahram,* "Frankly Speaking," 5 May 1972, where he denies those charges, in FBIS-MEA, 5 May 72, G1.
8. First, p. 214.
9. Twenty-third installment of Sadat's memoirs in *October,* D8.
10. See Chapter 3.
11. See Heikal, *The Road to Ramadan,* p. 81.
12. Ismail Fahmy, *Negotiations for Peace in the Middle East,* Johns Hopkins University Press, Baltimore, 1983, p. 104.

13. Twenty-third installment of Sadat's memoirs, in *October*, D10; see also Sadat's declaration on the establishment of FAR, Arab Republic of Egypt, Ministry of Information, State Information Service, *Speeches and Interviews by President Anwar El-Sadat, September 1970–December 1971*, n.p., n.d., p. 216.

14. Anwar El-Sadat, *In Search of Identity: An Autobiography*, Harper and Row, Publishers, New York, 1978, pp. 215–216.

15. Ibid., p. 217.

16. Twenty-third installment of Sadat's memoirs, in *October*, D10; also in an interview with high ranking Egyptian official who prefers to remain anonymous, January 1986. I was told that Qadhdhafi tried to keep Syria out of FAR. The official was present during the negotiations.

17. Speech of Qadhdhafi in Tripoli, 18 April 1971, in FBIS-MEA, 19 April 71, T6.

18. Iraqi News Agency, Baghdad, 22 July 1971, in FBIS-MEA, 22 July 71, T2.

19. Iraqi News Agency reporting text of *Al-Nahar* article, 30 July 1971, in FBIS-MEA, 30 July 71, T17. Ruth First claims that "loyal troops from the Suez Canal zone were sent to Sudan as well," p. 221.

20. Bayda Domestic Service, Qadhdhafi's speech at a public rally in al-Marj, Libya, broadcast live, 22 August 1971, in FBIS-MEA, 23 August 71, T7.

21. Ibid. Sudan was recognized as a de facto member of the Federation because of its membership in the Tripoli Charter.

22. First, p. 232.

23. See Lt. Gen. Saad el-Shazly, *The Crossing of the Suez*, American Mideast Research, San Francisco, 1980, pp. 130–149.

24. Ibid., p. 147.

25. See First, pp. 221–222; see also Numayri's discussion of his ties to the Arab East with Lebanese daily *Al-Nahar*, 25–26 October 1972 in *Al-Watha'iq al-'Arabiya 1972*, American University of Beirut, Beirut, n.d., pp. 574–578.

26. Muhammad Masmoudi in an interview on Paris Radio, 14 January 1974, in FBIS-MEA, 15 January 74, T10; an interview by *Al-Nahar* with Masmoudi on 17 January 1974, in FBIS-MEA, 17 January 74, T8.

27. I am discussing this issue at some greater length because this attempt at unity is not generally known by experts in the field.

28. *L'Action*, Tunis, 21 April 1972, p. 5, 4L, in FBIS-MEA, 26 April 72, T6–T7.

29. Ibid. T7.

30. Bourguiba's speech in ibid., T4.

31. *Le Matin*, Casablanca, 10 June 1972, in FBIS-MEA, 14 June 72, T1–T3.

32. Damis, *Conflict in Northwest Africa*, p. 18.

33. Ibid., p. 31.

34. Sadat, *In Search of Identity*, p. 233.

35. Tripoli Domestic Service, 27 July 1972, in FBIS-MEA, 28 July 72, T1.

36. Cairo Domestic Press Agency, 31 July 1972, in FBIS-MEA, 1 August 72, G3–G4.

37. Cairo, MENA, 2 August 1972, in FBIS-MEA, 2 August 72, T4.

38. For the reasons for this expulsion see Shazly, pp. 159–167; Heikal, *Road to Ramadan*, pp. 165–184; Sadat, pp. 225–234.

39. Sadat, p. 232.

40. See Heikal, *Road to Ramadan*, p. 191.

41. See statement issued on points of agreement between the two presidents on 18 September 1972, Cairo Domestic Service, 18 September 1972, in FBIS-MEA, 19 September 72, T1–T2.

42. Ibid., T2.

43. Heikal, *Road to Ramadan*, p. 191.

44. Sadat, p. 238.

45. As early as December 1972, *L'Opinion*, the organ of the Moroccan Istiqlal Party, noted that Libya "was increasingly isolated in the Arab world," in FBIS-MEA, 20 December 72, T5.

46. Chapman Pincher, "Egypt Gets Libya Planes," *Daily Express*, London, 10 April 1973, p. 1L, in FBIS-MEA, 11 April 73, T4–T5.

47. Ibid., T5.

48. Heikal, p. 197.

49. Cairo, Domestic Press Agency, 10 August 1972, in FBIS-MEA, 11 August 72, T1.

50. See Heikal's description of the march in *Road to Ramadan*, pp. 195–196.

51. See "51% Oil Nationalization," *Middle East Economic Digest*, 7 September 1973, p. 1023.

52. Proposal by Mamdouh Salem in "Documents," *Arab Report and Record*, 1–15 August 1973.

53. Ibid.

54. Bayda Domestic Service, 5 February 1972, in FBIS-MEA, 7 February 72, T4.

55. Speech by Qadhdhafi in Umdurman, Sudan, on 25 May 1972, in FBIS-MEA, 26 May 72, T1–T6.

56. Numayri's speech in Umdurman, Sudan, on 25 May 1972, in ibid., T9.

57. Umdurman Domestic Service, 20 September 1972, in FBIS-MEA, 21 September 72, T3.

58. Tripoli, Libya News Agency, 24 September 1972, in FBIS-MEA, 26 September 72, T4.

59. Qadhdhafi's speech at a public rally in Tunis, 16 December 1972, in FBIS-MEA, 19 December 72, T4–T10.

60. Interview with high Tunisian government official who prefers to remain anonymous, Tunis, June 1986.

61. Bourguiba's speech answering Qadhdhafi at public rally in Tunis, 16 December 1972, in FBIS-MEA, 19 December 72, T11.

62. Damascus MENA, 23 December 1972, in FBIS-MEA, 26 December 72, T6.

63. I William Zartman and Aureniano Buendia, "La politique étrangère Libyenne," in Maurice Flory (ed.), *La Libye Nouvelle*, CNRS, Paris, 1975, p. 114.

64. See Chapter 3.

65. John Cooley, *Libyan Sandstorm*, Holt, Rinehart and Winston, New York, 1982, p. 99.

66. Bayda Domestic Service, 28 August 1971, in FBIS-MEA, 30 August 71, T1.

67. President Francois Tombalbaye's interview with *Le Figaro*, in Fort Lamy, Chad, Paris AFP, 3 September 1971, in FBIS-MEA, 3 September 71, VI.

68. Neuberger, p. 26.

69. See Chapter 3.

70. See the description of the planned coup in Patrick Seale and Maureen McConville, *The Hilton Assignment*, Praeger Publishers, New York, 1973; see also Cooley, pp. 98–99.

71. *Jeune Afrique*, Paris, 23 December 1972, in FBIS-MEA, 18 January 73.

72. Fort Lamy Domestic Service, 26 December 1972, in FBIS-MEA, 29 December 72, V1.

73. Neuberger claims that Qadhdhafi promised Tombalbaye $93 million. Somehow that sounds excessive even in terms of promises that were not kept. Neuberger, pp. 27–28.

74. Bernard Lanne, *Tchad-Libye: La Querelle des frontieres*, Editions Karthala, Paris, 1982, p. 228.

75. Ibid. For the geographical location of those administrative units, see Socialist People's Libyan Arab Jamahiriya (SPLAJ), Secretariat of Planning, Census and Statistics Department, *Nata'ij al-Ta'adad al-'Am lil-Sukan*, Government Press, Tripoli, 1977, p. 38.

76. Lanne, p. 230.

77. Speech by Qadhdhafi broadcast on Tripoli Domestic Service, 7 October 1972, in FBIS-MEA, 12 October 72, p. 5.

78. Ibid.

79. Heikal, *Road to Ramadan*, p. 80.

80. Bayda Domestic Service, 24 February 1972, in FBIS-MEA, 25 February 72, T2.

81. Bayda Domestic Service, 11 July 1971, in FBIS-MEA, 12 July 71, T20.

82. Bayda Domestic Service, 10 July 1971, in FBIS-MEA, 12 July 71, T16.

83. KCA, Vol. 18, 4–11 September 1971, p. 2479.

84. Paris AFP, 10 July 1971, in FBIS-MEA, 12 July 71, T2.

85. Cairo, MENA, 14 July 1971, in FBIS-MEA, 15 July 71, T4.

86. *Le Matin*, Rabat, 24 March 1973, in FBIS-MEA, 28 March 73, T4.

87. Speech by Qadhdhafi broadcast on Tripoli Domestic Service, 11 June 1972, in FBIS-MEA, 12 June 72, T9.

# 5

## The Search for an Ally, 1973–1977

The smaller and less developed nations of the Third World face certain constraints that have a determining impact on their foreign policies. By and large, these nations are vulnerable to domestic upheavals when their regimes are unable to consolidate their power or establish their legitimacy. They are vulnerable to external intervention precisely because they are small, they are less developed, and they usually lack well-trained and well-equipped armed forces to protect the state from external threats. And finally events taking place in the larger system of states to which these smaller states belong can have serious destabilizing consequences for their own regimes.

As a small, less developed nation, Libya had always relied on a major ally to ensure its security externally and, to a lesser extent, internally. Under King Idris, the primary ally had been England and the secondary ally the United States. When Qadhdhafi came to power, Egypt became Libya's major regional ally. Egypt played the role of protector from external intervention and acted as a stabilizer of the domestic Libyan situation, especially in the first year after the coup.

The Arab-Israeli War of October 1973 changed all that. President Sadat of Egypt, with the support of a number of Arab heads of state, initiated the war but did not make Qadhdhafi privy to the preparations, organization, or launching of the operation. Qadhdhafi's exclusion dealt a very serious blow to his standing as an Arab leader. It was tantamount to dismissing his claims as a serious statesman who could be entrusted with the secret preparations of a major Arab war. It undermined his credibility and his legitimacy domestically and regionally. Furthermore, his behavior during and after the war did not endear him to Sadat, who withdrew all Egyptian forces from Libya in mid-1974. Thus, in the space of a few months, Qadhdhafi lost the legitimacy he had worked so hard to secure and the powerful ally that had protected his country and his regime since 1969.

His reaction was predictable. He made extensive use of revolutionary and pan-Arab ideological rhetoric to regain some of the legitimacy he had lost. Pitting himself against the traditional Arab leaders in the name of revolution and setting up a well-orchestrated confrontation with Egypt, he began playing David to Sadat's Goliath.

Then Qadhdhafi searched for an alternative regional protector, which he eventually found in 1975 in the state of Algeria. Until that time, however, he tried to unite with other minor powers and when he failed to do so turned to the Soviet Union as the external protector.

Finally, he began using subversion as a response to threats of isolation. Conflictual foreign policy actions became a means of retaliating against those states that he perceived as having rejected Libya's offers of union, harboring Libyan opposition organizations, or threatening the Libyan state with military intervention.

## The War of Ideology

Ideology was the principal means Qadhdhafi had at his disposal to legitimize his power domestically after he had been ignored and rebuffed by Sadat during the 1973 war. It was only by asserting a holier than thou attitude, by affecting a more radical, more ethical, and somewhat superior position to Egypt and Syria that Qadhdhafi could hope to regain some of the respect and domestic legitimacy that he had lost.[1]

When the October war was over Qadhdhafi payed a visit to the West, his first since he had assumed power. The visit, in November 1973, was necessary to counterbalance his postwar domestic and regional image as an unimportant and unreliable Arab leader. He went to Yugoslavia and France, presumably to sell oil and buy arms.[2] The choice of those two countries, however, was not accidental. He was playing the role of the major nonaligned Third World leader, wheeling and dealing with communist and capitalist countries alike. If the Arab world rejected him, he wanted to assure the Libyans that the rest of the world took him seriously.

During his tour he played to the mass media in his own inimitable way. He took part in a newspaper symposium in Paris on November 24 that included reporters from the *Times, Le Monde, La Stampa,* and *Die Welt;* reports of his activities and his press interviews flooded Europe for more than ten days. His performance was generally quite successful; *Die Welt* described him as "part Mao and part Ignatius Loyola, a man who wishes to change the world while infusing an ancient world religion with a new force of conviction."[3]

Qadhdhafi wanted to be considered a major Third World leader with a vision of a better world. He set himself up in the post–1973 war period as a revolutionary fighting for the Arab masses against the corrupt regimes of the Arab world. He thus assumed the position of the leader of an opposition movement within a wider state. The Libyan "revolution" became the spearhead of that movement, while the Arab world became the wider state against whose leaders Qadhdhafi pitted himself.

Qadhdhafi's projection of this image of the revolutionary leading a movement against a corrupt state recurs again and again in all of his major speeches and interviews after 1973. In an interview in 1974 with the Lebanese daily *Al-Safir*, Qadhdhafi discussed the difference between the ruler and the revolutionary. The ruler was a man of the present who neither cared about the future nor understood the past. The revolutionary, with whom Qadhdhafi identified, was a visionary who transformed the world around him through the force of his dreams for a better future.[4]

When discussing the Libyan revolution, Qadhdhafi spoke of it as a model for the Arab world that would lead to its transformation and the demise of weak and corrupt leaders: "The Libyan people invites the Arab masses to follow the same road of the popular revolution, and to establish the power of the people. It invites them to give up all dictatorial and democratic experiments which have failed and have paralysed the Arab masses."[5] Qadhdhafi represented Arab leaders as men with little integrity who were not serious about representing their people and represented himself as a man who had the interest of the masses at heart.

> I have attended a number of meetings and exerted all my efforts. . . .
> When you address kings and presidents, seriousness is out of place during the meeting. Therefore, we . . . address the nationalist forces in the Arab homeland. We address the masses, the Arab people, and the conscience of the Arab nation. In many cases, we do not believe that the Arab leaders represent the conscience of the Arab nation.[6]

Qadhdhafi then took on Egypt. Throughout this phase the Libyan mass media attacked Sadat, depicting him as a traitor who had sold out the Arab cause. If Qadhdhafi was to play the role of the righteous, nonaligned Third World leader fighting the battles of the Arabs single-handedly, then Sadat was to be the villain who had betrayed the Arab world, accepted a cease-fire with Israel, and moved from Egypt's traditional nonaligned position to the Western camp and into the arms of the United States.[7]

Qadhdhafi pursued his ideological rhetoric against Sadat and the Arab regimes throughout this period.[8] He also supported revolutionary movements in the Arab world such as the Dhufar revolutionaries against

Sultan Qabbus bin Said of 'Uman, the more radical elements of the Palestinian movement against the mainstream PLO,[9] the Frente Popular para la Liberación de Saguia el-Hamra y Rio de Oro (POLISARIO) against Morocco (although for different reasons, he could still justify his actions ideologically), the Progressive National Front for the Liberation of Tunisia against Bourguiba,[10] some of the Islamic groups such as the Takfir wal-Hijra against Sadat, and the opposition National Front against Numayri.

Not to be completely isolated in the region and in order to placate Sadat and deter him from attacking Libya, Qadhdhafi kept up attempts at reconciliation with Egypt. These attempts were demarcated by long periods of ideological warfare between the two countries, when Qadhdhafi would accuse Sadat of betraying the Arab cause.[11] Attempts at conciliation came to an end, however, once Qadhdhafi had secured his ties to Algeria and to the USSR in December 1975. From then on he no longer needed Egypt's protection and could proceed with an all out war of words and actions against his erstwhile ally.

## The Isolation of Libya in the 1973 Arab-Israeli War

There remains the question of why Libya was kept out of the preparations for the October 1973 war. In May 1974 passages from letters sent by Sadat to Qadhdhafi were published in *Al-Ahram* to explain to the Egyptians as well as to the rest of the Arab world the reasons for the deterioration of Egyptian-Libyan relations. In those letters, Sadat claims to have warned Qadhdhafi at an early stage of the impending battle. He accused the Libyan leader of having immediately gone public with this information and of having declared his opposition to the battle strategy proposed by Syria and Egypt.[12] That, concluded Sadat, was an act of sabotage, and it halted all further information concerning the war from reaching the Libyan leader.[13]

Sadat also claims that before the war he had asked Libya for an alternative port to Alexandria in case that city was bombed during the war, spare parts for the Mirages that Libya had already transferred to Egypt, and 4 million tons of oil during a period of one year to be stored in Egypt before the outbreak of the hostilities.[14] Qadhdhafi had apparently responded less than adequately to this request. He did prepare Tobruk as an auxiliary port to Alexandria, and Sadat acknowledged that the port had provided Egypt with important strategic depth. But Qadhdhafi had been reluctant to pay for the spare parts for the Mirage bombers, and Saudi Arabia had had to purchase them instead.[15] He had reneged on the oil delivery: Qadhdhafi had made an initial delivery of less than 1 million tons, but when the cease-fire was declared, he refused to deliver the rest of the oil, claiming that he would do so only if the battle was resumed. Algeria had to step in and double the amount of oil it was giving Egypt from 1 million to 2 million tons.[16] When the hostilities stopped, Libya also rescinded on a pledge it had made before the war to pay Egypt $60 million. Finally, Sadat accused Qadhdhafi of broadcasting a very demoralizing speech to the Egyptian armed forces, among others, on October 7, 1973, at the outbreak of the war. In this speech, Qadhdhafi criticized Egypt's military strategy and predicted the defeat of the Egyptian army.[17]

Thus, from Sadat's point of view, Libya had failed Egypt in its hour of need. The strategic alliance between Egypt and Libya that Nasir had sought through the Tripoli Charter and Sadat had pursued through the FAR had proved to be of much less value than they had anticipated. Consequently, in terms of Egypt's national interest Libya was no longer important, and unity prospects were shelved. Libya, however, would pursue the idea for two more years.

## Libyan Conflictual Behavior Toward Egypt

Libya's foreign policy behavior in the post–1973 war period must be understood in terms of the isolation of Libya in North Africa. Isolation weakened Libya because the country became more vulnerable to external intervention; isolation also undermined the regime in the eyes of Libyans, who perceived their leaders as unpopular and/or ineffective in the region. This perception was probably behind the two major attempted coups against Qadhdhafi during that period. The first took place in late January 1974 when military officers and soldiers who supported Egypt and wanted Libya to have close relations with that country tried to topple Qadhdhafi.[18] The second attempted coup, in August 1975, was even more serious because it was spearheaded by members of the RCC itself, Major Bashir Hawwadi and Major 'Umar al-Muhaishi. Both had been very close to Qadhdhafi. The reasons for the coup were rooted in Qadhdhafi's domestic policies,[19] as well as in his deteriorating foreign relations with Egypt and with various states of the Arab world.[20] The domestic situation was exacerbated further when in July 1975 an air-to-ground missile was fired by some army officers at Qadhdhafi's dais during a military parade,[21] and a plot by army officers to assassinate Qadhdhafi was uncovered a month later.[22]

During this period of isolation, Qadhdhafi's policy toward Egypt alternated between subversive actions and conciliatory initiatives. Having been ignored, Qadhdhafi resorted to subversive behavior against the state he perceived to be the cause of Libya's predicament. But he then attempted reconciliation and even talks of unity to ensure that Sadat would not lose patience and intervene militarily in Libya.

Subversive activities against Egypt began in mid-April 1974 when the Technical Military College in Cairo was reportedly attacked by twenty armed men belonging to an organization calling itself the Islamic Liberation Organization. It was headed by a man working for the League of Arab States who was carrying both a Libyan and an Iraqi passport and who was apparently financed and supported by Libya. The attack caused the death of eleven people and the wounding of many others.[23] The Libyan version of the story was "that the students of the technical military college carried out a mutiny in the college, arrested the guards . . . seized several rifles and attempted to proceed to the People's Assembly where President as-Sadat was to deliver his speech."[24]

Libya thus tried to discredit Sadat's regime by describing the attack as an attempt to overthrow the Egyptian president. This action was part of the ideological warfare Qadhdhafi was waging to substantiate his claims that Sadat was an unpopular, weak, and corrupt leader whose people wanted to overthrow him. 'Abdullah Sariyya, the ringleader of the operation, apparently stated during preliminary hearings of his confession that Qadhdhafi had wanted "to give the impression that he is the only one loyal to the Palestinian question and that President as-Sadat and other Arab leaders are disloyal."[25]

A year later, in mid-April 1975, Qadhdhafi made another attempt at destabilizing the Egyptian regime. Security forces in Egypt uncovered a plot by Libya aimed at training the tribes of the western desert in the use of arms for subversive activities.[26] Some of those tribes were of Cyrenaican origin and had migrated to Egypt during the previous century. The Egyptian government was very concerned about its western desert population and was quick to report on Cairo National Service radio that the tribal chiefs in areas such as Marsa Matruh, Alexandria, and Fayyum had sent cables pledging their allegiance to Sadat.[27]

The discovery of the plot did not deter Qadhdhafi from trying in July 1975 to stir up the tribes again.[28] Sadat was so disturbed this time that he paid a personal visit to that region a few days later. He promised the tribal leaders to turn Marsa Matruh into a free zone and allow them to import goods without any restrictions, to establish towns in the region and promote tourism, and to give university education to the tribal leaders' sons.[29]

Qadhdhafi's aim was again to create the impression that Egypt's rulers lacked legitimacy and that the tribes looked toward Libya for leadership and support instead. In March 1975, for instance, the Tripoli news service reported that Qadhdhafi was receiving messages from the tribes in Egypt:[30] "A message from the Farjan tribe in the governorate of

Minya in Egypt reads. 'We condemn the action and moves of defeatist reaction and we support you. We promise you to take up arms and be at your disposal in defense of our cause and Arabism and in support of right and religion.' "[31] Although these actions could not seriously affect the Egyptian regime, they were used by Qadhdhafi to create the image in Libya of a strong Arab leader who was sought after for his dedication to the Arab cause by groups beyond Libya's borders.

Libya's subversive foreign policy actions were not directed only against states but also against individuals and groups that threatened the Qadhdhafi regime while residing in those states. In April 1974 there was an attempt to assassinate Egyptian journalist Ihsan 'Abd al-Quddus. The would-be assassin was a Libyan from Tobruk who had been paid to kill the journalist.[32] Ihsan 'Abd al-Quddus, chief editor of the weekly *Akhbar al-Yawm*, was a very important Egyptian journalist and one of the major critics of the Libyan regime. He had often accused it of being a puppet of the Soviet Union, and his widely read articles undermined Qadhdhafi's claims to legitimacy.[33] Two other Egyptian journalists, 'Ali Amin and Mustafa Amin, who had been critical of Qadhdhafi were targeted for assassination as well.[34]

Qadhdhafi also used terrorism against the leaders of a new Libyan opposition movement that had been formed around 'Umar al-Muhaishi in late 1975 and was headquartered in Cairo.[35] In March 1976 Libya attempted to kidnap Muhaishi, who had been a major figure in the coup attempt of August 1975, and 'Abd al-Mun'im al-Huni, a former Libyan foreign minister who had defected to Egypt.[36] Muhaishi, who had remained silent until then, began a full-fledged media blitz against the Qadhdhafi regime. The press, radio, and television in Egypt and Tunisia carried daily criticism of Qadhdhafi's domestic and foreign policies. Muhaishi discussed the Libyan army and the manner in which it had been treated,[37] and by early April he was calling for the overthrow of the Qadhdhafi regime from Cairo and from Tunis.[38]

Qadhdhafi had not waited for that point to be reached before attempting to deal with Muhaishi. At first he had demanded that Tunisia hand him over,[39] but when Bourguiba refused, subversive actions against Tunisia began taking place. In early March 1976, 760 Tunisians were deported from Libya,[40] and more followed throughout the spring. Egyptian workers were harassed and expelled from Libya during March 1976 as well. By the end of that month a number of Libyans had been arrested in Tunisia on the charge of having attempted to assassinate major Tunisian political figures. Prime Minister Hedi Nouira, who had opposed the Tunisian-Libyan merger of January 1974 and was critical of the Libyan regime, was apparently one of the targets.[41] Qadhdhafi also threatened to incite the tribes in southern Tunisia and in Egypt's western desert against their respective governments.[42]

By August 1976 Qadhdhafi had launched a full-fledged campaign of subversive actions and sabotage to pressure Egypt to hand over the members of the Libyan opposition and to stop criticizing the Libyan regime. There were explosives placed in government buildings in Cairo[43] and on trains in Alexandria,[44] and there was even an attempt to hijack a plane on a domestic flight from Cairo to Luxor.[45] When Qadhdhafi was asked about those acts of terrorism, he reportedly answered, "When Muhayshi moved from Tunis to Cairo he brought the bombs with him."[46] Qadhdhafi thus related the acts of sabotage to the Libyan opposition, implying that the sabotage would be stopped if Muhaishi was handed over or otherwise silenced.

By that time Egypt had had enough of Qadhdhafi and had moved infantry, paratroops, and air defense forces to the western borders with Libya.[47] That action was apparently sufficient to diffuse the conflict until the resumption of hostilities the following year.

The final major subversive Libyan action against Egypt during that period occurred a year later in July 1977. An Islamic fundamentalist group, Takfir wal-Hijra, kidnapped and assassinated a former Egyptian cabinet minister and well-known religious figure, Shaykh Muhammad al-Dhahabi. The Egyptian authorities accused Libya of being behind the operation and of supporting and financing the organization. Libyan opposition members agreed.[48] According to the public military prosecutor, Libya's plan included more kidnappings and bombings, as well as the occupation of the radio and television building in Cairo; the plans were to culminate in a coup against Sadat.[49] It is not quite clear to what extent Libya was involved in the activities of Takfir wal-Hijra. The assassination of the Cabinet minister and the brouhaha that followed occurred almost simultaneously with the outbreak of the Egyptian offensive against Libya in the western desert in July 1977. Consequently, the Egyptian authorities may have exaggerated the Libyan role in order to justify a military attack against another Arab country.

## Attempts at Libyan-Egyptian Reconciliation

Qadhdhafi's subversive activities alternated with attempts at reconciliation with Egypt until the end of 1975. Being isolated in the region he could not afford to provoke Egypt to retaliate. Thus, the period from November 1973 to December 1975 was characterized by an oscillation between vehement criticisms and acts of subversion against Egypt and renewed attempts at revitalizing the moribund FAR and the merger talks between Libya and Egypt.

As early as November 1973, Jallud, Libya's prime minister, had called for "the merger unity between Egypt and Libya"[50] that would continue the war against Israel. On February 19, 1974, Qadhdhafi went to Egypt and addressed the Egyptian People's Assembly, which was meeting to honor the heroes of the 1973 war. In his speech he said, "I also convey to you the greetings of the Libyan people . . . who strongly believe that they are an extension of the Egyptian people and that the Egyptian people are an extension to them and that the Libyan and Egyptian land(s) are one stretch and that their destiny despite all events, is a joint one and our future is one."[51]

It is interesting to note that Sadat's speech, which followed Qadhdhafi's, made no mention of unity between Egypt and Libya. It appears, therefore, that it was Qadhdhafi who was pushing for a reopening of the unity talks. During his visit Qadhdhafi also signed a number of agreements that had been prepared by the various committees of the FAR before the war. These included the setting up of an agricultural development organization, a land transport company, a maritime transport company, and a reinsurance company.[52]

During that visit Egypt and Libya agreed to resume talks on the merger between the two countries and discussed holding an Arab summit conference in Tripoli that spring.[53] These talks of unity and reconciliation came in the wake of an attempted military coup against Qadhdhafi in January 1974. Analysis of this action by the Arab press indicated that the officers and soldiers arrested were supporters of Egypt and wanted closer Libyan-Egyptian ties.[54]

Libyan-Egyptian relations deteriorated again between April and August 1974, when Qadhdhafi resumed his criticism of the Egyptian leader and supported the attack on the Technical Military College. But in August 1974 a second attempt at reconciliation was made by Qadhdhafi, ostensibly after Shaykh Zayid Bin Sultan al-Nuhayyan of the United Arab Emirates intervened to mediate between Qadhdhafi and Sadat.[55] As a peace gesture Sadat returned to Libya 34 Mirage bombers that Qadhdhafi had been demanding since the war ended.[56] The Egyptian deputy prime minister, Mamduh Salem, visited Tripoli on the fifth anniversary of the Libyan coup and spoke of good bilateral relations and unity of purpose between the two countries.[57] By the end of September, Sadat was calling for the FAR Assembly Council to convene in October.[58] But disagreements between the two states prevented the convening of the assembly, and the war of words resumed in the Egyptian and Libyan press.

By early December 1974 a third attempt at reconciliation was underway. A delegation from the Libyan Arab Socialist Union went to Cairo and to Damascus with messages from Qadhdhafi calling for the reactivation of the FAR, as well as the merger between Egypt and Libya.[59] By mid-

December 1974 the navigation route between Alexandria and Libya was reopened after having been closed for over five months[60] as a result of one of the quarrels between Libya and Egypt. Libya also resumed aid to Egypt, which had stopped after the cease-fire in October 1973.[61] And in January 1975 a number of economic and development agreements were reached on land reclamation projects, agricultural projects, and joint companies for oil exploration and drilling.[62] This was one of the longest periods of reconciliation between Egypt and Libya following the October 1973 war, and the reconciliation lasted until the end of February 1975, when Qadhdhafi announced in a press interview with *Le Monde,* "This Federation [FAR] no longer exists except on paper."[63] This period was followed by one of the longest and most conflictual periods in the history of Libyan-Egyptian relations.

The fourth and last attempt at reconciliation took place in mid-October 1975 when the National Assembly of FAR met in Cairo.[64] Egyptian newspapers, which had been banned in Libya, were distributed again, and the vitriolic press diatribes between the two countries stopped. Economic and trade agreements were reached, and the same pattern of conciliatory gestures began to unfold again. But it was short-lived. Apart from a very brief attempt at reconciliation in late October–early November 1976, Libyan-Egyptian relations went from bad to worse until the final military confrontation of July 1977.

Qadhdhafi's foreign policy behavior toward Egypt combined subversive activities aimed at weakening and undermining Sadat's leadership in Egypt, while enhancing Qadhdhafi's own revolutionary image in Libya, with conciliatory moves aimed at placating Sadat and deterring him from attacking Libya. This pattern of behavior would be characteristic of Libya's foreign policy behavior in the region throughout this period.

### The Islamic Arab Republic

On January 12, 1974, Libya and Tunisia announced the merger of their two countries into the Islamic Arab Republic.[65] It appeared to most observers at the time to be a spur of the moment decision, an impulsive reaction to the breakdown in Egyptian-Libyan relations. When the merger did not materialize, many assumed that Bourguiba had simply realized his mistake in entering so hastily into a union agreement with Libya.[66]

The evolution and dissolution of that merger, however, were much more complex than such explanations imply. Although it is undeniable that Libya was primarily motivated to seek a merger with Tunisia in January 1974 because of faltering relations with Egypt, the merger itself was not a sudden, spur of the moment decision. Rather, it followed a pattern of alignments that was typical of intraregional relations in North Africa.[67]

On September 1, 1973, Bourguiba had paid a visit to Qadhdhafi on the fourth anniversary of the Libyan coup. It was later confirmed that the two leaders talked primarily about unity between Libya and Tunisia.[68] A week later at the fourth nonaligned conference in Algiers, Bourguiba called for a union among Tunisia, Algeria, and Libya.[69] Two weeks later in an interview with the Egyptian weekly *Al-Musawwar*, Bourguiba stated that he wanted to establish a united state in North Africa that would include Libya, Tunisia, Algeria, and Mauritania; the capital of this state would be Qayrawan in Tunisia.[70] He did qualify the statement, however, by saying that the merger would take place in stages. But his statements were strong enough to provoke a public reaction from Morocco. *Al-'Alam*, the organ of the Istiqlal party, commented, "The idea could cause us some anxiety . . . as it is evident to us that one of its consequences would be the miscarriage of the Arab Maghreb plan and the isolation of Morocco."[71]

Libya and Tunisia continued the discussions after the October 1973 war. Habib Bourguiba Jr. paid a four-day visit to Libya in mid-November 1973 and confirmed the strong ties between the two nations.[72] Joint development projects were planned by members of the Tunisian delegation that met with the Libyan minister of planning at the time of the visit. Tunisian-Libyan relations evolved and improved gradually until January 12, 1974, when the Tunisian-Libyan merger was declared.

By the time of the announcement of the formation of the Islamic Arab Republic, discussions about unity had been going on for four months. Thus, the assumption that the agreement was a spur of the moment decision on Qadhdhafi's part or a plot hatched by Bourguiba's entourage,[73] and financed by Qadhdhafi is unfounded.[74] The unity agreement was in conformity with the patterns of bloc formation that recur in North Africa.

The further assumption that the agreement broke down when Bourguiba realized he had been manipulated is even more unlikely. Despite his frail health, Bourguiba remained in firm control of Tunisia's foreign policy throughout his term in power. That he should enter blindly into such an agreement would have been without precedent. A more likely explanation is that Algeria intervened in the first twenty-four hours after the announcement and threatened Tunisia with military intervention if it went through with the union.[75] This explanation was confirmed by Qadhdhafi in an interview in May 1974. When he was asked if Algeria had prevented the formation of the Islamic Arab Republic, he replied, "This is true. . . They are strange people, brother. They do not establish unity and they do not allow others to establish unity."[76] Two years later,

'Umar al-Muhaishi, who had been a member of Libya's RCC until 1975 and then fled the country after attempting to overthrow Qadhdhafi, confirmed Algeria's threat to Tunisia. He said that Algeria considered the agreement a hostile action and began to mass troops on its borders with Tunisia.[77]

The Jarba agreement, as the merger treaty came to be known, was an example of a pattern of bloc formation that was dominant in the region for years. Alignments and realignments took place whenever any of the major powers was perceived as becoming too strong and therefore a threat to the other states in the region. The Jarba agreement also illustrated Libya's search for a regional ally. Despite the fact that Libya had begun searching outside the region for a protector when it lost Egypt, it also needed to strengthen its position regionally by developing alliances with other North African states.

But why did the merger fail if it took place within the parameters of North African alignments? The reason may be that the political environment in the region had changed between September 1973 and January 1974. In September 1973 when Bourguiba had originally proposed some form of union, Libya's impending merger with Egypt had been perceived as a threat by Tunisia and Algeria. Both had common borders with Libya and had no desire to see Egypt on their doorstep if the merger materialized. As in previous years,[78] the states of the Maghrib tried to draw Libya away from Egypt by offering Qadhdhafi the option of joining a North African federation of some kind that did not include Egypt. After the October war Libyan-Egyptian relations had deteriorated to such an extent that Algeria no longer feared a rapprochement between the two countries. Consequently, it saw no reason to pursue the union project with Libya any further. Nor would Algeria permit Tunisia to do so either, as a Tunisian-Libyan bloc was not a desirable regional development at a time when Algeria was preparing to confront Morocco over the Western Sahara issue.

Tunisia's calculations were somewhat different. Bourguiba was still apprehensive of a possible Libyan-Egyptian reconciliation, especially after Qadhdhafi's November 1973 visit to Egypt when he called for unity between Libyans and Egyptians. Even after the merger had floundered, Bourguiba himself proposed to Qadhdhafi, in April 1974, a resumption of unity talks if only Libya "dropped plans to federate with Egypt."[79]

Qadhdhafi would not accept the failure of the merger and insisted that the union had taken place. In January 1975 Libya made unilateral decisions concerning clauses on the legislative authority governing the union. It was to be a people's assembly composed of an equal number of members representing the various provinces and governorates in each country. Furthermore, the union's flag was decided upon, as was the rotation of the union's capital from Tripoli (the winter capital) to Carthage (the summer capital) to Qayrawan (the "honorary capital"[80]).

On Tunisia's side the matter remained unresolved. As the Tunisian foreign minister put it in March 1975, the Tunisian-Libyan union "is still at the point it was at the time of the Jerbah declaration. . . . No negotiations have taken place between Tunisia and Libya, nor has any referendum on their unity been organized. No constitutional amendment has taken place in Tunisia."[81]

The reason the Tunisians did not resolve the issue one way or the other is not hard to fathom. On the one hand, Tunisia could not consummate the merger because of Algeria's veto of the union. On the other hand, Tunisia did not want to anger Qadhdhafi by unilaterally abrogating the treaty and inviting serious economic and political retaliation from Libya. By keeping the issue unresolved, Qadhdhafi would still have the hope that the merger could come to life, and this would temper his actions against Tunisia.

Unable to coax Tunisia into finalizing the merger, Qadhdhafi opted to put pressure on the Tunisian authorities to accede to his demands. The issue of the continental shelf was brought up, apparently for the first time, in early August 1975. Until 1974 both Tunisia and Libya had been granting concessions for offshore exploration and drilling[82] without any major problem. The Tunisian prime minister, Hedi Nouira, however, claimed that the problem between the two states had existed for a number of years and that Libya and Tunisia had tried to negotiate an agreement but had failed. Tunisia's position was to resort to international arbitration, a position it held until June 1977 when Libya and Tunisia prepared a special agreement that they submitted to the International Court of Justice in December 1978.[83]

In order to push for unity, Qadhdhafi was creating a problem and offering a solution simultaneously: "The issue in the Jamahiriyah is not the continental shelf between us and Tunisia. We had proposed an integral unity between the two countries so that Tunisians and Libyans might share the oil."[84] In other words, Qadhdhafi was suggesting that he would not contest Tunisia's claims on othe continental shelf if Tunisia was willing to unite with Libya. He had thus created the problem of the continental shelf to bargain for something he really wanted—namely, the merger with Tunisia.[85] As in other instances, Qadhdhafi used Libya's capabilities to influence foreign policy. He failed, however, to get his merger.

## The Hassi Mas'ud Treaty

The search for a regional ally in the post–October war period was not confined to union overtures to Tunisia. Qadhdhafi also attempted to build links with Algeria, Morocco, and Sudan, as well as retain his ties to Egypt for as long as possible. The task was not an easy one, however. Morocco and Libya had broken relations over Libya's alleged support for the insurgents who had planned to overthrow King Hasan in 1971 and 1972. Algerian-Libyan relations had eroded after the attempted Jarba union with Tunisia. Qadhdhafi had juggled his relations with Sadat but had failed to achieve anything of significance there. And Sudanese-Libyan relations were strained, especially after Libya supported insurgents against the Numayri regime.

In its search for an ally, Libya looked east and west. Syrian-Libyan relations improved as those two countries' relations with Egypt deteriorated, and Libyan-Moroccan relations began to improve immediately after the October war. A brief statement from Rabat in mid-November 1973 announced that Libya and Morocco were expected to resume diplomatic relations in the near future.[86] By December 1974, Morocco and Libya were exchanging ambassadors. A month later Qadhdhafi was paying a secret visit to Morocco and reportedly offering his assistance to the king on the Spanish Sahara.[87] By mid-May 1975 Moroccan-Algerian disagreement over the Sahara had begun to take a turn for the worse, as Spain was announcing its plan to withdraw from the area.[88] Consequently, Libya's support for Morocco's stand was most welcome to King Hasan. By June 1975 the French press was reporting the formation of a Rabat-Tripoli axis.[89]

The axis, however, was short-lived. By October 19, 1975, when King Hasan organized his Green March on the Western Sahara, Libya had become critical of Morocco's role there. It is not beyond Algeria to have exerted pressure on Libya to change its stand on the issue. After all, in November 1975 Boumediene had asked Ould Daddah of Mauritania to choose between him and King Hasan. Boumediene had also threatened Mauritania with annexation if it chose to pursue the Moroccan course of action.[90]

On December 12, 1975, Boumediene paid a short visit to Libya, and on December 28 he and members of the Algerian Revolutionary Council met with Qadhdhafi and the members of the Libyan RCC in Hassi Mas'ud in Algeria to sign a mutual defense pact.[91] The brief communiqué that was issued to announce the new alliance stated that "the two presidents . . . agreed to confront existing challenges, whatever their nature and wherever they are and to consider any harm done to any of the two revolutions as harm done to the other."[92] With this clause

Algeria became Libya's major regional ally, and its principal protector in North Africa.

Algeria's role as Libya's protector was put to the test in July 1977 when Egypt launched a limited air and ground attack on Libya's radar installations, guerrilla training camps, and military airfields in the Cyrenaican desert, west of the Egyptian borders. Algeria did intervene on Libya's side to put an end to the confrontation. On July 24, 1977, Boumediene met with Sadat in Alexandria. It was reported that no sooner had the talks started between the two presidents than Egypt ordered the halting of the military operations against Libya.[93] John Cooley writes that Algeria did not merely mediate the conflict between Egypt and Libya but that "Boumediene gave some veiled hints that Algeria might have to intervene on the side of Libya if the Libyans invoked the 1975 defense treaty between the two countries."[94]

Whatever means Boumediene used, whether mediation or threat or both, it was Algeria's intervention on the side of Libya that put an end to the hostilities. Unlike the Soviet Union, Algeria, the regional ally, had been Libya's most effective protector against external intervention. Thus, the assumption that Libya needed a regional ally to defend it in case of war or military intervention proved to be justified in this case.

Libya demonstrated that it could be a staunch ally to Algeria as well. In its confrontation with Morocco over the Western Sahara, Algeria needed both financial and military aid. By the early 1980s, the POLISARIO, which numbered an estimated 7,000 armed fighters,[95] was being supplied by both Libya and Algeria with Soviet arms ranging from heavy equipment such as track-mounted SAM-6 missiles to lighter and more modern equipment.[96] The troops and the Saharan refugees received aid of various kinds from Libya, and a large number of families of POLISARIO fighters found refuge in Libya in the late 1970s.[97]

The Hassi Mas'ud Treaty between Libya and Algeria cemented the most important alliance in North Africa during the 1970s. Although the treaty received little serious attention either in the media or in scholarly works, it was responsible for the perpetuation of the war in the Western Sahara. It was also instrumental, in part at least, in stabilizing the Libyan regime during that period.[98]

## Libya and Sudan: An Uneasy Alliance

Libya's relation with Sudan was always to some extent a function of its relation to Egypt. When Egypt was closely allied to Libya, as in the early 1970s, ties to Sudan enhanced Libya's power and prestige in the region. An Egyptian-Sudanese-Libyan bloc was certainly a power to be reckoned with in Africa and in the Arab world. When Libyan-Egyptian relations deteriorated, however, close ties between Egypt and Sudan meant a double threat to Libya's security. To prevent the formation of a hostile Egyptian-Sudanese bloc on Libya's eastern border, Qadhdhafi would either try to pressure Sudan to break away from Egypt or try to form a union with Sudan to isolate Egypt.

When Egyptian-Sudanese relations improved in March 1974 and talks of economic integration between the two countries took place, the Libyan press vehemently criticized Numayri for his relation to Sadat.[99] By May 1974 Numayri was accusing Qadhdhafi of being behind another coup attempt and of harboring members of the Sudanese opposition, many of whom were against the Egyptian-Sudanese rapprochement.[100]

When that approach failed, Qadhdhafi sought to improve his relations with Sudan. In the early months of 1975 the two leaders began discussing economic and political integration between their two countries. They agreed to study a project aimed at integrating North Darfur province in Sudan with Kufra municipality in Libya to form a nucleus of "joint action" where all trade, customs, and transport barriers would be removed to allow Sudanese and Libyans to interact freely.[101] Rather than break away from Egypt, however, Numayri tried to reconcile Qadhdhafi and Sadat instead. The final attempt at an Egyptian-Libyan reconciliation in October 1975 was apparently mediated by Sudan.[102]

When this attempt at distancing Sudan from Egypt proved unsuccessful, Qadhdhafi again resorted to a conflictual policy, which backfired. In July 1976 another coup attempt took place in Sudan, the fifteenth by some counts since 1969,[103] and Libya was accused of direct involvement.[104] The coup attempt in fact had been carried out by members of the Sudanese opposition, the National Front, and Libya had provided only training and possibly financial assistance.[105] Egypt intervened with an alleged 15,000 troops to contain the abortive coup,[106] and by the end of July 1976, Egypt and Sudan had signed a joint defense pact.[107] This was precisely what Libya feared most, and the pact was immediately dubbed a "military alliance against the Libyan Arab Republic."[108]

## The External Alliance

In the aftermath of the 1973 war, Qadhdhafi began seeking an ally not only within the region but outside it as well. He needed an ally to take over the dual functions that Egypt had performed between 1969 and 1973—namely, to deter external intervention and to ensure the continuity of the regime. Libya's military forces in 1973 were much too weak to defend the country's extensive territory, and the regime had not yet developed a power base strong enough to neutralize domestic opposition.

The October war rendered external intervention in Libya a possibility to be reckoned with. To guard against such an eventuality, the Libyan government took a number of preventive measures. A few days after the outbreak of the war, the RCC issued a new law prohibiting the entry or residence of foreigners around the major oil areas without a special permit from the Ministry of the Interior.[109] This action underscored Qadhdhafi's fear of the possibility of sabotage of the oil fields during the war. At the height of the Arab-Israeli confrontation, the Libyan foreign minister issued a formal denial that any French-made Mirage planes bought by Libya had been used in the war.[110] This blatant lie masked Libya's fear of possible French retaliation against Libya for having failed to comply with the agreement not to use those planes for military purposes against Israel. On October 9, 1973, an official statement was issued that the Gulf of Sidra was " 'an indivisible part' of Libya and subject to Libya's 'full sovereignty.' "[111] This was the first time such a statement had been made by the Qadhdhafi government, and it demonstrated the RCC's fear of a possible threat to Libya's northern borders. And finally, in the aftermath of the war, when the Arabs imposed an oil embargo on the West, the possibility of Western intervention in Libya was openly discussed in the Western press and apparently by some high-ranking NATO commanders as well[112] and was reported in the Libyan mass media.

It thus became clear to the RCC during October and November 1973 that Libya had become extremely vulnerable to external intervention for its participation, albeit limited, in the war and in the oil embargo that followed. The RCC also realized that Egypt would be unable to defend Libya from a major attack because of Egypt's involvement in the war with Israel. At that point Libya turned to the USSR not merely for military assistance but for an alliance that would protect Libyan territory from external intervention.

Until November 1973, Qadhdhafi had been openly critical of communism and the Soviet Union.[113] In fact, as late as October 23, 1973, at the time of the Egyptian-Israeli cease-fire, Qadhdhafi had asserted in an interview with *Le Monde* that "the Soviet Union remains the main enemy of the Arab world."[114] He explained his rather extreme statement by saying that if the Soviets had not made such a fuss about their "miserable military supplies"[115] to the Arab states, the United States would not have provided all the assistance it did to Israel.

By November 12, 1973, however, the Libyan attitude toward the USSR had changed completely. Fear of Western reprisals for the Arab oil embargo may have been the primary reason for this overnight reversal in foreign policy. 'Abd al-Salam Jallud asserted in an interview with *Der Spiegel*, "We regard the superpower Soviet Union as an ally and friend. Our differences with the Soviet Union are differences between friends and nothing else."[116] Although Qadhdhafi remained somewhat less enthusiastic about the Soviet Union than Jallud did,[117] the turning point in Libyan-Soviet relations had been reached.

In January 1974 Jallud made a tour of the Eastern bloc states and invited them to buy Libyan oil at auctions in Libya. Major economic and military agreements were signed between the two countries, and Soviet military advisers began replacing Egyptian personnel.[118] In May 1974 Jallud visited the Soviet Union with a long shopping list of military hardware.[119] Although the Soviet Union had been selling arms to Libya since the 1960s, and in larger amounts after the summer of 1970, this was the beginning of a new phase in arms transfers that eventually made the USSR Libya's major arms supplier.[120]

Some military experts estimate that the USSR supplied Libya with more than two-thirds of all its military purchases during the period 1974–1978.[121] After 1975 the arms transfers to Libya increased tremendously, "with more money expended per year than was expended in the entire first five years of the decade."[122] The estimated value of those imports during 1974–1977 was $3.8 billion (in constant 1979 million dollars),[123] whereas the total military expenditures for that period were estimated at $7.2 billion (in constant 1982 million dollars), increasing significantly every year.[124]

By March 1974, however, the oil embargo had been lifted. The Kissinger shuttle diplomacy was in full swing and had already resulted in the January 1974 disengagement agreement between Egypt and Israel. The threat to Libya was no longer Western reprisals for the oil embargo but the new Egyptian-U.S. rapprochement. Qadhdhafi perceived this relationship as particularly threatening to Libya because of its proximity to Egypt. When describing Libyan-Soviet relations in May 1974, Qadhdhafi put it in the context of an external threat to the region: "The U.S.S.R. is certainly a friend. Our relations with it are good. Perhaps these relations are now stronger than before, particularly as both of us have come to realize the seriousness of the American offensive in the region."[125]

Qadhdhafi was thus acknowledging that Libya's relationship to the USSR was primarily strategic. But whereas the Soviet Union was interested in containing U.S. influence in the region, Qadhdhafi's principal fear was that Egypt, supported by the United States, would now turn against Libya and attack it. In fact, the fear of an Egyptian military intervention was so real during that phase that Bulgarians were hired, with the USSR's blessings, to build antitank fortifications in the western desert as a kind of Maginot Line to prevent a possible Egyptian invasion of Libya.[126]

By giving Libya arms and personnel, the Soviet Union was also providing a deterrent force to any would-be attacker on Libya's territory. But the USSR's role as protector was not tested until the spring of 1977, when it became apparent that Egypt was going to launch a military offensive on Libya's western borders. Ironically, this attack was prompted in part by the 1976 installation of Soviet radar close to the Egyptian-Libyan borders. This radar allowed Libya and the USSR to collect information not only on the Egyptian air defense system but on the activities of the U.S. and NATO forces in the Mediterranean.[127]

The USSR's reaction to the perceived Egyptian threat against Libya was to send a public message to Cairo, and to several other Arab capitals as well, accusing Egypt of having designs on Libya. The message stated that Egypt wished to control Libya's oil wealth and was planning to attack Libya in order to divert attention from its own domestic problems. The message warned of the possible repercussions of such an aggression and came very close to threatening Egypt: "If the Egyptian leadership drives the situation toward a clash with Libya, and if it continues in its efforts to attack the current regime in Libya, it must realize that full responsibility for the results, which are difficult to anticipate, rests upon Egypt."[128]

This statement was meant to frighten the Egyptian authorities and deter them from attacking Libya. It was also probably calculated to bring about Arab mediation or Arab pressure on Egypt to prevent the attack from taking place. The message, however, incensed the Egyptians, who lambasted the Soviet Union for weeks in their mass media.[129] Three months later, undeterred by Soviet warnings, Egypt attacked Libya and destroyed the Soviet-built radar installations in the Cyrenaican desert.

Although the Soviet Union became Libya's major international ally during that period, providing it with vast quantities of arms and attempting to defend it against external aggression, the USSR was not particularly successful in its role as Libya's protector. In fact, the Soviet Union may have been the indirect cause of the Egyptian military offensive.

Libya, however, did not forsake this alliance because despite its shortcomings, the alliance strengthened Libya's position regionally, internationally, and domestically. Libyans were bound to be impressed by the Soviets' interest in their country and to perceive their leaders as important and powerful men who had been capable of securing the patronage of a superpower. According to one member of the RCC, "We should not be remote from the Soviet Union because the stronger our friendship with the Soviet Union is . . . the more we can make big strides peacefully. It is a well-known fact that a weak party which has no strong and sincere ally cannot achieve anything."[130]

## An Independent Foreign Policy

This period witnessed the development of Qadhdhafi's own style of leadership, which dominated Libya's domestic and foreign policies. His flamboyant, apparently spontaneous style of ruling masked a shrewd, calculating mind that knew how to assess realistically a dangerous political situation and make the most of rather limited options. A Don Quixote in words, he was ruthless and pragmatic, using subversion to pressure governments and pursuing the Libyan opposition relentlessly until he had it neutralized.

By the end of this period, Qadhdhafi had become stronger than he had ever been. He had achieved his core goals by consolidating his domestic power and his regional and international alliances. For the rest of the decade those alliances would remain his basic protection in the region. Domestically, all voices of dissension had been silenced. Those in the RCC and the Libyan leadership who had opposed Qadhdhafi's policies toward Egypt and the rest of the Arab world had either fled or been executed. Those who remained had to toe the line behind the Libyan leader.

### Notes

1. See Zartman on the importance of appropriating, manipulating, and monopolizing ideological slogans, *International Relations of Africa*, p. 62.

2. Paris AFP, 25 November 1973, in FBIS-MEA, 26 November 73, T10.

3. *Die Welt*, Hamburg, 26 November 1973, in FBIS-MEA, 28 November 73, T19. See also coverage of the symposium reported in the *Times*, *Le Monde* and *Stampa Serra*, FBIS-MEA, 30 November 73, T16, T17.

4. Interview with Qadhdhafi in *Al-Safir*, Beirut, 28 April 1974, L.A.R., Arab Socialist Union, *Al-Sijil al-Qawmi, Bayanat wa Khutab wa Ahadith al-'Aqid Mu'ammar al-Qadhdhafi, 1973–1974*, The Arab Revolution Printing Press, Tripoli, n.d., p. 498.

5. Speech by Qadhdhafi on 1 September 1976, in Tripoli, in *Al-Sijil al-Qawmi, 1976–1977*, p. 195.

6. Qadhdhafi at a press conference in Paris, in FBIS-MEA, 26 November 73, T8.

7. See, for instance, Qadhdhafi's public telegram to Sadat in L.A.R., Secretariat of Culture and Information, *Al-Sijil al-Qawmi, Bayanat wa Khutab wa Ahadith al-'Aqid Mu'ammar al-Qadhdhafi, 1976–1977*, The Arab Revolution Printing Press, Tripoli, n.d., p. 467. See also Qadhdhafi's challenge to Sadat: "We are following the line of 'Abd al-Nasir. We are placing ourselves in the arena of challenge. With this challenge we want to challenge President as-Sadat. If he is a unionist and if he is in fact following the line of 'Abd al-Nasir, then let him prove it."

Speech by Qadhdhafi in Tripoli, Voice of the Arab Homeland, 25 July 1975, in FBIS-MEA, 25 July 75, I2.

8. See 'Abdallah Billal, *Qira'at fi Hadhihi al-Tahawwulat*, The General Company for Publication, Distribution and Advertisement, n.p., 1979, pp. 109–122. For a presentation of Qadhdhafi's revolutionary ideology, see M. El-Shahat (ed.), *Libya Begins the Era of Jamahiriyat*, International Publication House, Rome, 1978.

9. See Deeb and Deeb, *Libya Since the Revolution*, p. 136.

10. Rabat Domestic Service, 19 December 1974, in FBIS-MEA, 20 December 74, I7.

11. See, for instance, Qadhdhafi's speech at a public rally on 2 June 1977, in *Al-Sijil al-Qawmi, 1976–1977*, p. 751; see also an interview with a Lebanese weekly, *Al-Usbu' al-'Arabi*, republished in L.A.R., *Min Ahadith Al 'Aqid Mu'ammar al-Qadhdhafi fi al-Sahafa al-'Arabiya wal-'Alamiya*, The Arab Revolution Printing Press, Tripoli, 1975, pp. 55–56.

12. *Al-Ahram*, Cairo, 24 May 1974, in FBIS-MEA, 24 May 74, D2.

13. Twenty-eighth installment of Sadat's memoirs, "The Ice Thaws Between Moscow and Cairo," published in the Egyptian weekly, *October*, Cairo, 29 May 1977, pp. 11–15, in FBIS-MEA, 1 June 77, D5.

14. FBIS-MEA, 24 May 74, D3–D4.

15. Ibid., D4.

16. Ibid.

17. Thirty-second installment of Sadat's Memoirs, in *October*, Cairo, 26 June 1977, pp. 19–23, in FBIS-MEA, 6 July 77, D2.

18. Damascus MENA, Cairo MENA, 27 February 1974, in FBIS-MEA, 27 February 74, T2.

19. I analyze the domestic reasons for the 1975 coup in "Libya's Economic Development 1969–1986: Social and Political Implications," *Maghreb Review*, London, Vol. 11, Nos. 1–2, 1987, pp. 1–8.

20. Cairo MENA, 19 August 1975, in FBIS-MEA, 19 August 1975, I1.

21. Cairo Voice of the Arabs, 5 July 1975, in FBIS-MEA, 7 July 75, I6.

22. *Al-Jumhuriya*, Cairo 4 August 1975, in FBIS-MEA, 4 August 75, I1.

23. See Cairo MENA, 21 April 1974, in FBIS-MEA, 22 April 74, D12.

24. Tripoli Domestic Service, 22 April 1974, in FBIS-MEA, 23 April 74, D1.

25. Cairo MENA, 27 April 1974, in FBIS-MEA, 29 April 74, D7.

26. Cairo MENA, 21 April 1975, in FBIS-MEA, 22 April 75, D6.

27. Cairo Domestic Service, 20 April 1975, in FBIS-MEA, 22 April 75, D6.

28. Cairo MENA, 7 July 1975, in FBIS-MEA, 8 July 75, D1.

29. See speech by Sadat in Marsa Matruh, 14 August 1975, in FBIS-MEA, 15 August 75, D2.

30. Tripoli ARNA, 26 March 1975, in FBIS-MEA, 28 March 75, I3.

31. Ibid.

32. Cairo MENA, 7 August 1974, text of letter from Sadat to Qadhdhafi in FBIS-MEA, 7 August 74, D1.

33. See, for instance, 'Abd al-Quddus's article in *Akhbar al-Yawm*, 27 April 1974, in FBIS-MEA, 30 April 74, D6–D7.

34. *Al-Ahram*, Cairo, 30 March 1976, p. 5, in FBIS-MEA, 9 April 76, D6.

35. The Tajamu' al-Watani al-Libi, the Libyan National Grouping, was formed in May 1976 in Cairo. For an excellent discussion of the Libyan opposition, see Martin Sicker, "The Libyan Opposition to Qadhdhafi," in *Global Affairs*, Vol. 1, No. 3, Summer 1986, pp. 51–66; see also Lisa Anderson, "Qadhdhafi and His Opposition," *The Middle East Journal*, Vol. 40, No. 2, Spring 1986, pp. 225–237.

36. See "New Spotlight on the Libyan Opposition," in *The Middle East*, July 1984, p. 20.

37. A most revealing interview with 'Umar al-Muhaishi is in *Al-Ahram*, Cairo, 12 March 1976, in FBIS-MEA, 18 March 76, D1.

38. Muhaishi's call for revolt against the Qadhdhafi regime, Cairo Middle East Service, 3 April 1976, in FBIS-MEA, 6 April 76, D9.

39. Sicker, p. 53.

40. Tunis Domestic Service, 10 March 1976, in FBIS-MEA, 11 March 76, I1.

41. Press interview with Prime Minister Hedi Nouira, Tunis, 22 March 1976, in FBIS-MEA, 23 March 1976, I5–I6.

42. Tripoli Voice of the Arab Homeland, speech by Qadhdhafi, 31 March 1976, in FBIS-MEA, 2 April 76, I1.

43. Cairo MENA, 8 August 1976, in FBIS-MEA, 9 August 76.

44. Cairo Domestic Service, 14 August 1976, in FBIS-MEA, 16 August 76, D13.

45. Cairo Voice of the Arabs, 24 August 1976, in FBIS-MEA, 25 August 76, D1.

46. 'Abd al-Sattar al-Tawila, *'Aqid al-Qadhdhafi wa Misr*, Rose al-Yusuf Publications, Cairo, 1977, p. 118.

47. Cairo MENA, 12 August 1976, in FBIS-MEA, 13 August 76.

48. See *Al-Inqadh*, n.p., Vol. 3, No. 11, p. 92. This is the organ of the National Front for the Salvation of Libya, a Libyan opposition organization.

49. Cairo MENA, 20 July 1977, in FBIS-MEA, 21 July 77, D6.

50. *Al-Anwar*, Beirut, 25 November 1973, pp. 10, 12, in FBIS-MEA, 28 November 73, T21.

51. Qadhdhafi's speech at the Egyptian People's Assembly, Cairo, 19 February 1974, in FBIS-MEA, 20 February 74, G5.

52. Cairo Domestic Service, 20 February 1974, in FBIS-MEA, 21 February 74, T2.

53. *Al-Ahram*, Cairo, 22 February 1974, in FBIS-MEA, 22 February 74, G1.

54. Damascus MENA, Cairo MENA, 27 February 1974, in FBIS-MEA, 27 February 74, T2–T3.

55. Cairo Domestic Service, 19 August 1974, in FBIS-MEA, 19 August 74, D7.

56. FBIS-MEA, 29 August 74, D8.

57. Tripoli ARNA, 5 September 1974, in FBIS-MEA, 9 September 74, I2.

58. Cairo MENA, 26 September 1974, in FBIS-MEA, 27 September 74, D5.

59. Tripoli ARNA, 7 December 1974, in FBIS-MEA, 9 December 74, I2.

60. Baghdad INA, 14 December 1974, in FBIS-MEA, 16 December 74, D6.

61. Baghdad INA, 22 December 1974, in FBIS-MEA, 23 December 74, D10.

62. Tripoli ARNA, 30 January 1975, in FBIS-MEA, 31 January 75, I3.

63. Qadhdhafi's interview with *Le Monde*, Paris, 22 February 1975, pp. 1–2.

64. Cairo DPA, 13 October 1974, in FBIS-MEA, 15 October 74, D4.

65. See text of statement on the formation of the Islamic Arab Republic read by Tunisian foreign minister Muhammad Masmudi, and broadcast live by Tripoli Domestic Service, 12 January 1974, in FBIS-MEA, 14 January 74, T5.

66. See for instance, Wright, *Libya: A Modern History*, pp. 165–166.

67. The following section has appeared in *The Middle East Journal*, Winter 1989, Vol. 43, No. 1.

68. See Habib al-Chatti's interview with the Egyptian daily *Al-Akhbar*, 8 March 1974, in FBIS-MEA, 21 March 74, T5.

69. Bourguiba's speech at the fourth nonaligned conference on 7 September 1973, in the special issue on the conference, FBIS-MEA, October 73, p. 57.

70. Interview of Bourguiba with *Al-Musawwar*, Cairo, reported by Tunis Domestic Service, 20 September 1973, in FBIS-MEA, 21 September 73, T8.

71. See article in *Al-'Alam*, Rabat, 15 September 1973, in FBIS-MEA, 18 September 73, T7.

72. Tripoli Domestic Service, 17 November 1973, in FBIS-MEA, 19 November 73, T7.

73. Interview with former prime minister Bahi Ladgham, Carthage, Tunisia, June 1986.

74. The Tunisian foreign minister, Muhammad Masmoudi, appears to have been very close to Qadhdhafi. That agreement, however, had the blessings of Bourguiba, and in the final analysis, it was Bourguiba's decision to enter into the agreement.

75. This explanation was given to me by a number of Tunisian officials who prefer to remain anonymous, in Tunis, June 1986.

76. Interview with the Lebanese daily *Al-Safir*, reported by Tripoli Voice of the Arabs, 5 May 1974, in FBIS-MEA, 6 May 74, I7.

77. 'Umar al-Muhaishi's interview with *Al-Ahram*, 27 March 1976, in FBIS-MEA, 1 April 76, D7.

78. See Deeb, "Inter-Maghribi Relations," pp. 24–26.

79. Bourguiba's interview with the Austrian daily *Kurier*, Vienna, in FBIS-MEA, 18 April 74, I3.

80. Tripoli ARNA, 13 January 1975, in FBIS-MEA, 14 January 75, I7.

81. Habib Chatti's interview with *Le Matin*, 13 March 1974, in FBIS-MEA, 14 March 74, I6.

82. Mark B. Feldman, "The Tunisia-Libya Continental Shelf: Geographic Justice or Judicial Compromise?" in *American Journal of International Law*, Vol. 77, April 1983, p. 220.

83. See "Libya-Tunisia: Agreement to Submit Question of the Continental Shelf to the International Court of Justice," original text reproduced in *International Legal Materials*, Vol. 18, No. 1, January 1979, pp. 49–55.

84. Qadhdhafi's speech at a military parade on 2 June 1977, reported by Tripoli ARNA, 2 June 1977, in FBIS-MEA, 3 June 77, I7.

85. Interview with Dr. Habib Slim, director of the Political Science Department, Faculty of Law and Political Science, University of Tunis, June 1986.

86. FBIS-MEA, 16 November 73, T7.

87. *Al-Nahar*, Beirut, 22 January 1975, in FBIS-MEA, 24 January 75, I1. See also "La Libye regarde vers l'ouest," in *Maghreb-Machrek*, No. 70, October-December 1975, p. 8.

88. Paris AFP, 26 May 1975, in FBIS-MEA, 29 May 75, I9.

89. *Informations d'Outre Mer*, Paris, 25 June 1975, in FBIS-MEA, 3 July 75, I2.

90. I. William Zartman, *Ripe for Resolution, Conflict and Intervention in Africa*, Oxford University Press, Oxford, 1985, p. 34; see also Grimaud, p. 211.

91. Algiers Domestic Service, 28 December 1975, in FBIS-MEA, 29 December 75, I1.

92. Excerpt from the communiqué issued on the 28–29 December 1975, after talks between Boumediene and Qadhdhafi, in FBIS-MEA, 30 December 75, T1.

93. Cairo Domestic Service, 24 July 1977, in FBIS-MEA, 25 July 77, D24.

94. Cooley, *Libyan Sandstorm*, p. 122.

95. Richard B. Parker, *North Africa: Regional Tensions and Strategic Concerns*, Praeger, New York, 1984, p. 114.

96. Ibid.

97. I met a number of Sahrawi women whose husbands were fighting in the Sahara during my stay in Libya in 1977–1978.

98. There were two attempts at assassinating Qadhdhafi in 1976 and 1978.

99. Khartoum SUNA, 9 March 1974, in FBIS-MEA, 11 March 74, T7.

100. Interview with Numayri by the Lebanese newspaper *Al-Hayat*, reported on 4 May 1974, pp. 1, 7, in FBIS-MEA, 10 May 1974, I6.

101. Umdurman Domestic Service, 5 March 1975, in FBIS-MEA, 6 March 75, I6–I7.

102. *Al-Dustur*, Amman, 1 October 1975, in FBIS-MEA, 3 October 75, D9.

103. See Peter Bechtold, "The Contemporary Sudan," in *American-Arab Affairs*, Fall 1983, No. 6, p. 93.

104. William D. Brewer, "The Libyan-Sudanese 'Crisis' of 1981: Danger for Darfur and Dilemma for the United States," *The Middle East Journal*, Vol. 36, No. 2, Spring 1982, pp. 209–210.

105. Bechtold, "The Contemporary Sudan," p. 91.

106. *Al-Siyasa*, Kuwait, 21 July 1976, p. 1, in FBIS-MEA, 29 July 76, D3; see also Fahmy, p. 110.

107. See text of Joint Defense Pact in FBIS-MEA, 22 July 76, D1.

108. Tripoli ARNA, 25 July 1976, in FBIS-MEA, 28 July 76, I6.

109. See text of the RCC's law concerning oil areas, broadcast by Tripoli Domestic Service, 12 October 1973, in FBIS-MEA, 15 October 73, T3–T5.

110. Paris AFP, 15 October 1973, in FBIS-MEA, 16 October 73, T4.

111. Tripoli Domestic Service, 9 October 1973, in FBIS-MEA, 10 October 73, T8.

112. *Der Spiegel*, Hamburg, 12 November 1973, pp. 120–123, in FBIS-MEA, 13 November 73, T10.

113. Fahmy, pp. 133–134.

114. Eric Rouleau's interview with Qadhdhafi for *Le Monde*, Paris, 23 October 73, pp. 1, 6.

115. Ibid.

116. Interview with *Der Spiegel*.

117. See, for instance, his comments to the press during his Paris visit in November 1973, in FBIS-MEA, 30 November 73, T16.

118. See Lisa Anderson, "Qadhdhafi and the Kremlin," *Problems of Communism*, September–October 1985, p. 33.

119. Zartman, "Arms Imports—The Libya Experience," p. 15.

120. A special report on Libya, published by the U.S. Department of State, asserts, "In 1974 Qadhafi signed his first major arms agreement with the Soviet Union. The value of this contract—$2.3 billion—was almost $1 billion more than that of all the military agreements Qadhafi had signed up to that point." U.S. Department of State, Bureau of Public Affairs, Washington, D.C., Special Report No. 111, October 1983, "The Libyan Problem," p. 2. Anderson in her article "Libya and the Kremlin," using the same report, repeats the statement, p. 34. There is no evidence that such an agreement ever took place at that time, and given other glaring inaccuracies of the report, I seriously doubt the validity of that statement.

121. Haley, p. 66.

122. Zartman, "Arms Imports—The Libya Experience," p. 15.

123. My calculations are based on ibid.

124. U.S. Arms Control and Disarmament Agency, *World Military Expenditures and Arms Transfers 1973–1983*, Washington, D.C., 1985, p. 71. The figures are only estimates, and different sources, including the Arms Control and Disarmament Agency, give different figures for the same years.

125. Qadhdhafi's interview with *Al-Safir*, Beirut, broadcast on Tripoli Voice of the Arab Homeland, 5 May 1974, in FBIS-MEA, 6 May 74, I6.

126. *The Sunday Telegraph*, London, 27 April 1975, p. 2, in FBIS-MEA, 28 April 75, I3.

127. See Cairo MENA reports, 24 July 1977, in FBIS-MEA, 25 July 77, D24; also reports from Tel Aviv in ibid., N3.

128. Text of the note sent to the Soviet embassies and foreign ministries of several Arab countries, Cairo MENA, 27 April 77, in FBIS-MEA, 28 April 77, D1.

129. See, for instance, the commentaries on the Voice of the Arabs broadcast 28 April 1977, in FBIS-MEA, 29 April 77, D4.

130. 'Umar al-Muhaishi's interview with *Al-Ba'ath*, Damascus, 11 March 1975, p. 3, in FBIS-MEA, 20 March 75, I3.

# 6

## The Heyday of the Libyan Jamahiriya, 1977–1981

The isolation of Egypt in the Arab world in the wake of Sadat's visit to Jerusalem in November 1977, and more particularly after the Camp David Agreements of September 1978, strengthened Libya's regime. Not only was Egypt in no position to directly attack Libya;[1] the peace agreement with Israel alienated the rest of the Arab states and drew their leaders closer to the Libyan position. Qadhdhafi had been proven right in the eyes of those leaders for having criticized and opposed Sadat since 1973 and for having said all along that Sadat would make peace unilaterally with Israel and would betray the Arabs.

Furthermore, because Libya's alliances with Algeria and the Soviet Union remained strong despite the USSR's poor showing during the Egyptian-Libyan confrontation in the summer of 1977, Qadhdhafi did not require other allies, and calls for unions and mergers declined until 1980. When domestic and external pressures began building up again at that time, he resumed his search for states with which Libya could merge.

Because Qadhdhafi was feeling more secure throughout most of this phase, he began to capitalize on his newfound popularity in the Arab world and Africa by playing the role of statesman rather than that of revolutionary. He mediated conflicts, resolved pending problems with his neighbors, and in general sought to enhance his legitimacy by cooperating with rather than confronting other states in the region. Concomitantly, subversive and conflictual foreign policy actions diminished, as did his revolutionary rhetoric.

The thrust of Qadhdhafi's foreign policy during this whole period was to isolate Egypt in the Arab world and keep it out of Arab politics. So eager was he to mobilize Arab public opinion against Egypt that in March 1979 in Baghdad, his foreign secretary, 'Ali 'Abd al-Salam al-Turayki, stated that the struggle against Egypt should take precedence over that against Israel.[2]

Qadhdhafi's legitimacy was based during this period on his anti-Egyptian stand. In December 1977 he founded the Steadfastness and Confrontation Front with Algeria, Syria, the People's Democratic Republic of Yemen, and the PLO against Egypt. He held meetings in Tripoli and Benghazi with Arab heads of state who had previously shunned and been critical of Libya, such as King Khalid of Saudi Arabia; the purpose of these meetings was to isolate Egypt. To reduce the chance of Egyptian involvement in the region as much as to enhance his newly acquired legitimacy, Qadhdhafi began to mediate regional conflicts, such as that between Ethiopia and Somalia in March 1978.[3] He strengthened his ties to all the major Arab and African states neighboring Libya and toured the Arab east in an effort to mobilize support for his boycott of Egypt in June 1979 and to ensure that it would never threaten Libya's territorial integrity again.

A year after Egypt's attack on Libya, Qadhdhafi's fortunes had improved dramatically.[4] He was no longer a pariah in the Arab world, and his peers accepted him as a leader and a statesman in his own right. Unlike the October 1973 war period, they were now consulting him on all important matters regarding the Arab world and Africa.

## Qadhdhafi's New Ideology: A Change of Heart or a Change of Tactics?

The content of his ideological rhetoric during this phase underwent considerable change. The revolutionary element declined significantly in all of Qadhdhafi's speeches aimed at regional audiences (although domestically it increased markedly as he began to make some of the most drastic economic and social reforms of his tenure in power). This change became noticeable only after the Camp David Agreements. Until then the more conservative Arab states had not condemned Sadat or sided with the Steadfastness and Confrontation Front states.[5] Consequently, Qadhdhafi's conciliatory rhetoric appeared only when he felt he could rally states such as Saudi Arabia and the United Arab Emirates to his point of view.

In fact, Qadhdhafi's September 1, 1978, speech on the ninth anniversary of the Libyan coup was still very much in harmony with what he had been saying for the previous five years. The speech contained statements such as, "The revolutionary committees will spread everywhere throughout the Arab homeland to bring about a pan-Arab popular revolution and unify the Arab nation and solve its political problems."[6]

Following the Camp David Agreements of September 1978, Qadhdhafi, always the shrewd politician, reversed his ideological stands completely. Realizing that he could mobilize the support of the conservative Arab rulers to isolate Egypt in the region, he decided to change his tune. Revolution became diffused to mean a protest against Sadat's behavior rather than a specific movement aimed at overthrowing a political regime or system. Furthermore, Qadhdhafi, the so-called populist leader of the Arab masses against their corrupt rulers, began criticizing those very masses and praising their leaders.

Less than six weeks after the September 1 speech in which he had called for popular revolution in the Arab world, Qadhdhafi made a very different speech at a rally in Tripoli:

> We hail those Arab rulers, who have completely rejected what the Egyptian president dared to do. . . . But, while hailing Arab rulers on this occasion, I am not prepared . . . to hail the Arab peoples from the ocean to the Gulf. The reason is that Arab rulers have rejected what Egypt dared to do with the Israeli enemy, whereas the Arab masses—which seem to be turning into flocks of sheep—have not budged. . . .
>
> If the Arab masses do not rise and get angry at such a time, then when will they rebel and get angry?[7]

The only other Arab country that Qadhdhafi attacked in that speech was Morocco because of King Hasan's original support for Sadat's peaceful settlement with Israel. But even when Qadhdhafi criticized Morocco for receiving Sadat after the Camp David Agreements were signed and called for rebellion, he used the term again to mean a protest against Egypt rather than the overthrowing of the Moroccan monarch. Qadhdhafi said, "I am not saying that a revolution should take place in Morocco against the king. No I am not saying this. I am talking about a revolution against this dishonor which the Egyptian president brought to Morocco."[8]

As time passed, Qadhdhafi began to question his own notion of the necessity for a revolution in the Arab world, appearing disillusioned with the whole idea. In a speech on September 1, 1979, a year after he had called for popular revolution in the Arab world, he gave a very different speech. Addressing himself to the Libyan people as well as to the kings, princes, sultans, and presidents who were gathered in Benghazi to attend the ceremonies for the tenth anniversary of the Libyan coup, he said that Arab unity between states with different forms of political government was more important than revolution because "the model revolution has not succeeded. Most of the people's revolutions have relapsed. . . . Therefore the method of realizing Arab unity through the Arab reality we are living in remains strongly valid at this stage."[9] Throughout the speech he praised the conservative heads of state of Jordan and the Arabian peninsula, whom he had spent a whole decade insulting and whose overthrow he had called for on innumerable occasions.[10]

This ideological transformation was not focused only on the concept of revolution. Qadhdhafi began questioning other concepts as well. In the summer of 1979 he began a tour of the Arab world aimed at strengthening his ties with the major powers of the Arab east and at further isolating Egypt by calling for the moving of the Arab League's headquarters from Cairo to Tunis or Kuwait. In an interview with a Lebanese magazine on the eve of his departure, he discussed Arab politics. For the first time he talked of "Arab unity" not in ideological terms but in geopolitical terms: "The Libyans have no objection or reservation whatever with respect to the establishment of Arab unity, *but the geographical factor does not allow it.* Geographically unity between Syria and Iraq seems quite possible. Unity between Libya, Tunisia and Algeria is geographically possible."[11] Although Qadhdhafi would not often use the concept in this way, it is clear that he realized the difference between the use of a general and diffuse ideological concept of Arab unity and the more political and pragmatic functions of regional blocs.

Qadhdhafi also mellowed his anti-imperialist stand toward the United States and showed some reservations about the USSR, perhaps because most of the rulers to whom he was appealing happened to be close allies of the United States. He became more conciliatory toward the United States in the immediate aftermath of the Camp David Agreements. At an Arab-U.S. conference in Tripoli in October 1978, he addressed the U.S. delegation in rather mild terms: "This symposium must be a brick in a large structure which one day may be completed, because it is of no interest to Arabs and Americans to continue misunderstanding and hostility."[12] The next day at another symposium he was almost apologetic about Libya's relationship with the Soviet Union: "This U.S. policy is compelling the Socialist People's Libyan Arab Jamahiriyah, day after day, to resort to the Soviet Union and to be hostile to the U.S."[13]

Thus, not only was he questioning the necessity of revolution and anti-imperialism; he was also approaching the very core of Arab nationalist ideology—the idea of Arab unity—from a purely pragmatic and geopolitical point of view. In fact, in late spring 1980, when he was asked by a correspondent for an Italian magazine to define politics, instead of answering with some ideological slogan, as was his wont, he replied cryptically, "Politics mean the tackling of interests."[14]

## Political Reversals

By late summer and early autumn of 1980, however, the situation had changed both domestically and externally for Libya. There was an attempted tribal uprising in Cyrenaica led by a close associate of Qadhdhafi; the Libyan opposition in Egypt and elsewhere was calling for Qadhdhafi's overthrow; Sadat was on the offensive, had massed troops on Libya's borders, and had begun military maneuvers with the United States; and thousands of Libyan troops were engaged in a Chadian war against forces that had Egyptian, Sudanese, and French support.

The straw that broke the camel's back was the call to a jihad by Prince Fahd of Saudi Arabia when Israel declared Jerusalem the new capital of Israel.[15] Somehow that action in the wake of Qadhdhafi's other troubles was perceived as undermining his leadership. After all, he had been the one to call for revolutions, wars, and holy wars. He probably felt slighted and ignored, as in the case of the 1973 war, and so returned to his revolutionary rhetoric of the previous phase. In October 1980 while delivering a sermon on an Islamic religious feast, Qadhdhafi attacked Saudi Arabia. Referring to the U.S. AWACS that Saudi Arabia had just acquired,[16] he said, "Let Muslims everywhere know that Mecca, the holy Ka'ba, holy Al-Madinah, the prophet's tomb and the holy Mount of 'Arafat are now under the yoke of American occupation."[17] He called for a jihad to liberate Mecca, an apparent response to the prince's call for a jihad to liberate Jerusalem. Qadhdhafi then urged the Islamic "masses" to take up arms and fight, saying, "We feel the crusade wars have not ended since a new crusade has been launched by means of American planes and ships and is entrenching itself in Egypt, Somalia, Muscat, Oman, Saudi Arabia and Palestine."[18]

Revolution was back; so were calls for Arab unity. The Tripoli Domestic Service asked the Arab people to unite, saying they were "indivisible whatever the regional frontiers are."[19] Arab regimes were again lambasted and described as agents of imperialism,[20] and once more ideological rhetoric[21] became the focus of Qadhdhafi's speeches and Libya's media editorials and commentaries.

## Strategic Alliances and Mergers

There were five attempts at regional alliances, unions, and mergers during this phase of Libya's foreign policy in North Africa. Each occurred in a particular regional and political context. Furthermore, the primary determinants of these alliances were once again not so much ideological as pragmatic and were aimed at preserving Qadhdhafi's regime in power and defending Libya's territorial integrity.[22]

## The Steadfastness and Confrontation Front

The first attempt took place in early December 1977. Following Sadat's visit to Jerusalem, Qadhdhafi called for an Arab summit in Tripoli to discuss the implications of that visit for the Arab world. At that conference the decision was made to form the Steadfastness and Confrontation Front, an alliance of Libya, the PLO, and the more radical states in the Arab world, including Algeria, the People's Democratic Republic of Yemen (PDRY), and Syria. The front was opened to other countries of the region as well, but no other country joined, not even Iraq, which supported the front's stands.

The Steadfastness and Confrontation Front was a qualitatively different type of alliance from the Jarba union with Tunisia in January 1974 or the attempted merger with Egypt in 1973. The latter two involved economic, social, and political integration as well as mutual defense agreements and were to be headed by only one president. The Tripoli Declaration of December 5, 1977, which the front issued at the end of the conference,[23] implied that integration in any domain was not required of the signatories. Each leader was to continue dealing with the affairs of his own state unhampered by this agreement. The declaration did, however, include a mutual defense clause that stipulated that "members of the pan-Arab front consider any aggression against any member as an aggression against all members."[24]

The aim of the Steadfastness and Confrontation Front was primarily the isolation of Egypt in the Arab world. The first four decisions of the Tripoli Declaration were

1. To condemn President al-Sadat's visit to the Zionist entity since it constitutes a great betrayal of the sacrifice and struggle of our Arab people . . . [25]
2. To work for the frustration of the results of President al-Sadat's visit to the Zionist entity . . . [26]
3. To freeze . . . political and diplomatic relations with the Egyptian government . . . [27]
4. To decide not to take part in Arab League meetings which are held in Egypt . . . [28]

From Libya's perspective, this was a purely strategic alliance aimed at isolating Egypt in the Arab world. Libya's rationale was that a politically undermined Egypt would be too weak regionally to undertake any more attacks against Libya's borders. An Arab consensus would prevail to prevent an outcast Egypt from attacking one of its own members.

## The Unsuccessful Tripartite Agreement
## with Tunisia and Algeria

In June 1978 Libya invited Tunisia to enter into a tripartite federation that was to include Algeria.[29] This was a classic example of an attempt at merging and bloc formation when Qadhdhafi perceived his regime and/or his territory to be threatened.

The threats that made Qadhdhafi seek this federation with Algeria and Tunisia were both domestic and regional. The previous year Qadhdhafi had undertaken very drastic economic and social reforms in Libya, alienating almost every social group, tribe, and clan in his society.[30] Even members of the RCC and the *'ulamas* (men of religion) opposed those reforms.[31] As a result, in March 1978 another attempted coup took place against Qadhdhafi when the helicopter in which he was supposed to fly crashed, killing all passengers aboard.[32]

On the regional level the situation in Chad had deteriorated again. The Sabha accords had failed to impose law and order in that country, and President Felix Malloum had called in the French by invoking Chad's defense pact with France.[33] Egypt was apparently also supporting the anti-Libyan government in Ndjamena.[34] The French and Egyptian intervention in Chad was perceived by Qadhdhafi as an attempt to encircle Libya. Consequently, as early as February 1978 Qadhdhafi began saying that Libya and Tunisia were "one country, one nation and parts of the same body."[35] More visits were exchanged and more speeches made on the importance of unity and integration between countries of the Maghrib, until eventually in June 1978 Libya officially asked Tunisia to join this federation.[36] Tunisia's refusal was one of the major causes of the Libyan-sponsored military attack on Gafsa in Tunisia in 1980.[37]

Following the failure of this union attempt, Qadhdhafi knew a period of unprecedented popularity in the Arab world and Africa in the wake of the Camp David Agreements of September 1978. Almost all major Arab leaders, including King Khalid and Prince Sa'ud al-Faysal of Saudi Arabia, visited Libya between 1978 and 1979.[38] They were not just visits of protocol; they also involved consultations on intraregional affairs. The Saudi visit, for instance, was aimed at mediating the Moroccan-Algerian conflict over the Western Sahara in which Libya was involved. The Moroccans themselves were eager to open a dialogue with Libya regarding the future of the Maghrib.[39] Libya, Sudan, and Nigeria were attempting to solve the Chadian civil war, while Qadhdhafi was personally involved in mediating the Somali-Ethiopian conflict over the Ogaden.

Although the domestic scene was anything but peaceful, with two more alleged coup attempts reported in November 1978[40] and in March 1979,[41] Qadhdhafi enjoyed enough support in Africa and in the Arab world not to feel unduly threatened. Consequently, after the Camp David Agreements of September 1978 and until April 1980, there were no more attempts at unity with any of Libya's neighbors.

### Attempts at a Libyan-Algerian Merger

In the spring of 1980, however, the regional situation had changed again.[42] Egypt was taking the offensive and had massed troops on Libya's eastern borders. Sudan was resolving differences with Egypt and cooperating with it to support anti-Libyan factions in Chad. France was playing a very active role in Chad, and Libya's military forces were heavily engaged in the fighting there. More significantly, the Libyan opposition was organizing domestically and abroad and calling for the overthrow of the Qadhdhafi regime.

This was the type of situation that would induce Qadhdhafi to improve his relations with his neighbors and initiate new attempts at merging with states in the region to diffuse the threats to his regime. In late February 1980 the Algerian interior minister visited Libya, and he and his Libyan counterpart talked about forming a joint committee "to define stages for achieving the unity both countries [were] looking forward to."[43] The joint committee met in April 1980 at the height of the border crisis with Egypt.[44] It was clear that the move was intended to remind Libya's neighbor that Algeria was protecting Libya against any external military intervention. In June 1980 Algeria was warning Egypt not to attack Libya: "Algeria wishes to denounce these provocations and most forcefully condemn the invasion attempt which the Egyptian . . . army plans to carry out thereby threatening peace and security in the region. . . . Algeria declares its solidarity and stands on the side of the Libyan people."[45]

The union, however, never materialized. The aim of those union talks had been to raise the stakes of a possible Libyan-Egyptian confrontation to such a level that it would deter Egypt from attacking Libya. When the threat of such a confrontation receded, so did the prospects for a Libyan-Algerian merger.

### A Libyan-Chadian Merger

In January 1981 another union was announced, this time between Libya and Chad. The first article of the Chadian-Libyan agreement stated that both parties had agreed to work for complete unity, a unity of the masses in which wealth, power, and arms would be given to the people.[46] The longest of the articles of the agreement was devoted to a condemnation of Egypt and Sudan for their "imperialist, Zionist and reactionary" attempts at destabilizing the Chadian goverment. This article threatened

Sudan with dire consequences if it engaged in any further aggression against Chadian territory.[47] This merger was clearly intended to be a response to what was perceived in Libya as an Egyptian-Sudanese threat to Libya's southern borders. The merger was also imposed on a weak and divided Chad by a victorious Libya in order to legitimize the presence of its troops in that country and to ensure Libya's permanent control of the Aouzou strip.

### Treaty of Friendship and Cooperation

The last alliance in this phase took place in mid-August 1981 when the Treaty of Friendship and Cooperation was signed among Libya, the PDRY, and Ethiopia.[48] The Egyptians immediately denounced the treaty and accused the Soviet Union of being behind it. The timing of this alliance, they said, was significant because it took place when talks of Egyptian-Sudanese integration were underway, bolstered by extensive U.S. military and economic aid.[49] "This move is primarily aimed at encircling Egypt and Sudan to isolate them," Egypt claimed.[50] The timing also coincided with U.S. military maneuvers off the Gulf of Sidra, which Libya perceived as direct provocation.[51]

There is no doubt that the combined threats to Libya's borders precipitated the events that led to the declaration of the friendship treaty among Libya, Ethiopia, and the PDRY. The U.S. Sixth Fleet off the Gulf of Sidra threatened Libya's northern borders, an integrated Sudanese-Egyptian bloc represented a new danger to Libya's eastern borders, and the war raging in Chad appeared to threaten Libya's southern borders.

Whether the idea was promoted by the Soviet Union or not is difficult to say because of a dearth of reliable information. The Soviet Union, however, had a strategic interest in Ethiopia[52] and the PDRY, because their location on the Red Sea and the Gulf of Aden linked the Indian Ocean to the Suez Canal. A strong alliance among these three friendly states in the region would provide the Soviets with access routes from the Mediterranean to the Indian Ocean.

The significance of this alliance for the three states directly concerned was primarily in the projection of an image of their increased power in the region. For Libya the alliance meant a strengthening of ties with other pro-Soviet states and the assumption of a threatening stance to deter external intervention from the north, east, or south. In fact, nothing much was accomplished by this alliance, and although Libya and Ethiopia continued supporting rebels in southern Sudan, no treaty was needed to do so.

Thus, the various attempts at mergers and alliances undertaken by Libya during this phase were undertaken at times when Qadhdhafi felt

very threatened externally and domestically. The combined threat triggered a response to merge with other powers in the region. Domestic
unrest alone, or external opposition alone, was not sufficient to provoke
such a reaction.

A perception of threat, however, is not always enough to explain
certain alliances. The Chad merger, for instance, and the Steadfastness
and Confrontation Front were also determined to some extent by Libya's
desire to extend beyond its borders and increase its power and prestige
regionally.

Finally, alliances with states within the North African system were
not the only alternative Libya had to redress the regional balance of
power with it felt threatened. The treaty with the PDRY and Ethiopia
was an alliance with states outside the system to counterbalance threats
by states within the system.

## Conciliation or Subversion?
## The Case of Tunisia

After the failure of the Jarba union of 1974, Libyan-Tunisian relations
had become rather strained. Tunisia had accused the Libyan authorities
on numerous occasions of fomenting trouble in Tunisia, of training
Tunisians to perform sabotage in their own country, and of attempting
to assassinate Tunisian politicians. After Sadat's visit to Jerusalem,
however, Qadhdhafi's attitude changed. He had been granted the recognition he sought in the region as a result of having opposed Egypt
and foretold Sadat's unilateral moves toward the United States and Israel
in the wake of the October war of 1973. Having become more secure
on the regional level, Qadhdhafi became less revolutionary and more
conciliatory. He began playing the role of mediator of conflicts between
neighboring states and attempted to resolve disagreements between
himself and other regional leaders.

He started with Tunisia, trying to iron out some of the differences
that existed between the two states. A major bone of contention was
the continental shelf.[53] This was an area that extended beyond the Libyan
and Tunisian borders well into the Gulf of Gabes. It had been found
to be rich in oil reserves, and until 1974 several oil companies had been
given the right to drill and explore for offshore oil. After 1974, however,
Qadhdhafi started making a political issue out of the shelf in order to
pressure Tunisia into a union that it did not want. He claimed that most
of the continental shelf was an underwater extension of Libyan territory
and therefore that oil revenues belonged to Libya. Tunisia, for which
the continental shelf represented a very important potential source of

revenue, disputed Qadhdhafi's claims, maintaining that a large part of the continental shelf was a prolongation of Tunisian territory.[54] Tunisia asked Libya on several occasions to submit the matter to the International Court of Justice, but Qadhdhafi would not oblige; he insisted on tying the issue to a merger between the two countries.

On June 10, 1977, however, a special agreement to submit the matter to the International Court was signed in Tunis by Habib Chatti, the Tunisian minister of foreign affairs, and 'Ali 'Abd al-Salam Turayki, Libya's secretary for foreign affairs. It was not until December 1978, however, that the special agreement was submitted to the court[55] because Qadhdhafi did not actually decide to resolve the problem until after the Camp David Agreements of September 1978, when he felt secure in his newfound legitimacy in the Arab world. Had Libya remained an outcast in the region, it is very unlikely that the matter of the continental shelf would have been dealt with so peacefully and diplomatically.[56]

Throughout the spring of 1978 Libyan-Tunisian relations continued to improve. In May 1978 the Tunisian prime minister, Hedi Nouira, paid a three-day visit to Libya and signed a number of agreements on agricultural, industrial, and trade cooperation between the two countries. Speeches were made by both parties, and a joint communiqué was issued that emphasized the need to strengthen their relations and "resume the joint constructive action which proceeds from the old historic ties between the two sister countries, their common fate, and their aspiration for integration, cohesion and unity."[57]

By early June 1978 Tunisian-Libyan relations had improved to such an extent that Qadhdhafi felt that he could propose to Bourguiba the idea of a federal union that would also include Algeria.[58] Tunisia, however, was reluctant to enter into a federation with either regional power. An editorial in the Tunisian daily *L'Action* quoted the Tunisian prime minister as saying, "If we manage to lay the foundation stone, a strong foundation stone, of cooperation between our two countries, we will have strengthened our mutual understanding, strengthened the fraternity of our two peoples and opened up broad vistas for their joint future."[59]

Qadhdhafi had heard these words before. He realized that Tunisia was interested in economic cooperation with Libya but was not ready to make any political commitment. It was rejecting Libya's overtures while reaping huge benefits from bilateral trade, labor, agricultural, and industrial agreements. Scorned and humiliated again in his attempt to create a union with Tunisia, Qadhdhafi turned once more to subversion and sabotage.[60] During the summer of 1978 and until the Camp David Agreements, Libya waged a press campaign against Tunisia. The Tunisian daily *L'Action* was so incensed by the Libyan attacks that it even accused Jallud, Libya's second in command, of bribing French newspapers such as *L'Humanite* to criticize and insult Tunisia.[61] By early October 1978 relations had deteriorated to such an extent that accusations of Tunisians being trained in Libyan camps[62] and supplies of weapons from Libya being discovered in southern Tunisia were resumed.[63]

On January 27, 1980, sixty armed men entered Gafsa, a small southwestern town in Tunisia; attacked the army barracks, national guards, and police station; and took control of the town. They then attempted to foment an uprising against the Tunisian authorities.[64] The insurgency was put down after four days of armed clashes with the Tunisian armed forces, which had received French logistic support.

The Tunisian government's claim that Libya was behind the operation appears to be substantiated.[65] Libya apparently trained and armed the attackers and masterminded the plot. Significantly, Algeria was also implicated in the affair.[66]

No one is completely sure why this attack occurred. Nonetheless, there are two different although not mutually exclusive interpretations of the affair. Some North African specialists believe that Qadhdhafi wanted to bring down the Tunisian government in retaliation for the failure of the January 1974 merger. They refer to Qadhdhafi's September 1, 1978, speech in which he threatened Tunisia with popular revolution for having refused to unite with Libya. The quotation, however, could also be understood to refer to the later rejection of the union proposal with Algeria and Libya in May–June 1978: "Faced by a refusal to unite, from a very small minority, we find ourselves obliged to use new means to achieve popular revolution. In the future action will be taken to create popular revolutionary committees, working openly or covertly, depending on the circumstances of each country, in order to realize unity."[67]

Other scholars view the events as an Algerian strategy to pressure Tunisia to change its pro-Moroccan stand on the Western Sahara.[68] The proponents of this interpretation point to the fact that Gafsa is very close to the Tunisian-Algerian borders and rather far from Libya. Although this interpretation is a valid one, it does not account sufficiently for Libya's role in the attack.[69]

Taken together, however, the two interpretations give us a more complete picture of the reasons for the Gafsa attack. Whereas Libya was primarily motivated by a wish to retaliate for the rejection of its proposal for a federal union with Tunisia, Algeria's principal motive was to ensure that all minor states in the region stood on its side on the Western Sahara issue.

## The Case of Chad

As in the case of Tunisia, Libyan foreign policy toward Chad was conciliatory when Qadhdhafi was feeling secure and in control of the situation and acrimonious and subversive when he was not. From late 1977 until early February 1978, the insurgent forces supported by Libya fought the Chadian army and dislodged it from a large section of northern Chad, including Zouar, Bardai, Faya-Largeau, and the oases of Ounianga-Kebir and Fadi in the Tibesti.[70] Ndjamena subsequently broke diplomatic relations with Tripoli to protest its support for the insurgents. In mid-February Qadhdhafi, in his new role as mediator and conciliator, intervened and arranged for a cease-fire between the various forces of the insurgency and the Malloum government. Qadhdhafi then convened a minisummit in Sabha, in the southern province of the Fezzan in Libya, that was attended by the heads of state of Chad, Niger, and Libya and the first vice-president of Sudan. The agreements at the summit included the reestablishment of diplomatic relations between Tripoli and Ndjamena, the withdrawal of the Chadian complaint against Libya at the United Nations, the prohibition of any foreign intervention in Chad, the convening of a meeting between the various insurgent forces and the Chadian government in March 1978, and the creation of a military committee composed of Libyan and Nigerian officers to oversee the cease-fire and control the situation until national reconciliation was achieved.[71]

Hostilities between the government and the insurgent forces of the FROLINAT resumed one month later, however, and President Malloum accused Libya of fomenting the troubles.[72] The fact is that the Sabha accords had weakened the insurgents, who had been pressured by Libya to accept a cease-fire at a time when they were winning major battles against the regular Chadian army. It was they and not the Libyans who had decided to break the cease-fire. Libya's motives in trying to restrain them by calling for a cease-fire and the Sabha summit had been purely political. Not only did Qadhdhafi want to appear as the main mediator in the Chadian conflict; he also wanted Malloum to drop his complaints about Libya's claims to the Aouzou strip. Being in a very weak position, Malloum had apparently agreed if Libya convinced the insurgents to stop the fighting.[73] It was therefore not in Libya's interest at that time to reignite the hostilities, especially as they led Malloum to invoke Chad's defense pact with France, which in turn seized this opportunity to reestablish its declining influence in Chad.

French Jaguar bombers struck at the FROLINAT forces and halted their new offensive against the Chadian capital. The FROLINAT eventually succumbed to internal power struggles and split along ethnic lines. Malloum did not fare any better as riots against his junta broke out in southern Chad. By mid-1978, Hissene Habre, an anti-Qadhdhafi Muslim northerner and leader of the Forces Armées du Nord, which was supported by Egypt and the Sudan, had emerged as the strongman.

### The Rise and Fall of the Malloum-Habre Coalition

In order to reestablish some law and order, a coalition government was formed in August 1978 headed by Malloum, the Christian southerner, with Habre, the Muslim northerner, as prime minister. That government had the blessing of France as well as that of Egypt, Sudan, and Saudi Arabia.[74]

But to have an anti-Libyan government in Chad, supported by Egypt and Sudan and armed primarily by France, was the last situation that Qadhdhafi wanted on his southern borders. His reaction was to initiate subversive actions to destabilize the new anti-Libyan government. He began assisting the buildup of a pro-Libyan insurgent force headed by Ahmat Asil whose function was to create disorder in Chad and undermine the coalition government of Malloum and Habre. The government broke up in February 1979, not only because of Qadhdhafi's actions but also because of Habre's ambition to control the state. Military conflict erupted throughout the country and caused thousands of casualties.

With the fall of the Malloum-Habre coalition government, however, the threatening situation was over, and it was time for Libya to mediate the conflict again. In March 1979 a conference was convened in Kano, Nigeria, to try finding a way out of the Chadian conflict. Nigeria, Libya, Sudan, Cameroon, and Niger were all parties to the conference.[75] France apparently gave its blessing as well.[76] The various Chadian groups met and decided to form a transitional government in which all parties would be represented: the Gouvernment d'Union Nationale de Transition (GUNT).[77] The real power was invested in Goukouni Ouedeye as minister of the interior, and Hissene Habre, who became minister of defense. Libya apparently played an important role in mediating between the parties, as it had no desire to see another anti-Libyan government set up in Ndjamena.[78]

### GUNT and GUNT II

By May 1979 it was becoming evident to Qadhdhafi that Ouedeye and Habre were effectively sharing power and becoming too independent from Libya. They were dividing government positions between their own people and keeping out of office 'Abd al-Qadir Kamougé, a southerner and a Christian who headed the Forces Armées Tchadienne and was

Nigeria's favorite; and Asil Ahmat, Libya's man and head of the Conseil Democratique de la Revolution (CDR).[79] Nigeria and Libya were incensed and closed their borders with Chad.[80]

An independent government in Ndjamena was threatening to Libya because Chad could enter into defense pacts with other nations, make alliances with rival powers such as Sudan and Egypt, allow the Libyan opposition to operate in the north, and, most significantly, challenge Libya's claims to the Aouzou strip. Habre had already taken these actions, and apparently Ouedeye was also willing to challenge Libya. In an interview with *Africa Report,* Ouedeye was quoted as saying, "We have not changed our position regarding the occupation of Aouzou. It is an occupation."[81]

Libya's response was swift. Qadhdhafi increased his support for the various opposition groups to the GUNT, including the original FROLINAT headed by Muhammad Abba Siddiq,[82] the Vulcan Army headed by Abdallahi Adoum Dana, and the CDR headed by Asil Ahmat. All three men were Muslim northerners who immediately began fomenting trouble in the north. In June 1979 Libya and Nigeria formed an umbrella organization of all the opposition forces, the Front d'Action Commune Provisoir, as an alternative administration to the GUNT.[83] Through this front, Qadhdhafi was able to support southern Christian insurgents against the government. Here again practical considerations of Libyan interest took precedence over ideological support for Arab Muslim northerners in Chad.[84] Libyan forces and Libyan armored units launched a major attack in northern Chad with the support of this front. Despite France's logistic and military assistance to the GUNT, it collapsed by the end of July 1979.

To find a solution to the renewed violence and to choose a new government after the fall of the GUNT, all parties to the conflict returned to the conference table in August, this time in Lagos. Another coalition government, the GUNT II, was formed in November 1979 and included Libya's protégés: Ahmat as foreign minister, Siddiq as minister of the interior, and Kamougé as vice-president.[85] It was not difficult to predict what was going to follow: The pro-Libyan forces in the new government formed an alliance with each other and Ouedeye and under pressure from Qadhdhafi pushed the anti-Libyan Habre out of power. This in turn led to a civil war and a complete breakdown of the system that lasted until the end of 1980 and caused thousands of casualties and tens of thousands of refugees. Ouedeye then ordered French troops to withdraw from Chad and asked Libya to intervene.[86] It did, entering in full force in October 1980 and making heavy use of armored units and the air force.[87] By mid-November Libyan forces were occupying parts of northern Chad, and Ouedeye had launched a coordinated attack on Ndjamena.[88]

### The Rationales for Military Intervention

Having ensured the victory of Goukouni Ouedeye, Qadhdhafi then announced a Libyan-Chadian merger in January 1981 to consolidate and legitimize his power and the presence of his troops in Chad.[89] The merger was necessary to guarantee the supremacy of Libya's relationship to Chad. Qadhdhafi wanted to make sure that Libya, and Libya alone, could move its troops in and out of Chad at will and that no state, either in the Arab League or the OAU, could question his right to do so.

In December 1980 Qadhdhafi had admitted for the first time that Libyan forces were fighting in Chad at the request of the "legitimate Chadian government."[90] He asserted again that the Aouzou strip was Libyan: "Aouzou . . . is a Libyan oasis and its inhabitants would not understand if they were told that they are Chadians and not Libyans."[91] When asked why he was fighting in Chad, Qadhdhafi replied, "We do not accept encirclement by hostile regimes. We had a gentlemen's agreement with As-Sadat under the terms of which he promised not to intervene in Chad. However, he is helping Habre."[92]

It is difficult to accept at face value Qadhdhafi's assertion that he wished to protect his "Libyan" Muslim brethren in northern Chad against the Christian southerners[93] when he had no qualms whatever in backing Kamougé, a Christian southerner, who was allegedly responsible for the massacre of thousands of Muslim northerners.[94] Qadhdhafi, on the other hand, had always feared the presence of hostile forces on his southern borders. More than one attempt at overthrowing him had been launched from Chad. Consequently, one of the main reasons Libyan forces were in Chad was to ensure that only a pro-Libyan government would be in power, which would not permit Egypt, Sudan, or France to operate freely on Libya's southern borders. Thus, every time an anti-Libyan government, or even one that was too independent from Libya, came to power in Chad, Qadhdhafi engaged in a conflictual foreign policy of supporting, arming, and training groups opposing that government.

Controlling the Aouzou strip in northern Chad meant that no forces hostile to Qadhdhafi's regime could enter Libya from the south, that Libya's military power could be extended beyond its borders, and that Libya's leverage in its dealings with Western nations was heightened. Some experts on Libya have also argued that Qadhdhafi's interest in the Aouzou strip stemmed from his wish to gain control of its uranium reserves for economic as well as political reasons: "Quite simply, it is a question of consolidating Libya's position as an energy supplier generally. Its ability to supply energy to those who control the real levers of international power or international opinion . . . is as important as any issue involving Arab public opinion."[95]

Qadhdhafi's military intervention was therefore not merely a defensive action against the perceived threat of anti-Libyan forces in Chad. It was also an aggressive pursuit of his interest in extending Libya's influence and increasing his power and prestige by gaining control of strategic resources.

## The Case of Sudan

After Sadat's visit to Jerusalem in November 1977, Qadhdhafi's efforts centered around the isolation of Egypt in the Arab world. He did this by increasing his ideological rhetoric against Egypt and by improving Libya's relations with most of the Arab states, including Sudan. After being initially critical of Numayri for supporting Sadat's visit to Jerusalem,[96] Qadhdhafi changed his tactics. In February 1978 Sudan's first vice-president visited Tripoli to discuss bilateral relations.[97] At the end of the visit Sudan and Libya issued a communiqué affirming their joint policy on such general issues as "Arabism, Islam, African fraternity, socialism, unity, the liberation of Palestine, combatting colonialism and racism."[98] The communiqué also acknowledged Libya's fear of an Egyptian-Sudanese bloc but affirmed Sudan's peaceful intentions. The communiqué stated that "the joint defense agreement between Egypt and Sudan was a defensive one and not directed against the Jamahiriya."[99]

The two countries also agreed to resume diplomatic relations and allow their national carriers to fly again between the two countries.[100] By April 1978 Qadhdhafi had agreed to close down the training camps of the Sudanese opposition in Libya, and Numayri had decided to pardon them and invite them back to Sudan.[101] A year later 350 Ansar who had opposed Numayri did return to Sudan under a general amnesty.[102] Libya also resumed economic aid to Sudan and invited Sudanese workers to come to Libya.[103]

After the Camp David Agreements Sudan was in a quandary. A condemnation of the agreements would incur the wrath of Egypt, Sudan's main supporter and protector in the region; support of Egypt would cost Sudan the political and economic support of the rest of the Arab world.[104] For the next few months Sudan wavered between the two positions, supporting Egypt at times, but qualifying that support.[105] Sudanese-Egyptian relations gradually cooled until in December 1979 Sudan withdrew its ambassador to Cairo.

Libya took advantage of this situation by enticing Sudan with economic aid, with the closing down of training camps for the Sudanese opposition, with invitations to join Libya in finding a solution to the Chadian conflict, and so forth. Egypt fought back by proceeding with the integration plans between Egypt and the Sudan, seeking to establish a Nile basin organization made up of the states on the Nile,[106] and planning for the development of the Jonglei Canal in Sudan, which would have been an economic boon for the country.[107]

The exacerbation of the situation in Chad in the spring of 1980 and Libya's aggressive role in the civil war, however, began to threaten Sudan's security on its western borders. Consequently, Sudan turned to Egypt for protection, and relations between the two countries began to improve. Concomitantly, Sudan's relations with Libya began to deteriorate.[108] Mutual fear and suspicion were at the root of the conflict. Whereas Numayri feared the spillover of the Chadian civil war into Sudan (which had similar ethnic problems), Libya viewed Egypt's support for Habre, which was taking place via Sudan,[109] as an attempt to encircle Libya. According to Qadhdhafi, "The Chadian war . . . was being waged against the Libyan Jamahiriyah. We were forced to cross the border to defend ourselves."[110]

## Old Conflicts and New Threats in 1980

Despite Sudan's and Egypt's reconciliation and both countries' cooperation with France to support anti-Libyan forces in Chad—all of which should have triggered Qadhdhafi's usual response to threats—Qadhdhafi was uncharacteristically subdued in 1980. In fact, Qadhdhafi was simultaneously facing overwhelming domestic opposition and external opposition and consequently remained conciliatory in order not to exacerbate an already volatile situation. The crisis in Chad was very serious, and Libya had more than 5,000 regular troops fighting there,[111] and an estimated 14,000 at the height of the Chadian war.[112] Libya was suffering significant losses in labor and military equipment, Egypt had massed a large number of troops and was engaging in military maneuvers with the U.S. Air Force,[113] and Egypt had declared a state of emergency in the western desert and was threatening Libya with another punitive attack.[114] Exiled Libyans in Europe who opposed the Qadhdhafi regime had begun flocking to Cairo;[115] they saw Egypt as the only safe haven after they had been threatened with assassination if they did not return to Libya.[116] Some of them organized themselves into the Libyan Liberation Front[117] and called for the toppling of Qadhdhafi.[118]

In mid-August 1980 a major uprising took place in Tubruq, headed by Major Idris al-Shuhaybi, Qadhdhafi's right-hand man, on Libya's eastern borders with Egypt. Shuhaybi had the support of some of the main disaffected tribes of Cyrenaica.[119] This attempt to overthrow Qadhdhafi was the most serious since 1975, when members of the RCC had plotted to get rid of him.

Qadhdhafi faced war in Chad, a potential military attack by Egypt, and very serious opposition from Libyans inside and outside the country. Always cautious, Qadhdhafi was not about to make a bad situation worse by embarking on a conflictual course of action vis-à-vis his neighbors. On the contrary, his approach was conciliatory both to Egypt and Sudan. Libya offered Sudan $600,000 in material aid for refugees,[120] greater cooperation between the two countries in the military and economic spheres, assistance in land reclamation projects and in the grain cultivation program, and employment opportunities for Sudanese workers.[121]

Qadhdhafi's attitude toward Egypt was much the same. In an interview with *Die Deutsche Welle*, Qadhdhafi was quoted as saying, "We have no desire to send our forces beyond Chad. . . . We are in the process of ending all military confrontations including those with the army of As-Sadat, which is amassed in full force on our border. We will work seriously to eliminate military confrontation with Egypt."[122]

Despite the presence of Egyptian troops on Libya's eastern borders, Qadhdhafi reduced his own forces there and opened up Libya's borders to Egyptian civilians. On the borders large posters were set up that read, "The Jamahariya welcomes the Egyptian brothers on its soil unconditionally and without restrictions."[123]

Thus, when Qadhdhafi felt secure after Egypt's isolation in the aftermath of the Jerusalem visit and the Camp David Agreements, he pursued a conciliatory foreign policy toward Sudan, trying to woo it away from Egypt. When Qadhdhafi felt threatened externally and domestically, he continued to pursue a conciliatory policy in order to diffuse the danger to Libya's borders and to his regime.

## Notes

1. Egypt would have had considerable difficulty attacking or invading another Arab state in the wake of the peace treaty with Israel, although Egypt did continue to threaten Libya with retaliation.

2. Press conference held in Baghdad by Foreign Secretary 'Ali 'Abd al-Salam al-Turayki, 31 March 1979, in FBIS-MEA, 3 April 79, A1–A2.

3. Rome ANSA, 21 March 1978, in FBIS-MEA, 22 March 78, I2.

4. *The Guardian*, London, 8 May 1978, p. 20, in FBIS-MEA, 9 May 78, I1.

5. See below.

6. Qadhdhafi's 1 September 1978, speech, Tripoli Domestic Service, 1 September 1978, in FBIS-MEA, 5 September 78, I2.

7. Qadhdhafi's address at the 7 October Rally in Tripoli, in FBIS-MEA, 11 October 78, I2.

8. Ibid., I7.

9. Qadhdhafi's speech on 1 September 1979, delivered in Benghazi, Tripoli Domestic Service, 1 September 1979, in FBIS-MEA, 4 September 79, I4.

10. Ibid., I6.

11. Interview with Qadhdhafi for *Al-Mustaqbal*, 30 June 1979, pp. 26, 27, in FBIS-MEA, 3 July 79, I1. My emphasis.

12. Speech by Qadhdhafi at symposium on Arab-U.S. dialogue, in Tripoli, Tripoli Domestic Service, 11 October 1978, in FBIS-MEA, 12 October 78, I5.

13. Qadhdhafi's 11 October Address to the People's Dialogue session in Tripoli, Tripoli JANA, 12 October 1978, in FBIS-MEA, 13 October 78, I3.

14. Interview with Qadhdhafi for *Panorama*, Rome, in FBIS-MEA, 7 June 80, I2.

15. See text of call for a jihad by Crown Prince Fahd bin 'Abd al-'Aziz, reprinted in *Al-Anwar*, Beirut, 14 August 1980.

16. William B. Quandt, *Saudi Arabia in the 1980's: Foreign Policy, Security and Oil*, The Brookings Institution, Washington, D.C., 1981, p. 156.

17. Qadhdhafi's sermon in Zawila, Libya, 19 October 1980, in Tripoli Domestic Service, 19 October 1980, in FBIS-MEA, 20 October 80, I2.

18. Ibid., see for U.S.-Libyan relations, Lillian Craig Harris, *Libya: Qadhdhafi's Revolution and the Modern State*, Westview Press, Boulder, 1986, pp. 99–102.

19. Tripoli Domestic Service, 29 October 1980, in FBIS-MEA, 30 October 80, I1.

20. Voice of the Arab Homeland, 30 October 80, in FBIS-MEA, 31 October 80, I2.

21. See, for instance, interview with Qadhdhafi in *Der Spiegel*, 21 September 81, pp. 148–156, in FBIS-MEA, 22 September 81, Q1.

22. See Chapter 1.

23. See text of Declaration of Tripoli Conference, in Tripoli JANA, 5 December 1977, in FBIS-MEA, 5 December 77, A11–A15.

24. Article 10 of the Declaration of Tripoli Conference, in ibid., A14.

25. Ibid., A13.

26. Ibid.

27. Ibid.

28. Ibid.

29. See below.

30. For an analysis of those reforms see Marius Deeb and Mary-Jane Deeb, *Libya Since the Revolution: Aspects of Social and Political Development*, Praeger, New York, 1982, pp. 113–120; see also Marius Deeb, "Radical Political Ideologies and Concepts of Property in Libya and South Yemen," *Middle East Journal*, Vol. 40, No. 3, Summer 1986, pp. 445–461.

31. *Arab Report and Record*, 1–15 June 1978, p. 409.

32. Paris, AFP, 12 March 1978, in FBIS-MEA, 13 March 78, I2.

33. See below.

34. Tripoli Voice of the Arab Homeland, 13 February 1978, in FBIS-MEA, 14 February 78, I1.

35. Tripoli JANA, 7 June 1978, in FBIS-MEA, 8 June 78, I3.

36. Tripoli Domestic Service, 7 June 1978, in FBIS-MEA, 8 June 78, I3.

37. See below.

38. Tripoli Voice of the Arab Homeland, 29 September 1979, in FBIS-MEA, 1 October 1979, I1.

39. Rabat MAP, 15 September 1979, in FBIS-MEA, 17 September 79, I4.

40. Kuwait KUNA, 22 November 1978, in FBIS-MEA, 22 November 78, I3.

41. Cairo MENA, 7 March 1979, in FBIS-MEA, 7 March 79, D7.

42. See below.

43. Tripoli JANA, 19 February 1980, in FBIS-MEA, 20 February 80, I4.

44. Tripoli JANA, 5 April 1980, in FBIS-MEA, 7 April 80, I4.

45. Algiers Domestic Service, 19 June 1980, in FBIS-MEA, 20 June 80, I1.

46. See the text of the Chadian-Libyan Union Agreement of January 1981, in Michel N'Gangbet, *Peut-on encore sauver le Tchad?* Editions Karthala, Paris, 1984, Appendix 3, p. 115.

47. See Article 6 of the Chadian-Libyan Union Agreement in ibid., p. 116.

48. Aden Domestic Service, 17 August 1981, in FBIS-MEA, 21 August 81, C6.

49. Political Commentary on Cairo Domestic Service, 20 August 1981, in FBIS-MEA, 21 August 81, D3.

50. Ibid.

51. See statement issued by the People's Committee of the People's Foreign Liaison Bureau, in FBIS-MEA, 19 August 81, Q1. In fact, the downing of two Libyan Sukhoi planes by U.S. aircraft in the Gulf of Sidra in August 1981 occurred during U.S. military maneuvers.

52. See Zartman, *Ripe for Resolution*, p. 84. The USSR's role, however, is not clear; see Anderson, "Qadhdhafi and the Kremlin," p. 37; and Robert O. Freedman, *Soviet Policy Toward the Middle East Since 1970*, Praeger, New York, 1982, pp. 412–413. Moscow praised the treaty, describing it as "an important stage in strengthening the national liberation movement's solidarity and in stepping up their struggle against imperialism and reaction and for peace and progress." *Pravda*, Moscow, 23 August 1981, quoted in Freedman, pp. 412–413.

53. See brief discussion in Chapter 5.

54. See Feldman, pp. 222–224, for a discussion of the claims and contentions of the two states.

55. See the analysis of the special agreement by Lawrence L. Herman, "The Court Giveth and the Court Taketh Away: An Analysis of the Tunisia-Libya Continental Shelf Case," in *International and Comparative Law Quarterly*, Vol. 33, No. 4, October 1984, pp. 825–858; see also text of special agreement in *International Legal Materials*, pp. 49–55.

56. The Tunisians are still very unhappy at the way the International Court of Justice ruled on the matter. For them the issue is not yet settled.

57. Text of the joint Tunisian-Libyan communiqué, Tripoli Domestic Service, 15 May 1978, in FBIS-MEA, 16 May 78, I1.

58. Tripoli Domestic Service, 7 June 1978, in FBIS-MEA, 8 June 78, I3.

59. *L'Action*, Tunis, 10 June 1978, in FBIS-MEA, 29 June 78, I1.

60. Interview with Faraj al-Chayeb, chargé of foreign relations of the Dustur Party, Tunis, Maison du Parti, June 1986.

61. *L'Action*, Tunis, 8 August 78, pp. 1–2, in FBIS-MEA, 16 August 78, I1–I2.

62. *L'Action*, Tunis, 1 October 1978, in FBIS-MEA, 6 October 78, I3.

63. Ibid.

64. This is the Tunisian version of the events based on the confessions of the people arrested. As there is no other credible version of the events, I question here only the causes of the Gafsa attack. See Tunis TAP, 31 January 1980, in FBIS-MEA, 1 February 80, I10–I12.

65. *Le Monde*, Paris, 31 January 1980, pp. 1, 8.

66. Ibid.; also interviews with Habib Slim and Faraj al-Chayeb in Tunis, June 1986.

67. Qadhdhafi's 1 September 1978, speech, quoted in Sadok Belaid, "L'Operation de Gafsa de Janvier 1980 et ses enseignements," *Revue Tunisienne de Droit*, Vol. 11, 1979, Numero Special, p. 23. This appears to be the Tunisian government's viewpoint as well; see *Recent Developments in the Relations Between Libya and Tunisia*, Tunis, 4 February 1980, government pamphlet, Ministry of Foreign Affairs in Tunis, June 1986.

68. Although the Tunisian authorities officially denied any Algerian involvement, privately they confided that there had been an Algerian-Libyan connivance in the attack. Based on interviews in Tunis, June 1986.

69. Interviews with Faraj al-Chayeb and Habib Slim in Tunis, June 1986.

70. See for an analysis of Chadian-Libyan relations in 1978 H. Mammeri, "Le Colonel Kadhafi et la question Tchadienne," *Maghreb-Machrek*, No. 80, April–June 1978, pp. 11–13.

71. Ibid., p. 12; see also Tripoli JANA, 26 February 1978, in FBIS-MEA, 3 March 1978, I2.

72. Tripoli Voice of the Arab Homeland, 29 June 1978, in FBIS-MEA, 30 June 78, I3.

73. See Jonathan Bearman's interpretation of those events in *Qadhdhafi's Libya*, Zed Books, London, 1986, p. 213.

74. Neuberger, pp. 38–39; Bearman, pp. 213–214; for Egypt's role in Chad see *Arab Report and Record*, 15–28 February 1978, p. 126.

75. See N'Gangbet, pp. 111–113.

76. Neuberger, p. 43.

77. See N'Gangbet, pp. 111–113.

78. See message by Malloum to Qadhdhafi to thank him for his mediation, Tripoli JANA, 17 March 1979, in FBIS-MEA, 20 March 79, I2.

79. Bearman, p. 215.

80. Nigeria also withdrew its troops that were supposed to oversee the ceasefire in N'Djamena.

81. *Africa Report*, Vol. 23, No. 5, September-October 1978, in Neuberger, p. 40.

82. Tripoli JANA, 3 May 1979, in FBIS-MEA, 4 May 79, I2–I4.

83. See Bearman, p. 215.

84. Neuberger, p. 46.

85. Ibid.

86. Tripoli JANA, 5 April 1980, in FBIS-MEA, 7 April 80, I2.

87. Paris AFP, 6 November 1980, in FBIS-MEA, 7 November 80, S1; see also report in Paris AFP, 11 November 1980, in FBIS-MEA, 12 November 80, S1.

88. Paris AFP, 19 November 1980, in FBIS-MEA, 19 November 80, S2.

89. See text of Chadian-Libyan Union Agreement in N'Gangbet, Appendix 3, pp. 115–117.

90. Interview with Qadhdhafi in *Le Monde*, 2 December 1980, p. 7, in FBIS-MEA, 3 December 80, I1–I2.

91. Ibid., I2.

92. Ibid.

93. See Rene Lemarchand, "Libyan Goals, Objectives and Prospects in Africa," unpublished paper prepared for the Defense Academic Research Support Program Conference on Prospects for Africa, U.S. European Command, Stuttgart, Germany, April 1986, for a discussion of the cultural approach, pp. 2–3.

94. Neuberger, p. 46.

95. Nourredine Abdi, "Common Regional Policy for Algeria and Libya: From Maghribi Unity to Saharan Integration," in E.G.H. Joffe and K. S. McLachlan, eds., *Social and Economic Development of Libya*, MENAS, Cambridgeshire, 1982, p. 225.

96. See Qadhdhafi's interview with *Paris Match*, Paris, 15 December 1977, in FBIS-MEA, 16 December 77, I4.

97. Umdurman Domestic Service, 7 February 1978, in FBIS-MEA, 8 February 78, I4.

98. See text of Libyan-Sudanese communiqué, Tripoli Domestic Service, 8 February 1978, in FBIS-MEA, 9 February 78, I5.

99. Ibid.

100. Ibid.

101. Umdurman Domestic Service, 12 April 1978, in FBIS-MEA, 13 April 78, I2.

102. Khartoum SUNA, 28 May 1979, in FBIS-MEA, 30 May 79, I9.

103. Khartoum SUNA, 19 April 1978, in FBIS-MEA, 21 April 78, I3–I4.

104. See interview with Sudanese vice-president, General 'Abd al-Majd Khalil, in *Al-Sharq al-Awsat*, London, 2 October 1979, p. 2, in FBIS-MEA, 10 October 79, I8.

105. See for Khartoum's vacillating position, Khartoum SUNA, 20 October 1978, in FBIS-MEA, 20 October 78, I5; see also *Al-Ra'y*, Amman, 7 April 1979, p. 15, in FBIS-MEA, 9 April 79, I5; and Doha, QNA, 9 April 79, I6.

106. Khartoum SUNA, 14 January 1979, in FBIS-MEA, 16 January 79, I3.

107. See Bechtold, "The Contemporary Sudan," p. 98.

108. Muhammad Bashir Hamid in his article "The Findlandization of Sudan's Foreign Policy," in *Journal of Arab Affairs*, Vol. 2, No. 2, pp. 201–223, claims that Egyptian-Sudanese relations were strained in the spring of 1980 because

of a Sudanese-Ethiopian rapprochement. Evidence shows that relations between Egypt and Sudan were improving during that spring as illustrated by Numayri's decree in March 1980 amending an earlier immigration law to allow Egyptians to enter Sudan freely with only an identity card. See Khartoum SUNA, 29 March 1980, in FBIS-MEA, 2 April 80, I7.

109. Tripoli JANA, 5 April 1980, in FBIS-MEA, 7 April 80, I2.

110. Interview with Qadhdhafi in *L'Humanité*, Paris, 21 January 1981, p. 9, in FBIS-MEA, 27 January 81, I3.

111. See Mark Heller, ed., *The Middle East Military Balance 1983*, Tel Aviv University, Tel Aviv, 1983, p. 39.

112. Bearman, p. 217.

113. Cairo MENA, 19 June 1980, in FBIS-MEA, 19 June 80, D1.

114. See, for instance, the editorial in *Al-Ahram*, Cairo, 20 June 1980, pp. 1, 3, in FBIS-MEA, 25 June 80, D2–D3.

115. *Al-Majallah*, London, 21–27 June 1980, p. 7, in FBIS-MEA, 27 June 80, D5.

116. The deadline for their return to Libya was 11 June 1980, after which they would be assassinated. See interviews with *Panorama*, Rome, reported by Tripoli JANA, 7 June 1980, in FBIS-MEA, 9 June 80, I3–I4.

117. Cairo MENA, 29 June 1980, in FBIS-MEA, 30 June 80, D5.

118. A number of other opposition groups were founded in Cairo during the summer of 1980, among them the Libyan National Democratic Movement, the Libyan National League, and the Free Libyan National Movement, all asking Egypt to help them overthrow Qadhdhafi.

119. See for description of uprising Cairo MENA, 19 August 1980, in FBIS-MEA, 19 August 80, D11.

120. Khartoum SUNA, 31 August 1980, in FBIS-MEA, 4 September 80, I5.

121. Tripoli JANA, 18 February 1981, in FBIS-MEA, 19 February 81, I2.

122. Interview with Qadhdhafi in *Die Deutsche Welle*, reported in Tripoli Voice of the Arab Homeland, 15 February 1981, in FBIS-MEA, 17 February 81, I2.

123. *Al-Sharq al-Awsat*, London, 13 January 1981, in FBIS-MEA, 15 January 81, D8.

# 7

# Libya in the Post-Sadat Era, 1981–1985

During the 1981–1985 phase, changes in the North African system of states influenced the direction of Libya's foreign policy in the region. The death of Sadat removed the visible symbol of Libya's confrontation with Egypt. It became more difficult for Qadhdhafi to blame all the trials and tribulations of the Arab world on Egypt's peace treaty with Israel when the treaty's main architect was assassinated for it. An era of Egyptian-Libyan relations spanning more than a decade came to an end. The alliance with Algeria that had provided Libya with a regional protector since 1975 began to erode in early 1981, and Qadhdhafi found himself once more isolated in North Africa. Furthermore, the Reagan administration took a more aggressive stance toward Libya that involved deliberate military threats to Libya in the Gulf of Sidra, support for Libyan opposition abroad, a campaign of disinformation, and military support for regional governments antagonistic to Qadhdhafi.[1]

## Sadat's Death and Its Repercussions in Libya

The assassination of Sadat in October 1981 gave rise to anxiety in several quarters. The United States realized it had lost a very important ally in the Middle East and feared that this might weaken its position in the region. As General Alexander Haig, then U.S. secretary of state, explains in his memoirs:

> [I]t was possible to imagine Egypt, after Sadat, drifting back into the radical world with all the consequences that could follow: the dismantling of the peace process, a further loss of American prestige and influence, and a flight by the rest of the moderate Arabs into neutralism or accommodation with the forces they most feared—radicalism and the Soviet Union.[2]

As a consequence, the United States moved swiftly to strengthen its position in the region. After Sadat's funeral, Haig and Numayri met for an hour in Cairo to discuss Sudan's defensive needs. Khartoum announced two days later that "the U.S. has agreed . . . to supply Sudan quickly with all its defensive needs and that some equipment will immediately be delivered."[3]

In November 1981, the United States began a major joint military maneuver codenamed Operation Bright Star with Egyptian, Sudanese, Somali, and 'Umani forces to impress the regional powers with the continued U.S. presence and interest in protecting those states from external interference.[4] Part of the maneuvers took place in the western desert near Libya's borders.

Sudan had also been shocked by Sadat's death and feared that while Egypt was in the process of making the transition to a new successor, Sudan might be attacked by forces coming from Libya or Ethiopia or be exposed to domestic upheavals. Numayri consequently sought out U.S. military assistance and played up the Libyan threat to induce the United States to be more forthcoming in delivering military hardware. To bolster his allegations, Numayri announced that he was preparing to launch a preemptive attack against Libya to defend Sudan's sovereignty.[5]

On October 7, 1981, the day after Sadat's assassination, the Libyan opposition in Khartoum announced the formation of the National Front for the Salvation of Libya (NFSL), headed by a major critic of the Qadhdhafi regime, Muhammad Yusuf al-Maqarif. The aim of the organization was the overthrow of the Qadhdhafi regime and the search for a democratic alternative to his rule.[6] The front was the most important opposition organization yet to emerge against Qadhdhafi. Maqarif, the secretary general of the front, was the former Libyan auditor general and ambassador to India who defected to the opposition in July 1980.[7] The NFSL's members represented a cross-section of the best educated and most important families in Libya who held positions of power in the Libyan administration under the Qadhdhafi regime. Their defection during the years must have been a very serious brain drain from Libya, which could ill afford to lose them.[8] They were able to mobilize considerable domestic support for the front.

Libya's problems were compounded by the fact that relations with Algeria were deteriorating. Those relations had become strained after Libya's merger with Chad in January 1981 and declared intent to keep Libyan troops there.[9] Algeria felt uneasy about Libya's long-term intentions not only in Chad but in the neighboring states of Mali and Niger as well.[10] Furthermore, Libya's military presence in Chad could lead to a French military intervention in that region close to the Algerian borders (an intervention that did take place in 1983).

The strain in Libyan-Algerian relations was also caused by Libya's growing influence over the POLISARIO in the Western Sahara. This undermined Algeria's role in that area and allowed the POLISARIO to operate against Moroccan forces unchecked by Algeria. That, in turn, exacerbated tensions in the region and brought the possibility of a direct confrontation between Algeria and Morocco somewhat closer.[11]

Finally, Algeria and Libya did not see eye to eye with respect to the Fez I decisions taken by the Arab heads of state concerning the Arab-Israeli problem. Although both states were members of the Rejectionist Front, Algeria appears to have been more conciliatory and closer to the PLO than were Libya and Syria, which refused any form of compromise with Israel.[12]

Qadhdhafi perceived this situation—deteriorating relations with Libya's major ally and protector, joint U.S.-Egyptian maneuvers on Libya's borders, Sudan's threat of war, and an opposition organization calling for the overthrow of the Qadhdhafi regime—as threatening Libya's territorial integrity and the very survival of his regime. As a result, the state-controlled mass media reported that the "military aid which the United States gives Sudan is aimed at preparing aggression against Libya"[13] and described the Bright Star maneuvers as "an exercise for the invasion of Libya."[14] The panic reached the point where the Libyan radio broadcast "that an offensive plan aimed at the leader of the revolution will be executed between 10 and 15 November. This will coincide with the provocative military maneuvers which the forces will carry out west of Egypt."[15]

Qadhdhafi reacted predictably to these threats. He had to pacify the forces that threatened his regime and defuse a very dangerous situation. Using a variety of channels in Algeria, Italy, and Yugoslavia, he let it be known that he wished to reopen a dialogue with the United States.[16] He also tried to improve his relations with the Western world in general and with Italy in particular.[17] His attempts at conciliation, however, did not meet with much success.

Concomitantly, he tried to adopt a more friendly attitude toward Egypt, fearing that under U.S. influence Hosni Mubarak might attack Libya. The Libyan secretary of justice made a statement to the Kuwaiti paper *Al-Watan* that Libya had no wish to enter into war with either Sudan or Egypt and that the Libyan People's Congresses had decided to "prevent any confrontation between the Libyan and Egyptian armies."[18]

Qadhdhafi's most important conciliatory gesture, however, was ordering Libyan troops in Chad to withdraw immediately, before Operation Bright Star began. There was little Libyan publicity for this action, and news of the withdrawal came from French, Egyptian, and Sudanese sources.[19] The withdrawal took place officially in response to a call by the Chadian government for the complete pullout of Libyan forces from Chad.[20] The Chadian government, however, had asked Libya to withdraw its troops on a number of occasions, but to no avail.[21] The decision of oblige at that time was therefore not a response to any call by the Chadian authorities but rather was motivated by purely Libyan interests.

With the United States, Egypt, and Sudan preparing joint military maneuvers in the western desert, the regional situation had assumed a rather threatening outlook. The forces of these powers, unlike those of the Chadian government, could easily drive Libya out of Chad or even use the presence of Libyan troops there as a pretext to attack Libya directly.[22] Consequently, Qadhdhafi ordered the pullout of his forces to prevent potential aggression against Libyan territory from any or all of these three powers as well as to pacify Algeria, which had objected to Libya's role in Chad. The People's Foreign Liaison Bureau announced on November 11, 1981, a few days before the joint military maneuvers were to begin, that Libya had evacuated the towns of Iriba and Gnereda in eastern Chad. "Libya is no longer responsible for the defense of these regions. . . . Libyan forces have now completed their mission; they are adopting a neutral position between the Chad factions and they will not be biased on one or the other side."[23]

At the same time the Libyan mass media continued to denounce an imminent U.S. invasion of Libya. Articles and editorials with titles such as "Beware—America Is Coming"[24] were being published daily, announcing that the world was on the brink of war.[25]

Throughout those early months following Sadat's death, when the whole region appeared to be in a state of heightened alert, Qadhdhafi kept a very low profile, trying to mend his relations with his neighbors and to diffuse potential threats to his regime and to his country. As early as mid-1981 a Libyan-Moroccan rapprochement began that would eventually lead to the resumption of diplomatic relations between those two nations.[26] Qadhdhafi also paid a visit to Algeria and to Tunisia in January and February 1982,[27] as a result of which Tunisia and Libya renewed economic and political ties that had been all but frozen since the Gafsa affair in January 1980.[28]

## Libya's Isolation in the Arab World and Africa

By the end of July 1982, the danger of direct U.S., Egyptian, or Sudanese attack on Libya had receded. But a new situation began to unfold that threatened Libya with regional isolation. In August 1982 when the annual OAU summit meeting was to take place in Tripoli, twenty-one African nations refused to attend. In the absence of the quorum of thirty-four states required by the OAU Charter, the summit could not convene.[29]

The main issues of discord were: the admission of Saharan Democratic Arab Republic into the OAU, Libya's role in Chad, and the choice of Tripoli as the meeting place for the OAU summit.[30] Some states, such as Egypt (and perhaps Tunisia and Somalia), did not attend to prevent Qadhdhafi from becoming the chairman of the OAU that year.[31] Libya claimed, correctly, that Western powers and the United States in particular had exerted pressure on several African nations not to attend the OAU summit meetings.

This ostracizing of Libya in Africa was followed by the country's isolation in the Arab world. In September 1982 the Arab heads of state gathered in Fez to confer on the political situation in the region in the wake of the Israeli invasion of Lebanon. They discussed the September 1, 1982, Reagan plan as well as King Fahd's plan for a solution to all the conflicts in the area and formulated a number of resolutions. Algeria and Libya did not attend, and Egypt was not invited. The Fez II summit, as it came to be known because it took place a year after a similar meeting in Fez, proposed a number of resolutions that proved to be unacceptable to Algeria and Libya.

Algeria made no official statement, but the Algerian daily *Al-Sha'b* commented, "The Arabs have surrendered all their cards to the United States."[32] Libya's People's Foreign Liaison Bureau issued a formal statement that Libya "disowns the Fez resolutions and declares that our country is not closely or distantly connected with these resolutions . . . which went so far as to recognize the Zionist enemy."[33] Qadhdhafi's criticism of the Fez summit resolutions (which had been accepted by all parties attending including Syria and the PLO) resulted in his isolation on the Arab regional level.

Egypt, on the other hand, was consolidating its relations with Sudan. A month after the Fez II meeting Egypt and Sudan announced the integration of their two countries.[34] The charter of the *Takamul* project, as the new alliance came to be known, spoke of a "unity of history" that "the eternal Nile forged."[35] There was no mention of a greater Arab unity, a concept that had always been used when such integrations or unions were formed in the Arab world. The omission was intended to allay the fears of the southern Sudanese, who viewed with suspicion all calls for Arab unity, and may also have been made to demonstrate to the other Arab states that Egypt could still form powerful alliances and blocs in the region in spite of these states' attempts at isolating Egypt.

The integration charter placed a great deal of emphasis on national security and stated that Egypt and Sudan needed to "implement a single defense and security strategy"[36] and coordinate their military and foreign policies. A Nile Valley parliament[37] would supervise the process of integration.[38] When explaining the joint Egyptian-Sudanese security arrangements, Egyptian field marshall 'Abd al-Halim Abu Ghazaleh stated:

> It is noted that there is a foreign military will that is manipulating the situation and directing events in certain Arab countries, such as Libya and South Yemen. Their aim is controlling the Bab El-Mandeb Strait in order to block the Red Sea, which is a vital waterway for Egypt and Sudan. It is where the most important Egyptian and Sudanese ports lie and through which ships pass to the Suez Canal.[39]

The integration was thus perceived by Egypt and Sudan as a defensive alliance against external control (presumably Soviet) of strategic waterways in the region. Egypt had dropped the Arab unity rhetoric and was calling its alliance what it was: an integrative alliance between two regional powers set on defending their security.[40]

As in earlier periods when Egypt, under Nasir, had entered a union with Sudan and Libya, the Maghrib decided to close ranks against this new bloc, which it perceived as changing the regional balance of power. Beginning in early 1983 and throughout that spring, inter-Maghribi relations improved markedly. In February 1983 King Hasan and Shadli Bin Jadid met to discuss the normalization of relations between their two countries.[41] They later signed a number of agreements on the movement of residents between Morocco and Algeria and reopened their borders to traffic.[42]

The most important regional agreement that took place in the Maghrib, however, was that between Algeria and Tunisia. On March 19, 1983, the Treaty of Brotherhood and Concord[43] was signed by Bourguiba and Bin Jadid[44] along with a border agreement that settled a dispute between Tunisia and Algeria.[45] This alliance was an attempt by Algeria to strengthen its position in the region.

Fearing isolation in North Africa in the wake of this second bloc formation on the country's borders, Libya sent 'Abd al-Salam Jallud, Qadhdhafi's right-hand man, to Algeria to attempt to join the Maghribi alliance. On his return, the Libyan press reported that an agreement providing for the resumption of "the integrationist and unionist action between the two fraternal countries"[46] had been reached between Algeria and Libya. Algeria, however, denied these claims.[47] Apparently nothing much had been achieved by the visit, and for the next four years Algeria prevented Libya from joining the alliance. The official reason given was that Libya had not settled a border dispute over Ghat on the southwestern border of Algeria.

Between the summer of 1982 and the spring of 1983, the Libyan regime faced increased opposition. The NFSL was active publishing pamphlets, newsletters, and magazines in English, French and Arabic. These attacked Qadhdhafi and listed the human rights violations of his regime. The NFSL made the same case in international meetings.[48]

In April 1983 internal dissent against Qadhdhafi's policies took the form of armed clashes between members of the revolutionary committees and university faculty and students on various campuses in Libya, including those in Tripoli, Benghazi, and Sabha.[49] The clashes occurred as a result of Qadhdhafi's directives to the revolutionary committees to purge the universities of opposition elements.[50] State retribution was brutal. Twenty-five students and professors were allegedly killed in the purges, and many more were arrested and imprisoned.[51]

In May 1983 another assassination attempt on Qadhdhafi occurred, apparently by a member of the PLO. Libya accused the would-be assassin of having ties to the United States and Israel and called the attempt a "political operation aimed at destroying the only voice of opposition."[52]

Cumulatively all these political developments seriously undermined the Libyan regime. Qadhdhafi's failure to secure the chair of the OAU and to convene the meeting of the African nations in Tripoli was a severe blow to his prestige domestically and regionally. His political isolation in the Arab world following the Fez summit and his ineffectiveness in changing the course of events in the region did nothing to enhance his popularity in Libya. Domestic and external Libyan opposition to his policies only exacerbated further an already difficult state of affairs.

But it was the formation of two blocs on Libya's eastern and western borders that constituted the greatest threat to the nation's sovereignty and to the regime. Egypt and Sudan had set up an integrative union that had a common defense policy, which was partly directed against Libya, and Algeria and Tunisia had an alliance from which Libya was excluded. Sandwiched between two blocs that he could not join, isolated from the nations of Africa and the Arab world, Qadhdhafi found himself in a critical situation.

## Unions and Mergers:
## Libya's Search for New Allies

Throughout this period, therefore, Libya sought to unite with one or another neighbor in order to break out of this isolation and strengthen the regime's position at home and abroad.

## Attempts at Unity with Algeria

The first attempt at unity took place in January 1982 in the aftermath of Sadat's death. The region was in a state of heightened tension, and Qadhdhafi feared a Sudanese-Egyptian-U.S. attack against Libya.[53] On January 18, 1982, Qadhdhafi paid a visit to Algeria. He spent three days in political discussion, at the end of which he announced that he was negotiating a merger with Libya's powerful neighbor.[54] The Algerian domestic service reported the discussions as merely concerning cooperation between the two countries.[55] From the way the visit was reported by both countries, it was evident that Qadhdhafi was seeking unity, while Algeria seemed much less receptive to the idea. In spite of Algeria's reluctance, Morocco became worried about the possible repercussions of such an alliance on its borders. The Moroccan press wondered aloud, "If the new Libyan-Algerian concord will mean that Libya and Algeria will once again return to an alliance against Morocco and its unity and whether this means that Libya is retracting the pledge made at the Nairobi conference to support Morocco's efforts to establish peace in northwest Africa."[56]

## Overtures to Tunisia

Because of Algeria's lack of interest, however, nothing came of those talks. Disappointed with the visit to Algeria,[57] the Libyan delegation headed by Qadhdhafi paid a surprise visit to Tunisia on the way back to Libya. Amid a great deal of confusion, the Libyan leader apparently held a two-hour discussion with the Tunisian prime minister, Muhammad Mzali, on mutual trade and economic relations.[58] Political matters were set aside, however, until another meeting held a month later.

On this second visit, the issue of integration between the two countries was brought up. Qadhdhafi appeared on Tunisian television and announced, "I consider the foundation stone for Arab unity to be the economic factor, particularly the economic integration which has now been determined between Libya and Tunisia."[59]

Having been rebuffed in Algeria when he proposed a merger, Qadhdhafi steered away from this notion and spoke only of economic integration. He knew that concept would be more acceptable to the Tunisians, who were dependent to some extent on the Libyan economy for employment, investment, and trade. The response was most favorable, especially as the offer was accompanied by the signing of numerous trade, labor, industrial, and cultural agreements.[60] Prime Minister Mzali expressed his support for the idea of economic integration, which he contrasted to the more global merger concept. He said he hoped the problems that existed between Libya and Tunisia would be "resolved on the basis of work to ensure a complementary union between the two countries, considering that a merger-type union belongs to future generations."[61] Finally, full diplomatic relations between the two countries were reestablished, after having been all but frozen since the 1980 Gafsa affair.[62]

After those two visits a hiatus of almost ten months occurred before the question of unity and integration was brought up again. In December 1982 following the Egyptian-Sudanese integration treaty, Libya began discussing the issue of economic integration with Tunisia but without any concrete result.[63] It was only after Algeria and Tunisia set up their own alliance in March 1983 that Qadhdhafi began to pursue more vigorously the idea of a merger with Tunisia.

In July 1983 when Mzali and a Tunisian delegation paid a visit to Tripoli, Qadhdhafi called for unity again but in a rather indirect manner, so as not to be rebuffed. He said, "We do not mean . . . to impose a veto on the mass movements in Libya and Tunisia which aim at quick work for unity, with intensive steps to attain unity, integration and to eliminate borders and obstacles between the two countries."[64]

Mzali's answer was cautious. Tunisia needed the trade and economic agreements with Libya but did not want to commit itself to any merger with that state. So the Tunisian prime minister spoke of "existing cooperation" and "steps along the path of unity," but he let it be understood that unions and mergers were to take place only in the distant future.[65]

In December 1983 Mauritania joined the Tunisian-Algerian alliance, and Libya was again refused participation.[66] Qadhdhafi realized then that he could not join any of the alliances in the region and that he had become completely isolated in North Africa.

### The Libyan-Moroccan Federation

It is possible to understand the Libyan-Moroccan federation that was set up in August 1984[67] in the context of these changing regional alliances in North Africa.[68] Although the treaty took everyone by surprise, Richard B. Parker questions whether it was as spontaneous an action as Qadhdhafi and King Hasan claimed it was or whether the project had not been long in the offing.[69]

In fact, a rapprochement between Libya and Morocco had been taking place since mid-1981 and had culminated in the full resumption of Libyan-Moroccan diplomatic relations in December 1981 after a decade of antagonism between the two countries. In June 1981, a week before the OAU summit meeting in Nairobi, Qadhdhafi sent a special Libyan envoy accompanied by two PLO representatives to Rabat to begin talks on restoring diplomatic relations between the two countries. It is unlikely that the king would have agreed to this proposal unless he had received strong assurances from Libya that it would limit support for the POLISARIO. It was very significant that the special Libyan envoy entrusted with this mission was Colonel Mas'ud 'Abd al-Hafiz, the commander of the Sabha Military Region, which was the base from which arms and ammunitions were provided to the POLISARIO camps in the Tindouf region of Algeria.[70] In return King Hasan, who had been very strongly against Qadhdhafi's candidature to the OAU chair in 1982, did not oppose it when the issue was brought up at the Nairobi summit in June 1981.[71]

But the relations with Morocco went no further until March 1983, when the Algerian-Tunisian Treaty of Brotherhood and Concord was announced. Then there was a flurry of activity initiated by Qadhdhafi's cable of congratulations to King Hasan on the annual occasion of Throne Day.[72] In mid-June 1983 Qadhdhafi promised again to withdraw Libya's support for the POLISARIO. This move was probably due as much to his wish for reconciliation with Morocco as it was to spite Algeria, which had excluded Libya from the alliance with Tunisia. Qadhdhafi's action also occurred at the time of the OAU summit meeting in Addis Ababa when Qadhdhafi was denied the chair of the organization and was once again isolated and humiliated on the African regional level.[73] The official statement made to the Libyan news agency JANA concerning the withdrawal of Libyan support to the POLISARIO was somewhat ambiguous:

> Libya discharged its duty in full with regard to Saguia el Hamra and Rio de Oro until they were liberated from years of Spanish colonization through the struggle of the POLISARIO and until the issue was placed in the hands of the OAU. . . . Now that the OAU is responsible for tackling this issue, and now that relations between Morocco and Algeria have been restored, Libya declares that there has not been a Moroccan-Libyan problem or difference.[74]

But this statement was understood by all parties concerned to mean that Qadhdhafi would no longer support the POLISARIO.[75] At the end of June 1983 Qadhdhafi paid a visit to Rabat, where instead of finding a grateful monarch for his stand on the POLISARIO, he was received rather coolly.[76] It was reported that King Hasan, who was in close contact with France and the United States concerning the Chadian situation, warned Qadhdhafi that the Moroccan army might be sent into Chad.[77] This was a ploy to ensure that Qadhdddhafi would indeed stop sending arms and financing the POLISARIO. At this juncture Qadhdhafi was ready to abide by his promise to Morocco, as he no longer had any allies in the region. An agreement was reached that held for more than a year, with neither Hasan sending the army into Chad nor Qadhdhafi sending arms to the Western Sahara.[78]

A more ominous deal was struck during that visit as well: to turn over some members of the Libyan opposition to the Libyan authorities. The deal was implemented in the summer of 1983.[79] Members of the Libyan opposition had sought refuge in Morocco during the previous few years, including 'Umar al-Muhaishi, who had attempted to overthrow Qadhdhafi in 1975. These opposition figures were reportedly executed once in the hands of their government.

Negotiations continued between the two countries throughout 1983 and the early months of 1984. In August 1983 cooperation talks began when the Arab Libyan-Moroccan joint committee met in Tripoli to "improve cooperation in the economic, political, and social fields."[80] A number of joint Libyan-Moroccan subcommittees were set up to deal with such issues as the exchange of labor, trade, security, and culture.[81]

In January 1984 when the Arab-Libyan committee met in Rabat, a number of documents on cooperation between the two countries were signed by King Hasan. Those agreements dealt with exemption of custom duties between Libya and Morocco, the setting up of joint holding companies, the joint marketing of goods inside and outside their respective countries, and the facilitation of tourism between Libya and Morocco. Very important labor agreements were also signed that allowed skilled and unskilled Moroccan workers and professionals to seek employment in Libya.[82]

The whole framework of the August 1984 treaty between Rabat and Tripoli had been worked out during a period of more than eighteen months. There was nothing spontaneous or unpremeditated in that treaty. It was calculated to achieve the maximum benefits for both parties.

What was in fact achieved by the Arab-African federation between Libya and Morocco? Geopolitically it redressed the regional balance of power. It created a third axis joining the two states that had been isolated and had felt threatened by the Egyptian-Sudanese alliance and the Algerian-Tunisian-Mauritanian alliance.[83] Qadhdhafi broke out of his regional isolation and was able to acquire new legitimacy both domestically and in the Arab, African, and Islamic worlds by being allied to the Sharifian monarch, who was believed to be a descendant of the Prophet Muhammad, was a founding member of the OAU, and was a principal ally of the Western powers in North Africa. He was also protecting Libya from external threats by means of the mutual defense article in the treaty according to which Libya and Morocco were to cooperate closely to maintain the independence of the two countries.[84]

Finally, the turning over of the members of the opposition to the Libyan authorities weakened the resistance to Qadhdhafi's regime and discouraged the opposition from operating from neighboring states.

The benefits accrued to Morocco, which have been discussed at length by a number of authors,[85] were many and included political and military benefits from the withdrawal of Libyan support for the POLISARIO and the strengthening of Morocco vis-à-vis Algeria, the country's main rival in the region. In fact, Algeria was furious at the creation of the Arab-African federation, and the Algerian mass media blasted the union, accusing it of being aimed against Algeria: "Morocco wants to make the agreement a framework for an alliance policy based on confrontation."[86] The federation also offered new prospects for an ailing Moroccan economy that included major trade agreements and employment opportunities for a large number of Moroccan workers.

## A Return to Sabotage and Subversion

Between March 1983 and June 1984, Libyan subversive activities increased markedly after a hiatus of almost two years. Sudan became a primary target of Libyan sabotage because it was perceived as threatening Libya's security by supporting Habre in Chad, giving asylum to the Libyan opposition, and being party to a defensive alliance with Egypt. In March 1983, Sudan arrested fifty-six people on charges of plotting to carry out sabotage acts in various cities and towns of the country, including Khartoum, Umdurman, Kasla, and Kuduki.[87] Those persons were apparently supported by Libya and were trained in Libyan camps for the specific purpose of creating disturbances in Sudan.[88] A few weeks later Sudanese authorities impounded a motorized barge in Port Sudan that was carrying weapons and explosives hidden under foodstuffs, and Libyan agents who had been arrested led the Sudanese authorities to other hidden consignments of weapons on a Red Sea island.[89]

During this period, Libya began supporting the Sudan People's Liberation Movement (SPLM), which had been formed in May 1983.[90] It is not clear when Libya first began supporting those southern Sudanese insurgents against the Numayri regime, but by the spring of 1984, they appeared to be well armed and well trained, with a contingent operating from bases in Ethiopia[91] and another in Equatoria in southern Sudan.[92] Libya provided the SPLM with Soviet arms, financial assistance, and logistical supplies.[93] Libya's and Ethiopia's support for the SPLM headed by Colonel John Garang de Mabior was crucial in eventually bringing down the Numayri government in April 1985.

In March 1984 Libya was accused of bombing the Umdurman radio station in Sudan and of hitting civilian targets.[94] This action was prompted by the NFSL opposition group's broadcasts from Umdurman inciting Libyans to rebel. The bombing was meant to silence the Libyan opposition and to threaten Sudan with further air raids if it did not put an end to those broadcasts.[95]

Egypt also became a target of Libyan subversive activities for its support of the anti-Libyan government in Chad, for its provision of safe haven to Libyan dissidents, and for its masterminding of the *Takamul* integration project with Sudan. In March 1983 Egyptian authorities reported the arrest of several persons accused of attempting to carry out acts of sabotage in Egypt.[96] Libya had allegedly recruited them to create disturbances in big cities as well as in areas near the Libyan-Egyptian border.[97] A group calling itself the Revolutionary Committee was arrested in April 1983 as it was attempting to form underground organizations in Egypt to undermine Mubarak's regime. The organization was apparently made up of a number of Libyan agents who had been paid large sums of money to form revolutionary committees among young Egyptians.[98]

In July 1984 Egypt accused Libya of mining the entrance and exit of the Red Sea. For more than a month ships of every nationality had been damaged by mysterious explosions as they sailed back and forth from the Red Sea to the Suez Canal.[99] The Egyptian authorities traced the mining to a small cargo ship, the *Ghat*, owned by the Libyan General Maritime Transport Company of Tripoli, which had sailed through the Red Sea and the Suez Canal in early July and apparently mined the area.[100]

The principal reason for this action appears to have been the defection of a Libyan pilot in June 1984. He had flown to Egypt and had asked for political asylum there, joining the many Libyans who had sought refuge in Cairo and had become members of the Libyan opposition in exile.[101] The mining of the Red Sea was apparently in retaliation for Egypt's granting political asylum to the pilot.[102] In September 1984 Qadhdhafi offered Mubarak the carrot after the stick: namely, $5 billion for the return of the pilot and some form of assurance that Egypt would abbrogate its peace treaty with Israel.[103] He made a similar offer to Numayri to extradite members of the Libyan opposition operating in Sudan.[104]

Tunisia was not immune to Qadhdhafi's retaliatory subversive policies during that year. In January 1984 armed commandos who came from Libya blew up the pipeline joining the Tunisian oil port of Al-Sukhayra with the oil field of 'Ayn Amenas in Algeria.[105] It was a symbolic action aimed at expressing Libya's displeasure at being excluded from the

Algerian-Tunisian Friendship Treaty. Insult had been added to injury when Mauritania joined the Algerian-Tunisian Treaty of Brotherhood and Concord in December 1983,[106] while Libya's request to do likewise had been turned down by both Algeria and Tunisia. The official reasons given for refusing to include Libya in the alliance had been that it had not settled its border disputes with Algeria in Ghat in southwest Libya,[107] or with Tunisia over the continental shelf.[108]

## The Libyan-French Imbroglio in Chad

It was in Chad, however, that Libya's policy became most conflictual. In February 1983 Chadian authorities began warning the West of a potential Libyan attack against Chad. Idris Miskin, the Chadian foreign minister, claimed that Qadhdhafi had recruited a mercenary force of Chadians living in Libya, as well as 500 Katangans and 300 Central Africans, to fight in Chad,[109] whose northern region Libya was already occupying.[110]

A few weeks later *Agence France Presse* reported that Qadhdhafi was trying to impose on Habre's government a treaty to settle the border issue between Libya and Chad, set up a strategic alliance between the two countries, and proclaim Chad's Arab character. In return, Qadhdhafi was prepared to recognize officially Habre's government as the legitimate government of Chad.[111] The Chadian authorities had misgivings about the Libyan proposals[112] and decided to refuse the treaty and instead seek the support of the OAU, the United Nations, and a number of neighboring states and Western governments.[113]

Qadhdhafi was furious with the decision and declared that the Chadian government would pay a high price for seeking U.S. assistance.[114] In June 1983 fighting broke out in northern Chad between the government forces of Hissene Habre and those of former president Goukouni Ouedeye. Faya-Largeau was attacked by Ouedeye's forces with Libyan air and artillery support.[115] A few days later this very important northern town fell under Ouedeye's attacks.[116] His forces then moved east and stormed the town of Abeche, a Habre stronghold close to the Sudanese border.[117]

Although Habre was losing ground to Ouedeye's forces, he was not about to give up power that easily.[118] He turned to France, which had been supplying him with arms, and asked it to intervene directly in Chad and give his army air support to counter Libya's air attacks on Faya-Largeau.[119] Ten days later French paratroopers and military personnel arrived in Chad.[120]

Their arrival coincided with U.S. Navy military exercises in the Mediterranean off the Gulf of Sidra.[121] The simultaneous presence of French forces on Libya's southern borders and the U.S. Navy on the northern borders was perceived in Libya as threatening its security. The Libyan Foreign Liaison Bureau accused the United States of aggressive intentions against Libya,[122] and Qadhdhafi tried to dissuade France from sending troops by threatening it: "Frankly, I do not think France would be crazy enough to send troops to Chad. It would be political suicide. French prisoners would be taken, there could even be massacres. The very regime of Mitterrand would be threatened."[123]

When that threat did not work, Egypt joined in and openly supported Habre's proposal for a multinational force to be stationed in Chad.[124] This infuriated Qadhdhafi, who saw Egypt's involvement as further proof of its support for Western, and especially U.S., interests in the region.[125]

Morocco also chose this moment to threaten Libya in Chad. King Hasan apparently warned Qadhdhafi, who was visiting Morocco in early July 1983, that he supported Habre's government against the Libyan-backed Ouedeye forces and that he was prepared to send in the Moroccan Army to defend Habre.[126] Hasan was really exerting political pressure on Libya in order to stop the flow of Libyan arms to the POLISARIO in the Western Sahara. Thus, by moving into Chad to topple an unfriendly government, Qadhdhafi had precipitated a crisis involving both the Western powers, which in the final analysis constituted a much greater threat to the Libyan regime than Habre's government did, and regional powers, some of which had remained neutral in the conflict until that time.

While external threats to the Libyan regime were mounting, Qadhdhafi found an unexpected regional ally. Algeria, which had distanced itself from Libya since 1981, had become worried about the French presence in Chad. But it was Morocco's threat to send in the army that moved Algeria to action. Shadli Bin Jadid sent a cable to OAU chairman Mengistu stating that "Algeria considers the problems in Chad to be issues that concern Chadians alone. . . . Therefore all African and non-African countries must refrain from any initiative that could (complicate?) a problem that harms the sovereignty and independence of not only Chad, but of the whole continent."[127]

Algeria's tilt toward the Libyan position became more pronounced in August 1983 when the semi-official Algerian daily *Al-Sha'b* questioned the legitimacy of the Habre government: "And if we were to raise the question of legitimacy, then the side now in power in Ndjamena would be farther from legitimacy than any other parties."[128] Algeria was thus indirectly endorsing Libya's own position in the conflict in Chad and giving Libya some credibility on the international scene.

There was a brief lull in the fighting between Habre and Ouedeye in September and October 1983 when at the French-African summit in Vittel Habre called for reconciliation among the various warring parties in Chad.[129] Habre also spoke of trying to find a solution to the Chadian problem with Libya.[130] Sporadic fighting resumed, however, soon after the Vittel conference as a result of the failure of negotiations with Libya. The Chadian foreign minister in an interview with a French radio program said "We have made the first step. . . . We have begun talks with Tripoli. Unfortunately they ended in failure due to Libyan diktat."[131]

The armed clashes were followed by another truce between the parties, and a project for national reconciliation was drawn up[132] but was never implemented. Fighting resumed once more in January 1984 with the Ouedeye forces, supported directly by Libyan forces,[133] attempting to cut a major north-south road in the northwestern part of the country.[134] The southern leader, Kamougé, an erstwhile Libyan protégé, changed sides again and joined Habre's forces.[135] By the end of January, General Jean Poli, chief of the French Operation Manta in Chad, put it succinctly: "The North is being annexed by Libya."[136]

### Opposition to Qadhdhafi's Policies in Chad

The Chadian war, however, was becoming increasingly unpopular among Libyans, who could not understand why they were fighting there or forget the 1,500 Libyan soldiers who had been killed during the Libyan military intervention in the early 1980s.[137] Consequently, Qadhdhafi found himself obliged to justify the Libyan presence in Chad by claiming that it was to protect Libya from external threats. In a statement that summed up the Libyan government's perception of threat to its southern borders, Qadhdhafi explained:

> The wars taking place in Chad every now and then are directed against Libya through Chad. Let us take, for example, the Sudan. The government of Sudan does not differentiate much between Habre and Goukouni. But it wants to fight Libya through Chad. Thus it supports the side which Libya does not support. Had Libya been against Goukouni, Sudan would support him. . . . Egypt's stand on the side of Habre is exactly like that of Sudan; it is supporting Sudan and the war against Libya through Chad. . . . The United States, which brought arms and trainers and which was about to occupy Chad, cares nothing about Chad or Habre. It realizes he is not a strong ally. But America is also fighting Libya through Chad. . . . France does not want the United States to take the initiative from it in Africa. For this reason France intervened in Chad. It was also prompted by the fear of losing its friends in Africa who are afraid they will meet a fate similar to that of Habre.[138]

Qadhdhafi was thus facing strong opposition to his policies in Chad domestically, regionally, and internationally. It was the combined threat of this opposition that led Qadhdhafi in the last year of this phase to make a complete *volte-face* and change his regional policy from a basically conflictual one to a more conciliatory policy. At the end of April 1984 in a replay of the November 1981 scenario, he announced that he would withdraw his troops from Chad if France would do the same. In an interview with French television, Qadhdhafi declared, "If the Libyan presence in Chad serves as a pretext for the presence of French troops in that country . . . I declare that we are ready to withdraw from Chad so that there no longer exists any justification for the French Government, vis-a-vis French public opinion, to maintain a military contingent there."[139]

Five days later, Defense Minister Charles Hernu declared that France wanted to withdraw its troops from Chad as soon as possible, and a Franco-Libyan dialogue began on the simultaneous withdrawal of Libyan troops from Chad.[140] The discussions were long and tortuous, occupying the better part of that year. There were lulls that lasted for weeks and even months; then the dialogue would resume and things would appear to be moving, only to be stalled again. Finally, in mid-September 1984 an agreement was reached between Libya and France on a simultaneous withdrawal of forces starting on September 25.[141]

The Chadian authorities were worried, however, and warned the French that they were making a tactical error in withdrawing and in trusting Qadhdhafi's word. The presence of French troops in Chad had somewhat stabilized the situation in that country and had been a boon to its economy.[142] The Chadians did not want to lose the French presence in exchange for an uncertain future.

### Qadhdhafi's Manipulation of the Chadian Situation

The Chadians' worst fears proved to be justified: France pulled out, but Libya did not. Despite numerous warnings from Chadian authorities about the continued presence of Libyan troops in Chad, France withdrew its own troops. On November 10, 1984, Libya and France issued a joint statement to the effect that the withdrawal of both their forces had been completed in accordance with the Tripoli agreement of September 17, 1984.[143]

By the end of December 1984, fighting had resumed in Chad,[144] and it was apparent that the game was on again, but with a major difference: The French were out, and the Libyans were back in the saddle. Qadhdhafi's conciliatory attitude in May 1984 had effectively diffused the perceived threats to Libya's southern borders. He had managed to manipulate the situation in such a way that he had removed the most serious challenge to his borders and regime without having to withdraw his own forces.

In an interview at the end of January 1985, Qadhdhafi made a statement on Chad: "We shall not allow anybody to fight us from Chad or use that country to launch attacks against us. Furthermore, we are opposed to the installation of a regime hostile to Libya's security and the security of our borders."[145] Qadhdhafi then called Habre's government hostile to Libya and predicted that it was going to fall.[146] A few days later there was an assassination attempt against Habre. Chadian authorities requested the members of the U.N. Security Council to condemn Libya, which Chad accused of being behind the assassination attempt.[147]

Qadhdhafi's conciliatory action had been a purely tactical foreign policy maneuver to diffuse domestic and external threats to his regime and territory. Having manipulated France into withdrawing from Chad, Qadhdhafi began dealing with the regional threat by attempting to topple the Habre regime and reinstate a government more to his liking.

## Qadhdhafi's Ideological Confrontation with the United States and the Arab World

During this phase Qadhdhafi's ideology was again revolutionary and directed primarily against the United States rather than against Egypt, as in the previous periods. Sadat's assassination had stolen Qadhdhafi's thunder and had made it very difficult for him to continue accusing Egypt of selling out to Israel when the chief architect of the Camp David Agreements had been killed for his actions. All Qadhdhafi could do was call for the abrogation of the treaty as a condition for Egypt's return to the Arab fold. That, however, was not the type of heroic stand that could mobilize the Libyan masses behind him.

### Qadhdhafi Meets U.S. Attempts at Destabilization

The United States provided Qadhdhafi with the perfect dragon against which to play his role of the knight in shining armor. With the coming to power of Ronald Reagan, a whole new policy was adopted by the U.S. administration to combat international terrorism. Qadhdhafi was selected as the policy's prime target.[148]

According to a Libya expert who based his work on interviews with senior U.S. officials,[149] the Libyan regime was to be destablized by means of economic and military sanctions and threats including the banning of Libyan oil imports to the United States,[150] "the calculated use of the threat of U.S. military intervention against Libya,"[151] support for a strike force against Libyan forces in Chad by Egyptian and Sudanese troops,[152] and a strategic display of air power by means of military maneuvers such as Operation Bright Star.[153] Finally, a major campaign of disinformation was to be waged against the Libyan regime to portray its members as "international outlaws deserving of harsh punishment."[154]

Although facing serious external threats to his regime and to Libya's borders, Qadhdhafi was shrewd enough to capitalize on this new situation by playing the role of the revolutionary who was fighting a foreign oppressor. Moreover, he could substantiate his claims that the United States was threatening Libya because a U.S. task force was cruising in and around the Gulf of Sidra, U.S. AWACS were flying in Libyan airspace, military maneuvers were taking place in the western desert with Egyptian and Sudanese forces, and the U.S. president was blasting Qadhdhafi in speeches whenever possible.

During the early months after the crises of Sadat's death and Operation Bright Star, Qadhdhafi kept a very low profile, giving no interviews or major speeches. It was not until mid-December 1981 that his new ideological strategy began to unfold. In an interview with British television network ITV, Qadhdhafi was accused of "confronting Western interests at every turn."[155] Qadhdhafi was quick to point out that "the size of Libya and its capabilities simply do not match such accusations. They are merely justifications for aggression against Libya, prompted in the first place by the wealth of Libya and its strategic position."[156]

This statement contained the crux of Qadhdhafi's ideological position during the rest of this period. Libya was not attacking Western interests because it was too small and too weak to do so (gone were the days when Qadhdhafi would change the world with his Green Book). It was the West that was attacking Libya, not to retaliate for anything Libya was doing but in order to take control of its oil wealth. He made reference to Libya's strategic location almost as an afterthought, just in case someone pointed out that the West could get its oil elsewhere.

In mid-June 1982 when there was renewed talk of U.S. military maneuvers off the coast of Libya, Qadhdhafi began to play the heroic leader besieged by powers much greater than himself. "If the Americans hold their maneuvers, it will mean war. We are fearful for peace but we are not afraid of facing the Americans."[157] By late February 1983 when the U.S. Sixth Fleet was stationed in the Mediterranean not too far from the Libyan coast, Qadhdhafi rallied the Libyans around his regime by saying that the United States was on the verge of attacking Libya and they had to defend themselves: "We refuse to submit or yield. . . . We should be prepared to endure even death before submitting."[158]

Qadhdhafi's rhetoric became even more heroic the following year as he rallied the Libyans around his leadership: "It is enough that we challenge and fight the biggest power on earth—the United States—in defense of the Arab nation, the Gulf of Sidra and the cause of freedom everywhere in the world."[159] That stance was repeated again and again in different speeches throughout the next two years.

Another aspect of the attack on the United States was that it was a "crusading" force bent on subjugating the Muslims of the Arab world. Qadhdhafi used this tactic to mobilize Libyans around their faith, with himself in the role of defender of the faithful: "We openly accuse the West of engaging in historic terrorism against us, which may have paved the way for a fresh crusade campaign."[160]

In Rabat in July 1983 Qadhdhafi described the United States as the "real enemy of the Arabs and Islam, and its is the one who is seeking to destroy Arab existence. . . . It has a new crusade. The crusade war has not ended."[161] In September 1983 on the fourteenth anniversary of the Libyan revolution, Qadhdhafi spoke of the "invading American imperialist crusading forces which desecrate its land."[162]

By appearing to defend Libya against the threat of a superpower aggression, he was resurrecting the charismatic figure of his youth who could challenge any danger to his country. He was also appealing to the religious feelings of Libyans by portraying the struggle against the United States as one against a Christian invader.

### Qadhdhafi's Attacks on Arab Leaders

Qadhdhafi's revolutionary role was not confined to his attacks against the United States; it was also directed against the Arab rulers. Once again he put himself forward as the representative of the Arab masses against their corrupt rulers. Having been excluded from the *Takamul* alliance and the Brotherhood and Concord Treaty, as well as ignored by the summit leaders at Fez, Qadhdhafi turned vindictively against other Arab leaders. In September 1982 after the Fez conference, Qadhdhafi sent a message to the Arab heads of state asking them to reconsider their resolutions and to question the assistance they were giving to the United States by selling it oil. Contrasting himself to the Arab rulers, he wrote, "And I am not responsible to the United States because I am not a U.S. employee with the grade of king, president or amir in the Arab region."[163]

He was thus accusing them of being puppet governments and was questioning their integrity and their legitimacy. He followed that statement with a threat: "I bring you the good news that the Arab revolutionaries will in the end be forced to make a serious decision. If we Arabs must sink, then we must sink by our own decision and not by that of our enemies. By God, I have warned you."[164]

Qadhdhafi openly called for revolution against the leaders of the Arab world at a meeting of the various Arab opposition movements held in Tripoli in February 1983.[165] At the end of March he was still railing against Arab rulers: "Those traitors, the rulers of the Arab nation, what justification have they to agree to capitulate and to recognize Israel in Fez?"[166]

Qadhdhafi, who had been promoting Maghribi unity throughout 1982 as he searched for an ally on his western borders, suddenly changed his tune in June 1983. As he was not part of the Algerian-Tunisian alliance, Maghribi unity became something to be criticized and put down. At a press interview he said that all calls for regional alliances were to be fought because they served only the interests of the colonial powers, which sought to divide the Arab world.[167] When Qadhdhafi was involved in such regional alliances, however, he described them as a first step to complete Arab unity.

## The Rhetoric of Conciliation

Whether Qadhdhafi called for unity or for revolution was a function of Libya's security and recognition in the region. Whenever Qadhdhafi felt threatened or isolated in the Arab world, he lashed out against Arab leaders and called for their overthrow.

When, however, he became more secure with a major ally or protector in the region, his tone changed completely, and he no longer called for revolution, pan-Arabism, or pan-Islamism. He became the shrewd, pragmatic, and Machiavellian leader he really was. In his September 1, 1984, speech, after the setting up of the Arab-African federation between Libya and Morocco, Qadhdhafi did use revolutionary rhetoric criticizing U.S. imperialism and Zionism. But he refrained from attacking Arab rulers. On the contrary, he was most conciliatory toward Saudi Arabia, for instance. He, who a few months earlier had called for the overthrow of the Saudi regime, was now inviting it to join the federation: "Thus in this stage when a kingdom unites with Jamahiriyah to face up to the challenges we would not exclude the possibility that Saudi Arabia, as a kingdom, might also join [the] unity."[168]

But it was in his approach to religion and politics that Qadhdhafi's change in ideological stand after the setting up of the Federation with Morocco was most startling.[169] He who had supported Khomeini's Islamic Republic and had called for jihad,[170] now took a very cold and pragmatic view of the relation between state and religion:

> Prophecy has nothing to do with politics or the state. The Islamic state that was set up was created by those who came after the Prophet. This was a civil, subjective authority and was not holy because the Prophet had no deputies. The question of religion has nothing to do with politics. Religion in the first place is believing in the supernatural; it is belief in God, in the day of reckoning and so on. . . .

There is no morality in politics. Politicians lie to each other. . . . When we deal with politics the supernatural becomes irrelevant. It is impossible to deal with politics and compare these with the supernatural. Therefore, the political factor and all that is related to it is a subjective problem facing the human communities on this planet—a problem they have the right to resolve the way they deem fit.[171]

## Conclusion

Although by the end of this phase, Qadhdhafi had become more secure because of his regional alliances and more confident in his relations to the states of North Africa and the rest of the Arab world, he continued to face serious domestic problems. In April 1984, Ahmad Ahwas, the head of the military wing of the NFSL, wrote an article in the opposition magazine *Al-Inqadh* calling Libyans to organize and resist the Qadhdhafi government from within the state.[172] A supplement to that issue announced that there was going to be an increase in operations taking place inside Libya to topple the regime.[173]

On May 8, 1984, eight commandos of the NFSL attacked Qadhdhafi's own headquarters, the Bab al-'Aziziya barracks outside Tripoli, in order to assassinate him.[174] The operation was to have been led by Ahmad Ahwas, but he was killed in an armed clash with Libyan security forces near Zawara two days earlier.[175] Consequently, the attack was hastily organized and executed because it was feared that Qadhdhafi's intelligence agencies would discover the presence of the NFSL's commandos who had managed to infiltrate back into Libya.[176] The attempted coup failed.

Whatever other effect the attack on Bab al-'Aziziya had on the internal situation in Libya, it demonstrated that Qadhdhafi could be vulnerable in the very barracks where he lived and from which he operated. The attack also ushered in a qualitative change in the means used by the Libyan opposition to overthrow the Qadhdhafi regime.[177]

Despite a rather difficult phase in its internal affairs and international relations, the Qadhdhafi regime outlived those of its neighbors. Numayri was overthrown after a year of bloody unrest for his domestic policies; Sadat was assassinated primarily for his foreign policies. Qadhdhafi remained in power, kept control of the domestic situation, and was comfortable in the region with a very powerful ally.

Mere luck, petrodollars, and an East German secret service are not sufficient to explain the longevity of his regime. It was Qadhdhafi's successful manipulation of ideology, his great flexibility in foreign policy behavior, and a shrewd understanding of regional politics that ensured his survival in North Africa. His knowledge of the balance-of-power game in the region ensured that he was always allied to one side when the other was against him. As long as he was allied to Algeria, he could afford to be critical of kingdoms and shaykhdoms and play the role of socialist revolutionary. But when Algeria was no longer interested in Libya, Qadhdhafi renewed his ties with Morocco and modified his political stands on monarchical regimes.

It was also his understanding of the forces that operated on his eastern borders that made him enter into an alliance with Ethiopia and South Yemen to create an axis against the Egyptian-Sudanese bloc. Those alliances enhanced Qadhdhafi's legitimacy and increased his political leverage vis-à-vis his neighbors.

## Notes

1. See Hayley, pp. 247–249; and *Le Matin*, Paris, 3 August 1981, p. 10, JPRS, NE/NA Report No. 2418, 21 October 1981, p. 34.

2. Alexander M. Haig, Jr., *Caveat, Realism, Reagan and Foreign Policy*, Macmillan Publishing Co., New York, 1984, p. 172.

3. Khartoum SUNA, 12 October 1981, in FBIS-MEA, 13 October 81, Q8.

4. See Hayley's discussion of U.S. policy in the region in general and toward Libya in particular, p. 249.

5. Cairo Domestic Service, 13 October 1981, in FBIS-MEA, 13 October 81, Q9.

6. See for a discussion of the aims of the front, the National Front for the Salvation of Libya, *Libya: Daring to Hope Again*, pamphlet, published in Munich, April 1974, pp. 10–12.

7. See for his background, the National Front for the Salvation of Libya, *The National Front for the Salvation of Libya: A Program of Struggle to Topple the Gadhafi Regime and Lay the Foundation for Constitutional Democratic Rule in Libya*, pamphlet, published in Chicago, September 1986, p. 2.

8. Some of the other important members of the NFSL included Ahmad Ibrahim Ahwas, 'Abd al-Salam 'Ali 'A'ila, Ibrahim 'Abd al-'Aziz Sahad, Ghayth 'Abd al-Majid, 'Ashur Shams, Mahmud Nakku'a, Muhammad al-Duwayk, 'Ali Abu Za'kuk, Muhammad Sayfat, Muhammad 'Ali Yahya, Muhammad Fayez Jabril, Brik Suwaysi and 'Ali Zaydan. Ibid.

9. Damis, *Conflict in Northwest Africa*, p. 111.

10. Ibid.

11. Ibid., p. 110.

12. Abdelaziz Dahmani, "Algerie: La Nouvelle Diplomatie," *Jeune Afrique*, No. 1093, 16 December 1981, p. 31.

13. Tripoli JANA, 14 October 1981, in FBIS-MEA, 15 October 81, Q6.

14. Ibid.

15. Tripoli Voice of the Arab Homeland, 3 November 1981, in FBIS-MEA, 4 November 81, Q1.

16. Rome ANSA, 26 October 1981, in FBIS-MEA, 27 October 81, Q1.

17. Ibid.

18. Kuwait KUNA, 18 October 1981, in FBIS-MEA, 23 October 81, Q2.

19. Paris AFP, 3 November 1981, in FBIS-MEA, 4 November 81, S1; Khartoum SUNA, 3 November 1981, in FBIS-MEA, 4 November 81, Q1; Cairo MENA, 3 November 1981, in FBIS-MEA, 3 November 81, D2.

20. Cairo Domestic Service, 30 October 1981, in FBIS-MEA, 2 November 81, D7.

21. *Libya-Sudan-Chad Triangle: Dilemma for United States Policy,* Hearings Before the Subcommittee on Africa of the Committee on Foreign Affairs, House of Representatives, 97th Congress, 1st session, October 29 and November 4, 1981, U.S. Government Printing Office, Washington, D.C., 1982, p. 61.

22. This was Sudan's approach to launching its preemptive war against Libya, based on the fact that Libyan forces in Chad threatened its national security.

23. Tripoli JANA, 11 November 1981, in FBIS-MEA, 12 November 81, Q1.

24. Tripoli JANA, 9 November 1981, in FBIS-MEA, 12 November 81, Q1.

25. Ibid.

26. "Confidential," *Jeune Afrique,* No. 1092, 9 December 1981, p. 42.

27. *Le Monde,* Paris, 26 January 1982, p. 6; see also Kuwait KUNA, 25 February 1982, in FBIS-MEA, 26 February 82, Q1. Ambassadors had been withdrawn at the time of the Gafsa affair and diplomatic representation had been reduced to the level of chargé d'affaires.

28. Paris AFP, 3 March 1982, in FBIS-MEA, 4 March 82, Q21.

29. See John Damis, "The OAU and Western Sahara," in I.W. Zartman, ed., *The OAU After Twenty Years,* Praeger Publishers, New York, 1984, p. 281.

30. Jean-Emmanuel Pondi, "Qadhafi and the Organization of African Unity," in René Lemarchand, *The Green and the Black: Qadhafi's Policies in Africa,* Indiana University Press, Bloomington, Indiana, 1988, pp. 146–147.

31. Paris AFP, 1 August 1982, in FBIS-MEA, 2 August 82, P3.

32. Quoted by Paris AFP, 11 September 1982, in FBIS-MEA, 13 September 82, Q2.

33. Tripoli Voice of the Arab Homeland, 11 September 1982, in FBIS-MEA, 13 September 82, Q4.

34. See text of Egyptian-Sudanese integration charter, published in *Al-Ahram,* Cairo, 10 October 82, pp. 3, 10.

35. Ibid. in FBIS-MEA; for other aspects of the *Takamul* agreement see "Interview with Boutros-Boutros Ghali," in *American-Arab Affairs,* No. 6, Fall 1983, pp. 26–27.

36. See text of Egyptian-Sudanese integration charter.

37. See Chapter 6. For a geopolitical view of the integration treaty and the Nile Valley Parliament see the article by Egypt's minister of state for foreign affairs, Boutros-Boutros Ghali, "La Diplomatie Egyptienne Durant la Periode Post-Sadatienne," in *Studia Diplomatica,* Vol. 36, No. 1, 1983, pp. 15–17.

38. See text of Egyptian-Sudanese integration charter.

39. 'Abd al-Halim Abu Ghazaleh speech at the Nile Valley Young Parliamentarian's Conference, *Al-Ahram,* Cairo, 25 October 82, p. 3.

40. Both Egypt and Sudan were prepared to lay a trap for Qadhdhafi in 1983 by luring him to bomb Sudan. Then after invoking their mutual defense

treaty, Egypt, with U.S. AWACS assistance, would have bombed Libya's air force. The plan was foiled by U.S. press leaks. *The Washington Post*, 12 July 1987, pp. A1, A25.

41. See the description of the meeting in which the Algerian leader and his delegation had lunch with King Hasan and his delegation in a tent on Moroccan soil, and then all had tea together in a tent erected on Algerian soil. Rabat Domestic Service, 27 February 1983, in FBIS-MEA, 28 February 83, Q1.

42. Rabat Domestic Service, 7 April 1983, in FBIS-MEA, 8 April 83, Q3. For an analysis of the subject of their discussion see Zartman, *Ripe for Revolution*, p. 57.

43. Or as it was called Le Traité de Fraternite et de Concorde.

44. See text of Algerian-Tunisian treaty in *L'Action*, Tunis, 21 March 83.

45. See text of Algerian-Tunisian communiqué issued on 20 March 1983, Algiers Domestic Service, 20 March 1983, in FBIS-MEA, 22 March 83, Q1.

46. Tripoli JANA, 27 March 1983, in FBIS-MEA, 28 March 83, Q2.

47. Paris AFP, 29 March 1983, in FBIS-MEA, 30 March 83, Q1.

48. See, for instance, the pamphlet published by the Committee for the Day of Solidarity with the Libyan People, *Watha'iq Tudin al-Qadhdhafi*, n.p. n.d. (1983?), which lists Libya's human rights violations since 1969 and is subtitled *Memorandum Addressed to International Organizations* (in English and Arabic). Maqarif, the NFSL leader, had started that practice as early as June 1981, when he presented a paper at the OAU summit meeting in Nairobi entitled *Mudhakkara Muqadama ila Mu'tamar al-Qimat li Munadhama al-Wihda al-Afriqiya al-Mun'aqad bi Madina Nairobi-Kenya*; see also NFSL, *Memorandum Presented to the 69th Annual Session of the International Labour Organization*, Geneva, June 1983.

49. *Akhbar al-Yawm*, Cairo, 23 April 1983, p. 1, in FBIS-MEA, 27 April 83, Q3. Student clashes with the authorities in April 1983 may also have been related to the anniversary of police repression of student in April 1976. *Shuhada' Libya*, Washington, D.C., Vol. 7, No. 20, April 1987.

50. Ibid.

51. Ibid.; see also NFSL pamphlet with the names of some of the students and teachers who were executed and imprisoned without trial, *Watha'iq Tudin al-Qadhdhafi*, pp. 15, 20–21.

52. Tripoli JANA, 10 May 1983, in FBIS-MEA, 11 May 83, Q1.

53. See above.

54. Tripoli JANA, 21 January 1982, in FBIS-MEA, 22 January 82, Q1. See also Tripoli Voice of the Arab Homeland, 21 January 1982, in FBIS-MEA, 21 January 82, Q1.

55. Algiers Domestic Service, 20 January 1982, in FBIS-MEA, 21 January 82, Q1.

56. Rabat MAP, 25 January 1982, in FBIS-MEA, 26 January 82, Q3.

57. *Le Monde*, Paris, 26 January 1982, p. 6.

58. Ibid.

59. Tripoli JANA, 27 February 1982, in FBIS-MEA, 2 March 82, Q5.

60. Tunis TAP, 1 March 1982, in FBIS-MEA, 2 March 82, Q12–13. Those agreements, however, were not always honored by the Libyan authorities and

were in turn used as bargaining chips to extract political concessions from the Tunisian government. Interview with Tunisian Foreign Ministry Councillor, Ridha bi Slama, Tunis, 11 June 1986.

61. Kuwait KUNA, 25 February 1982, in FBIS-MEA, 26 February 82, Q1.

62. Tunis TAP, 3 March 1982, in FBIS-MEA, 4 March 82, Q21.

63. Apparently Mzali spoke of the necessity to find some practical steps to implement the integration program between the two countries at an economic meeting in Tripoli. Tripoli JANA, 1 December 1982, in FBIS-MEA, 3 December 82, Q1.

64. Tripoli Domestic Service, 19 July 1983, in FBIS-MEA, 20 July 83, Q2.

65. See Mzali's speech in Tripoli, 20 July 1983, in FBIS-MEA, 21 July 83, Q4.

66. See above.

67. See joint communiqué issued by Tripoli and Rabat announcing the formation of the federation, Tripoli Domestic Service, 14 August 1984, in FBIS-MEA, 15 August 84, Q1.

68. See Jean Leca, "Le Traite instituant l'Union Arabo-Africaine," Dossiers et Documents, *Maghreb-Machrek*, No. 106, October-December 1984, pp. 99–100.

69. Richard B. Parker, "Appointment in Oujda," in *Foreign Affairs*, Vol. 63, No. 5, Summer 1985, pp. 1098–1099.

70. Rabat Domestic Service, 17 June 1981, in FBIS-MEA, 18 June 81, Q6–Q7; see for an analysis of the reasons for this rapprochement *Al-Sharq al-Awsat*, London, 19 June 1981, pp. 1–2, in FBIS-MEA, 24 June 81, Q2; see also Muhammad Selhami, "Libye: Ce qui a changé," *Jeune Afrique*, No. 1082, 30 September 1981, pp. 41–42.

71. Paris AFP, 28 June 1981, in FBIS-MEA, 29 June 81, P1.

72. Rabat Domestic Service, 24 March 1983, in FBIS-MEA, 25 March 83, Q2.

73. See Zartman, *Ripe for Resolution*, p. 58.

74. See text of statement in Tripoli JANA, 16 June 1983, in FBIS-MEA, 17 June 83, Q1.

75. See Parker, "Appointment in Oujda," p. 1102. The author also claims that POLISARIO sources have maintained that Libya cut off the supply of arms to the Western Saharans but continued to give them financial assistance, fn., p. 1102.

76. Paris AFP, 1 July 1983, in FBIS-MEA, 5 July 83, Q3. Even the traditional Arab embrace was replaced by a brief handshake between Hasan and Qadhdhafi.

77. Ibid.

78. See Zartman, *Ripe for Resolution*, p. 58; also Mark Tessler, "Continuity and Change in Moroccan Politics, Part I: Challenge and Response in Hasan's Morocco," *UFSI Reports*, Africa, No. 1, January 1984, p. 7.

79. See Parker, "Appointment in Oujda," fn. 6, p. 1106; also *Al-Inqadh*, No. 11, November 1984, p. 20.

80. Excerpt from speech delivered by Moroccan interior minister Driss Basri, in Tripoli, Tripoli JANA, 3 August 1983, in FBIS-MEA, 4 August 83, Q3.

81. Ibid.

82. Rabat Domestic Service, 26 January 1984, in FBIS-MEA, 27 January 84, Q2–3.

83. See Leca, pp. 99–100.

84. See Article 9 of the Treaty Instituting the Union Between the Kingdom of Morocco and the Libyan Jamahiriya, text in *Maghreb-Machrek*, No. 106, October-December 1984, p. 102.

85. For example Zartman, *Ripe for Resolution*, p. 59; and Parker, "Appointment in Oujda," pp. 1100–1101.

86. Algiers Domestic Service, 11 September 1984, in FBIS-MEA, 13 September 84, Q1.

87. Cairo MENA, 9 March 1983, in FBIS-MEA, 10 March 83, Q3.

88. See *Akhir Sa'a*, Cairo, report on Libya's plots to subvert the Numayri regime, 16 March 1983, pp. 16, 17, in JPRS NE/NA, Libya, 17 May 1983, p. 26.

89. Khartourm SUNA, 13 March 1983, in FBIS-MEA, 14 March 83, Q4.

90. See Ann Mosely Lesch, "Rebellion in the Southern Sudan," *UFSI Reports*, No. 8, Africa, January 1985, p. 11.

91. Rick Wells, "Nimeiry Under Siege," *Africa Report*, May-June 1984, p. 61.

92. Lesch estimates that by December 1984 the SPLA had 10,000 men under arms, p. 12.

93. See Eric Rouleau, "Sudan's Revolutionary Spring," translated from French in *Merip Report*, No. 135, September 1985, p. 9.

94. For a full report on the Libyan air raid on Umdurman see "Al-Ghara al-Jawwiya al-Ghadira 'ala al-Sudan," in *Al-Inqadh*, No. 8, April 1984, supplement, p. 4. See also Khartoum SUNA, 16 March 1984, in FBIS-MEA, 19 March 84, Q6.

95. Mary-Jane Deeb, "Qaddafi's Calculated Risks," in *SAIS Review*, Vol. 6, No. 2, Summer-Fall 1986, p. 160.

96. *Al-Safir*, Beirut, 21 March 83, p. 12.

97. Ibid.

98. Cairo MENA, 30 April 1983, in FBIS-MEA, 2 May 83, D3.

99. For a description of the mining of the Red Sea see David Blundy and Andrew Lycett, *Qaddafi and the Libyan Revolution*, Little, Brown and Co., Boston, 1987, pp. 154–155.

100. See the long report on the mining of the Red Sea, " 'Ghat' wa Rihlatiha al-Ghamida," in *Al-Inqadh*, No. 11, November 1984, pp. 38–41.

101. Ibid.

102. In July 1987 the same thing happened. Libyan pilots fleeing the war in Chad sought political asylum in Egypt, and brought their aircrafts with them. Immediately afterward, Libya began subversive activities in Egypt that were seen by the Egyptian authorities as a form of pressure to have the pilots and their planes returned to Libya. *Al-Wafd*, Cairo, 23 July 1987, pp. 1, 4.

103. Cairo MENA, 5 September 1984, in FBIS-MEA, 6 September 84, D1.

104. Paris Radio Monte Carlo, 19 February 1985, in FBIS-MEA, 20 February 85, Q5.

105. Tunis Domestic Service, 9 January 1984, in FBIS-MEA, 10 January 84, Q3.

106. Algiers Domestic Service, 13 December 1983, in FBIS-MEA, 14 December 83, Q1.

107. For a discussion of the border issue between Libya and Algeria, see Lotfi Karim Charffi, "Des Equilibres Diplomatiques et Militaires au Maghreb, 1960–1985," thesis for the Diplome d'Etudes Superieures, Institut d'Etudes des Relations Internationales, Paris (1986?), pp. 59–60.

108. Paris AFP, 19 December 1983, in FBIS-MEA, 20 December 83, Q1. In fact the continental shelf had been settled by the International Court at the Hague in 1982, but Tunisia never accepted the verdict. See Chapter 6.

109. Paris AFP, 10 February 1983, in FBIS-MEA, 11 February 83, S1.

110. Cairo MENA, 18 February 1983, in FBIS-MEA, 18 February 83, Q3.

111. Paris AFP, 10 March 1983, in FBIS-MEA, 11 March 83, Q3.

112. Ibid.

113. Paris AFP, 18 April 1983, in FBIS-MEA, 18 April 83, S1.

114. Tripoli JANA, 28 April 1983, in FBIS-MEA, 29 April 83, Q1.

115. Paris AFP, 23 June 1983, in FBIS-MEA, 24 June 83, S2; and Paris AFP, 24 June 1983, in FBIS-MEA, 24 June 83, S2.

116. Paris AFP, 25 June 1983, in FBIS-MEA, 27 June 83, S1.

117. Paris AFP, 27 June 1983, in FBIS-MEA, 27 June 83, S2.

118. Ibid., S3.

119. Paris AFP, 31 July 1983, in FBIS-MEA, 1 August 83, S2.

120. FBIS Middle East and South Asia Review, Daily Report, 11 August 83, p. 1.

121. Tripoli JANA, 7 August 1983, in FBIS-MEA, 8 August 83, Q1.

122. "Statement by Foreign Liaison Bureau on U.S. Aggressive Intentions Against Libya," Tripoli JANA, 7 August 1983, in FBIS-MEA, 8 August 83, Q1.

123. Paris AFP, 30 June 1983, in FBIS-MEA, 1 July 83, Q3.

124. Tripoli JANA, 30 June 1983, in FBIS-MEA, 1 July 83, Q1.

125. Ibid.

126. Paris AFP, 1 July 83, in FBIS-MEA, 5 July 83, Q3.

127. Excerpt from the text of the cable sent by Shadli Bin Jadid to Haile Mariam Mengistu, 9 July 1983, in FBIS-MEA, 11 July 83, Q1.

128. Algiers APS, 13 August 1983, in FBIS-MEA, 16 August 83, Q1.

129. Paris Domestic Service, 6 October 1983, in FBIS-MEA, 6 October 83, S1.

130. Ibid.

131. Paris International Service, 19 October 1983, in FBIS-MEA, 20 October 83, S2.

132. See "Projet de Convention Nationale de Reconciliation," 10 December 1983, in N'Gangbet, Appendix 5, pp. 127–135.

133. Paris AFP, 4 January 1984, in FBIS-MEA, 5 January 84, S2–3.

134. Ibid., S3.

135. Ibid.

136. *Le Monde,* Paris, 18 January 1984, pp. 1, 3.

137. *Le Monde,* Paris, 12 May 1984, pp. 1–3.

138. Speech by Qadhdhafi to the General People's Congress meeting in Tripoli, 15 February 1984, in FBIS-MEA, 17 February 84, Q4–5.

139. Interview with Qadhdhafi on French television, Channel One, Paris AFP, 30 April 1984, in FBIS-MEA, 1 May 84, Q1.

140. *Le Monde*, Paris, 12 May 1984, pp. 1, 3. In fact it had been Mitterrand's position from the start of his administraiton that in order to get the Libyans out of Chad, a settlement had to be negotiated in which France and the OAU played an active role. See Hearings Before the Subcommittee on Africa, *Libya-Sudan-Chad Triangle*, October 1981, pp. 36–37.

141. Tripoli JANA, 17 September 1984, in FBIS-MEA, 17 September 84, Q1.

142. Paris International Service, 20 September 1984, in FBIS-MEA, 21 September 84, S2.

143. See text of statement in Tripoli JANA, 10 November 1984, in FBIS-MEA, 13 November 84, Q1.

144. Paris AFP, 27 December 1984, in FBIS-MEA, 28 December 84, S1.

145. Paris AFP, 21 January 1985, in FBIS-MEA, 22 January 85, Q1.

146. Ibid.

147. Ndjamena Domestic Service, 31 January 1985, in FBIS-MEA, 5 February 85, S1.

148. See Ellen Laipson, "U.S. Policy in Northern Africa," *American Arab Affairs*, Fall 1983, No. 6, pp. 51–54.

149. Hayley, pp. 248–249.

150. In the late 1970s Libya's oil exports to the United States constituted 10 percent of the U.S. total oil imports and approximately 5 percent of total U.S. supply. See *Review of Recent Developments in the Middle East 1979*, Hearings Before the Subcommittee on Europe and the Middle East of the Committee of Foreign Affairs, House of Representatives, 96th Congress, 1st session, 26 July 1979, "Libya," p. 83.

151. Hayley, p. 249. For a discussion of foreign policy toward Libya see Harris, pp. 99–102.

152. Hayley, p. 249.

153. Ibid.

154. Ibid. See also Bob Woodward's article, "Gadhafi Target of Secret U.S. Deception Plan," *The Washington Post*, 2 October 1986, p. A1.

155. Qadhdhafi's interview on London ITV Television Network, 10 December 1981, in FBIS-MEA, 11 December 81, Q5.

156. Ibid.

157. Interview with Qadhdhafi on Vienna Domestic Service, 18 June 1982, in FBIS-MEA, 21 June 82, Q4.

158. Qadhdhafi's speech at a meeting of the General People's Congress in Tripoli, Tripoli Domestic Service, in FBIS-MEA, 23 February 83, Q3.

159. This is presumably a direct quote from Qadhdhafi's press conference on 1 June 1983, Tripoli JANA, 2 June 1983, in FBIS-MEA, 3 June 83, Q1.

160. Interview with Qadhdhafi on French television, Channel One, in FBIS-MEA, 10 February 83, Q2.

161. Qadhdhafi's address to the Moroccans, Tripoli Voice of the Arab Homeland, 1 July 1983, in FBIS-MEA, 5 July 83, Q4.

162. Speech by Qadhdhafi, in Tripoli, on fourteenth anniversary of Libyan revolution, 1 September 1983, in FBIS-MEA, 2 September 83, Q1.

163. Text of message sent by Qadhdhafi to the Arab heads of state, published in *Al-Zahf al-Akhdar*, 27 September 1982, p. 1.

164. Ibid.

165. Qadhdhafi's speech at Opposition Movements Conference in Tripoli, Tripoli JANA, in FBIS-MEA, 2 February 1983, Q3.

166. Qadhdhafi's speech at the Jamal 'Abd al-Nasir Air Base, Tripoli Domestic Service, in FBIS-MEA, 28 March 83, Q6.

167. Press conference interview with Qadhdhafi in Tripoli, Tripoli JANA, 2 June 1983, in FBIS-MEA, 3 June 83, Q1.

168. Qadhdhafi's speech on fifteenth anniversary of Libyan revolution, on 1 September 1984 in Tripoli, Tripoli Domestic Service, 1 September 84, Q6.

169. For some of Qadhdhafi's views on Islam, see, for instance, Mu'ammar al-Qadhdhafi, *Al-Sijil al-Qawmi, Bayanat wa Khutab wa Ahadith*, Vol. 2, 1970–1971, Tripoli, n.d., pp. 117–118.

170. For an analysis of the role of Islam in Qadhdhafi's ideology see Marius K. Deeb, "Islam and Arab Nationalism in Al-Qaddafi's Ideology," *Journal of South Asian and Middle Eastern Studies*, Vol. II, No. 2, Winter 1978, pp. 12–26.

171. Interview with Qadhdhafi in *Al-Safir*, Beirut, 21 March 1985, pp. 8, 9, in FBIS-MEA, 29 March 85, Q3.

172. "Al-Ma'rakat fi al-Dakhil, Mata wa Kayfa?" in *Al-Inqadh*, No. 8, April 1984, pp. 56–58.

173. Muhammad Yusuf Al-Maqarif, "Al-Mufaj'a ha ta'ti min dakhil Libya," supplement of *Al-Inqadh*, No. 8, April 1984, pp. 12–13.

174. *Al-Inqadh*, No. 9, January 1984, pp. 12–17.

175. Paris AFP, 8 May 1984, in FBIS-MEA, 9 May 84, Q1.

176. *Al-Inqadh*, No. 9, January 1984, pp. 12–13.

177. See Marius Deeb and Mary-Jane Deeb, "Libya: Internal Developments and Regional Politics," in David H. Partington, ed., *The Middle East Annual: Issues and Events Vol. 4- 1984*, G. K. Hall & Co., Boston, 1985, p. 139.

# 8

## Libya in the Aftermath of the U.S. Bombing, 1986–1989

In January 1986 the Reagan administration ordered the freezing of Libya's U.S. assets in retaliation for terrorist attacks at the Rome and Vienna airports.[1] Against the advice of U.S. intelligence agencies, the White House chose to confront Libya militarily in the following months. The White House's actions apparently were the result of pressures and frustration with the U.S. inability to deal effectively with international terrorism.[2] In March 1986 there was a serious U.S.-Libyan confrontation in the Gulf of Sidra. The United States sank two Libyan navy patrol boats[3] after they fired SA5 missiles on U.S. ships that were carrying out naval exercises in the Gulf.[4] In April 1986 following the bombing of a West Berlin discotheque patronized by U.S. military personnel,[5] U.S. war planes hit various targets in Libya, including airfields, guerrilla training camps, government posts, and Qadhdhafi's headquarters at the Bab al-'Aziziya barracks.[6]

The U.S. attack on Libya that had been announced so often before by Qadhdhafi had finally taken place in much the same way that the Egyptian attack on Libya in 1977 had come about. Qadhdhafi reacted predictably: He adopted a conciliatory attitude and began mending his fences with his neighbors. During the months following the attack, he attempted to create a number of unions with states in the region, removed trade and other barriers between Libya and neighboring states, allowed the free passage of Libyans to Tunisia, and invited North Africans to come and work in Libya. In the case of Sudan this conciliatory approach had started a year earlier after the ousting of Numayri. Qadhdhafi was also able to diffuse domestic opposition by undertaking some major economic and political changes in Libya.

International reaction to the U.S. raid, although somewhat subdued, was a significant factor in boosting Qadhdhafi's position in the region and preventing a coup from occurring in the immediate aftermath of the attack. Regionally, there was a show of support for Libya; a number of Arab states condemned the raid.[7] Although the Soviet Union had done nothing to protect Libya from the U.S. attack, it canceled a meeting between Foreign Minister Edvard Shevardnadze and Secretary of State George Shultz in protest.[8] Gorbachev also sent a message to Qadhdhafi reaffirming the USSR's commitment to Libya's defense.[9] A number of Western European states were critical of the U.S. action, and there was a major debate in the U.N. Security Council concerning the legality of such an action against Libya. Cumulatively those actions may well have helped Qadhdhafi survive the spring and summer of 1986.

### The Libyan Opposition and Changes
### on the Domestic Front

Qadhdhafi's regime also faced difficulties on the domestic front. There was another assassination attempt against the Libyan leader in November 1985, this time by Colonel Hasan Iskhal, who was close to Qadhdhafi and a member of his tribe as well. In February 1987 nine youths who had been accused of assassinating Ahmad Misbah al-Urfali, a member of the security forces of the regime, were publicly executed, and their executions were televised.[10]

By and large, however, there was less domestic unrest than had been expected after the U.S. bombing. The explanation for this may not be too difficult to find. Libyans were shocked by the bombing of their country and more particularly by the fact that a number of civilian sites had been hit. They did not turn against Qadhdhafi and may even have rallied around their leader when he portrayed himself and his family as the primary target of the attack. Furthermore, if any group within the army or outside it had attempted to overthrow the regime at that time, the group's members would have immediately been labeled "puppets of the United States" and would have lost all credibility and legitimacy in the eyes of fellow Libyans.

The Libyan opposition abroad was also rather quiet as it did not wish to be seen condoning the U.S. military attack on Libya. In fact, many of its members were very critical of the raid.[11] Furthermore, the opposition could not operate in Sudan under the new regime of Sadiq al-Mahdi or trust Morocco to provide a safe haven for opposition members, and although Sadam Husayn of Iraq harbored a number of Libyan dissident groups, they lacked the freedom to be active there.

Qadhdhafi, however, was aware that it was only a matter of time before domestic opposition resurfaced. With his acute sense of timing, he began freeing political prisoners in March 1988. Those released numbered 400 and included the leaders of the 1969 Libyan coup who had shared power with Qadhdhafi for a brief period of time: Musa Ahmad and Ahmad al-Hawwaz.[12] The move to free political prisoners was marked by a dramatic television performance showing Qadhdhafi bulldozing the walls of a prison. The move was extremely popular in Libya and did much to diffuse the growing resentment among Libyans for his domestic policies and for the losses suffered by the Libyan army in Chad. He also invited members of the Libyan opposition abroad to return to Libya, promising to give them back their confiscated property and to allow them to live peacefully in their home country. The response was cautious optimism, but only a few members of the opposition groups returned to Libya.

Qadhdhafi also undertook a major program to liberalize the economy in the spring of 1988. He allowed the relaxation of strictures on domestic private enterprise. In an official statement the General People's Congress announced that it was everyone's right to choose his or her own profession, even if that included private enterprise. Some small and medium-sized agricultural and industrial concerns were even turned over to the private sector.[13] Within a short time the *suqs* (traditional marketplaces) began to flourish in the major cities and smaller towns. The goods available for purchase increased markedly, especially after the opening of borders with Tunisia and the removal of trade restrictions between the two countries.

By the end of 1988, when the reforms had proved to be more cosmetic than real and the economy had continued to deteriorate, domestic dissatisfaction began to manifest itself in demonstrations and protest on university campuses and then throughout the country. By January 1989 unrest had spread throughout Tripoli, Benghazi, Ajdabiya, and Al-Kufrah. The government forces responded with force, cracking down on university students in December 1988 and then arresting demonstrators throughout the country. The revolutionary committees targeted the mosques because they harbored dissidents and were the loci of opposition to government policies. In December 1988 and January 1989 a number of mosques were raided by security forces and revolutionary committees during the time of prayer. The clashes between worshipers and government forces were especially violent at the mosques of 'Ali Bin Abi Talib in Tripoli and al-Salmani in Benghazi.[14]

## Qadhdhafi and Mahdi

After the fall of Numayri in Sudan, Libya moved to consolidate its relations with the new regime. That many members of the transitional government had been close to Libya, which had offered them political asylum while they plotted to overthrow Numayri, made matters easier.

Two weeks after the coup, diplomatic relations between Tripoli and Khartoum were formally restored.[15] Sudan immediately expelled the Libyan opposition and closed down its military training camps.[16] In return, Libyans stopped supporting the SPLM of Garang in southern Sudan. Libya's Jallud invited Garang to join the transitional Sudanese government of Siwar al-Dhahab.[17] A year later Libya was providing planes and military equipment to bomb the southern Sudanese rebels' strongholds.[18]

Qadhdhafi was again changing his foreign policy to serve his interests. To ensure the expulsion of the Libyan opposition in Sudan that had threatened his regime since 1980, he was ready not only to stop aiding his erstwhile allies of the SPLM but to turn against them and provide the planes and the weapons to destroy them. His support for the SPLM had never been based on revolutionary principles, as he had claimed, but had been primarily a matter of expediency. Garang's movement had been useful to Qadhdhafi as long as it fought a government that he perceived as threatening Libya's regime and borders, but the movement became dispensable when that government changed and became friendly to Libya.

During the first three years of the post-Numayri era, Libya and Egypt jockeyed for influence in Sudan,[19] while Prime Minister Mahdi attempted to steer an independent course in both domestic and foreign policy. The close ties between Cairo and Khartoum under Numayri had been perceived in Libya as threatening its regime and its territorial sovereignty. Consequently, after the fall of Numayri, Qadhdhafi saw his chance to strengthen Libyan-Sudanese relations and effect a distancing between Egypt and Sudan.

A defense agreement with Libya was signed by Sudan,[20] while the *Takamul* agreement with Egypt, which included a mutual defense clause, was downgraded.[21] Libya also began to finance all major candidates in the Sudanese parliamentary elections of 1986[22] and invited the Sudanese to work in Libya. It began funneling substantial economic aid to that impoverished country and gave Sudan 2.2 million barrels of oil to stave off shortages during election week.[23] In return for economic and military aid, Libya asked Sudan to break off diplomatic relations with Egypt, the United States, and Chad[24] and to grant Libyan troops transit rights on their way to Chad.[25] Egypt, however, fought back, giving Sudan a $10 million military grant including armored cars, ammunition, and guns as well as volunteering to mediate with Ethiopia to stop its support for the SPLM.[26] This was done in an effort to offset Libya's growing influence in Sudan and to strengthen Egyptian-Sudanese relations, which had been rather strained after Numayri sought refuge in Cairo.

After the Sudanese parliamentary elections of April 1986, Prime Minister Mahdi announced the continuation of the policy of friendly relations with Libya, although he qualified it by saying, "The important thing is that the interest of our country and our foreign policy should not have its headquarters in either Washington or Tripoli. We expect both countries to respect our principles and interests."[27]

To bolster Qadhdhafi's position regionally after the military confrontation in the Gulf of Sidra between the U.S. Navy and Libyan patrol boats in March 1986, a Libyan delegation was sent to Sudan seeking unity between the two countries.[28] The head of the Libyan delegation announced after the visit, "There is going to be political unity and economic integration" between Libya and Sudan.[29] The Sudanese, on the other hand, were respectful but noncommittal.

The civil war in Sudan between government forces and the southern forces of Garang continued unabated throughout this phase, however, and Mahdi became more dependent on Libya for oil and for weapons.[30] With a weak and divided government in Khartoum Qadhdhafi was able to pursue his policy of rapprochement with Mahdi and in October 1988 announced another proposal for the unity of Sudan and Libya. This time the unity proposal was signed in Tripoli by delegations from the two nations, but it was never ratified by the Sudanese parliament.[31] A number of parties in Sudan strongly objected to the unity project, among them the powerful Democratic Unionist Party and the communist party.[32]

By the spring of 1989 the Sudanese situation had deteriorated further, and the army was demanding the ouster of Mahdi for his ineffective conduct of the war in the south. To pacify the army the Sudanese government reportedly signed a $250 million arms deal with Libya to provide the armed forces with tanks, aircraft, and artillery after they suffered serious military setbacks against the forces of Garang.[33]

Egypt, on the other hand, stopped its attempts at coopting the Sudanese leadership and openly criticized it, calling for its replacement with a more effective government. In March 1989 Egyptian officials were predicting that Mahdi's government would be dissolved soon, and they were hoping for a more effective administration to resolve the problem of the south.[34]

On June 30, 1989, a military coup overthrew Mahdi's government. Fifteen middle-ranking officers headed by 'Umar Ahmad Hasan Bashir led the bloodless military takeover. Although Egypt denied any involvement in the coup, it welcomed the change in leadership and immediately sent medical supplies and 20,000 tons of gasoline to the new Sudanese government.[35]

The early statements on foreign policy made by the new head of state represented a change of policy toward Egypt. Bashir expressed a wish to "affiliate" with Sudan's northern neighbor, which could have meant joining the Arab Cooperation Council, of which Egypt, Iraq, Jordan, and North Yemen were members. In spite of his assurances to the Libyan government that he wished to maintain good relations between their two countries, ties between them deteriorated after Mahdi's ouster.

## The Dissolution of the Arab-African Federation

Since the U.S. bombing of Libya, Qadhdhafi has faced other problems on the regional level. On August 29, 1986, Morocco announced that it was abrogating its treaty of union with Libya[36] because of an August 27 Libyan-Syrian communiqué strongly critical of the visit of the then Israeli prime minister, Shimon Peres, to Morocco on July 22–23, 1986. Some observers saw this as a preemptive move on the part of Morocco "in anticipation of a Libyan cancellation of the treaty."[37]

This is an unlikely interpretation of the events. If Libya had planned to break the union with Morocco, it would have done so in the immediate aftermath of the Peres visit, as Syria had. It would not have waited more than five weeks before abrogating the treaty.[38] The Libyan reaction to the visit had been only a pro forma criticism not meant to undermine the union. In fact, in mid-August a statement broadcast by the Jamahiriya News Service assured its Libyan audience that all was well with the Arab-African federation between Libya and Morocco and made no mention of the Peres visit.[39]

The view that Morocco, not Libya, had wanted to break relations is shared by a number of regional observers.[40] Evidence for this view is not hard to find. Morocco had significantly improved its position vis-à-vis the Western Sahara in the previous five years, and because of the fall of the oil prices and the various economic embargoes against Libya, that country was no longer able to give substantial military aid to the POLISARIO. Furthermore, because of the strong U.S. action against Libya caused by its alleged involvement in international terrorism, the alliance was proving to be a liability and detrimental to Morocco's prestige regionally and internationally.

Libya, on the other hand, had no reason to break the treaty with Morocco. It needed this alliance even more after the U.S. raid than before. Morocco remained a channel of communication with the Western world that Qadhdhafi needed as well as a counterbalance to the existing Algerian-Tunisian-Mauritanian bloc.

A year later, Qadhdhafi was still upset about the abrogation of the treaty, which had left him without a major ally in the region, thereby further weakening him after the confrontation with the United States. Commenting on King Hasan's behavior, Qadhdhafi complained, "The

[Moroccan] people set up the union through a referendum. If he was sensible he would have sought the people's opinion once again on the abrogation of the union. How can you seek the people's opinion in the beginning on the creation of the union and then renounce the union on the radio on your own? This is insane."[41]

Relations between Libya and Morocco remained cool after the abrogation of the treaty but did not deteriorate too drastically. It was therefore relatively easy for the Moroccan and the Libyan leaders to reconcile publicly in June 1988 at the Arab summit in Algiers. In October Libya was appointed for a period of two years to the chair of the Union of Maghriban Economic Chambers. The union, based in Casablanca, includes a number of commissions that deal with trade, industry, transport, finance, and investment among the states of the Maghrib.[42] King Hasan of Morocco described Libyan-Moroccan relations in an interview reported at the end of November 1988 in the following terms: "Our bilateral relations are excellent and so are our personal relations. Myself and Col. al-Qadhdhafi do not share the same views on issues, be they on the Mediterranean or international matters. . . . However, each one of us respects the matters on which we agree."[43]

## New Attempts at Unity

Following the confrontation with the United States and after the dissolution of the Arab-African federation, Libya began searching for new regional allies. As early as November 1986 there were talks of unity between Libya and Algeria.[44] Throughout the first six months of 1987 negotiations took place, and on June 29, 1987, while addressing the People's National Assembly in Algiers, Qadhdhafi called for unity between Libya and Algeria.[45] He justified that unity not only in general ideological terms, as was his wont, but in terms of regional security as well: "If our nations remain small, paper states, we will not survive in this era, which is dominated by giants and large political groupings."[46]

Relating the union attempt to the U.S. raid on Libya in April 1986, Qadhdhafi continued:

[W]e have been able to absorb the international reality that our era is one of large international groupings. As for the small states, they can no longer survive. The United States cannot gather 170 aircraft and attack the Soviet Union because the latter is strong, but it attacked Libya . . . even though the Soviet Union constitutes more danger to it than Libya. In this era, the small nations are trampled underfoot.[47]

These statements reveal Qadhdhafi's perception of Libya's vulnerability and demonstrate that his primary objective in conducting foreign policy is the survival of the state. Unity for Qadhdhafi is a means of survival; by allying Libya to other states he hopes to deter aggression.

The Algerian leadership was interested in the idea. Rabah Bitat, chair of the National People's Assembly of Algeria, related Qadhdhafi's visit to the escalation of conflicts in the region,[48] and added, "[W]e are working toward overcoming obstacles in order to build unity of the greater Maghrib."[49]

A secret agreement was negotiated between Qadhdhafi and Bin Jadid during the summer of 1987. Details of the agreement reached the Western press. There was to be no fusion between the two states, and matters related to defense and foreign policy were to be dealt with separately by each state. Unified political institutions were, however, to be created at five different levels and to be headed by a council whose presidency would rotate between Qadhdhafi and Bin Jadid.[50] Qadhdhafi wanted to make the agreement public immediately, but Algeria stalled and insisted to postpone the announcement until November 1, 1987, its national day.

The accord was never announced, however, probably because of strong U.S. pressure on Algeria not to set up any form of union with Libya. In February 1988, in a rare interview with U.S. journalists, Bin Jadid issued an appeal to the United States to stop opposing Algeria's attempt to "neutralize" Libya by accommodating it and attempting to bring it into a regional grouping that would include other states in North Africa.[51]

Libya did not give up the desire to be allied with Algeria that easily. Qadhdhafi began to moderate his statements on foreign policy issues, negotiated a cease-fire and then resumed diplomatic relations with Chad, and attended the Arab summit in Algiers in June 1988, the first time in many years. By the end of June 1988 he had an agreement with Algeria that was a substantive accord, even though it was not as clear on the issue of union as Qadhdhafi may have wanted.

On June 29, 1988, a press statement issued in Algiers confirmed the unity project between the two countries and that it would be submitted to the people of Algeria and Libya for discussion. The project was presented as a step in the direction of the creation of the Arab Maghrib, which itself was part of the general effort to promote Arab unity. The press statement also included more specific elements, such as freedom of movement for Libyans and Algerians between the two countries, the removal of custom duties, and the launching of regular maritime services between Libyan and Algerian ports. The press statement also made public the setting up of a number of joint Algerian-Libyan companies for the exploration and production of oil, for transport, for construction, and for other purposes including health, education, and banking.[52]

Relations soured temporarily in November 1988 when Algeria restored full diplomatic relations with Egypt. Qadhdhafi was furious and criticized

Algeria very strongly for that action.[53] Since then, however, Libyan-Algerian relations have been excellent, especially since the formation of the Arab Maghribi Union.

## Improved Relations with Tunisia

Qadhdhafi did not limit his union overtures to Algeria. When President Bourguiba of Tunisia was removed from office in November 1987, Qadhdhafi moved rapidly to improve relations with the new Tunisian head of state, Zayn al-'Abidin Bin 'Ali. Diplomatic relations, which had been broken in the summer of 1985, were officially restored at the end of December 1987, and since then Libyan-Tunisian political, economic, and social relations have been excellent.

Politically, the ties between the two countries were presented to their people and to the region as a whole in a somewhat different light. Whereas Bin 'Ali discussed them within the larger context of a Greater Arab Maghrib, the Libyans immediately began talking of bilateral unity between the two countries.[54] Each state had its own political agenda. Tunisia faced serious economic problems at home, and Libya offered the possibility of alleviating them without requiring the Tunisian government to make too many structural changes in its economy. Libya's most urgent need was for allies in the region.

Although the issue of unity was not settled one way or the other, other matters were. Visa requirements between Libya and Tunisia were lifted in February 1988, and in April borders were declared open to all who wished to travel between the two countries. On that occasion Qadhdhafi made a televised speech at Ra's Jabir on the Libyan-Tunisian border, where he declared the abolition of "man-made borders between the one and only Arab people in Tunisia and Libya."[55] He added, "Let it be understood that this measure of removing the borders between us drawn by French and Italian colonialism does not categorically violate national sovereignty, territorial integrity, or respect for the regimes in any part of the Arab homeland, in particular I am talking about the Tunisian and Libyan Arab sides."[56]

The qualifying statements were obviously meant to quell the fears of those Tunisians who may have seen the abolition of boundaries as an attempt by Qadhdhafi to annex Tunisian territory. These statements reveal, however, another aspect of the dilemma of unity for leaders like Qadhdhafi who have made it part of their ideological formulation of foreign policy: the dilemma of unity at the expense of the sovereignty of the state. It has been my contention throughout this book that for Qadhdhafi the state has always been more important than any form of union between Arab or Maghribi nations. His rather curious formulation of the issue expresses the view that the abolition of boundaries is a *symbolic* declaration of friendship and alliance that has nothing to do with the actual abolition of borders between states.

The result of those new initiatves was that Libyans began flocking to Tunisia in large numbers to buy goods that were unavailable on the Libyan market. Between April when the borders were opened and July 1988, Libyans spent by some estimates $250 million in Tunisia.[57] On the other hand, an estimated 10,000 Tunisian workers went to Libya to take over new jobs.[58] Many new joint ventures between Tunisia and Libya were set up, and the two governments agreed on joint exploitation of the continental shelf oil reserves, which had been a bone of contention between the two heads of state.

Politically this rapprochement with Tunisia acted as a safety valve for domestic discontent. Because of the economic shortages created by government policies, mismanagement, and decline in revenues, Libyans from all walks of life had become very dissatisfied with the regime. The opening up of Tunisia and the timely political and economic reforms preempted the type of upheaval that took place in Algeria in October 1988 and that could have seriously undermined the Libyan regime.

## The Arab Maghribi Union

Qadhdhafi's search for regional allies came to a successful conclusion when the Arab Maghribi Union among Algeria, Morocco, Tunisia, Libya, and Mauritania was proclaimed in Marrakesh on February 17, 1989.[59] The union was formed in response to external economic and political challenges to the region as a whole. The general economic situation had deteriorated markedly since the mid-1980s because of the fall of the price of oil, drought conditions followed by a plague of locusts that destroyed much agricultural produce (especially in Tunisia and Morocco), and a mounting external debt that affected all five states of the Maghrib, including Libya. In addition, the 1986 inclusion of Spain and Portugal in the European Community threatened to undermine North African exports of agricultural goods to Western Europe.

Politically, the union was set up to provide a framework for negotiating a settlement of the Western Sahara conflict between Algeria and Morocco, to mobilize support for the leadership of a number of Maghribi states that were facing domestic unrest and criticism, and to free Tunisia and Mauritania from Algerian dominance in the Brotherhood and Concord Alliance of 1983. Most significantly, however, the union was set up to create a counterbloc to Egypt, which returned to the Arab fold in 1988. Egypt, again one of the principal Arab powers in the Middle East, further strengthened its position by setting up a bloc of its own with Iraq,

Jordan, and North Yemen on the eve of the declaration of the Arab Maghribi Union.

Libya was included in the Maghribi alliance because it constituted a natural buffer zone between a powerful Egypt and the rest of North Africa. Libya was also included to ensure that it would not join Egypt again in an alliance that would change the balance of power in the region. Furthermore, with Qadhdhafi allied to the other states of the Maghrib, there was less likelihood of his working to undermine the union and to carry out acts of subversion against any or all of those states.

Qadhdhafi was brought out of his regional isolation when Libya joined the union. Not only did this enhance his position in the Arab world; it also strengthened him domestically. More confident of his acceptance on the regional level, he was able to crack down on domestic opposition with greater force.

## The Chadian Equation

During the fall of 1986, Qadhdhafi turned his attention to Libya's southern borders, where reconciliation was apparently taking place among the various Chadian factions.[60] From Libya's perspective, reconciliation in Chad meant a government in Ndjamena independent of Tripoli that could freely enter into regional alliances, allow foreign powers to operate from its territory, and threaten Libya's southern borders. It has been the contention here that if the Chadian government were not pro-Libya, Tripoli would not permit the various factions to reconcile and would perpetuate the conflict to ensure Libyan control over the situation. Thus, from November 1986, when Ouedeye's forces allied themselves with Habre's, Qadhdhafi began building up his forces in northern Chad and passed to the offensive.[61] In early December 1986, Libya launched a massive air and ground attack on Bardai, Zouar, Wour, and other smaller Chadian towns and occupied them.[62]

By the end of December, however, the Chadian forces began to claim victories in northern Chad[63] and during the next three months pushed the Libyan and pro-Libyan forces out of every town they occupied. By the end of March 1987, the Chadian forces had captured the Libyan base of Ouadi Doum, the last large Libyan stronghold in northern Chad.[64] They found extensive supplies of weapons and military equipment including L-39 bombers, MI-24 combat helicopters, T-55 tanks, and multiple rocket launchers that had been left behind by the retreating Libyan forces.[65] Although French and U.S. logistic support had helped the Chadian government forces gradually turn the tables against the Libyans,[66] the Chadians' themselves inflicted heavy losses on the Libyan army. This was a very serious defeat for Libya that resulted in the further demoralization of the armed forces. A cease-fire proposed by the OAU was finally agreed upon in September 1987 and was by and large respected by all parties concerned.

The OAU continued to mediate the conflict, but progress appeared to be stalled with no imminent resolution of the conflict in sight. As late as April 1988, Qadhdhafi was putting unacceptable conditions for peace to the Chadian government. These included the recognition of Libya's sovereignty over the Aouzou strip, the withdrawal of foreign forces from Chad, and the release of Libyan prisoners.[67] Chad saw no reason to accept those conditions, and negotiations reached a stalemate.

On May 27, 1988, the *New York Times* carried a rather startling article that began, "Libya's leader, Mu'ammar el-Qaddafi, has declared an end to the 20 year old war in Chad and said he would recognize the current Government of that country."[68] Five months later, in October 1988 both Tripoli and Ndjamena were announcing the restoration of diplomatic ties between the two countries.

This turnabout in Qadhdhafi's position on Chad was both tactical and strategic. On May 3, 1988, French cooperation minister, Michel Aurillac, had made this public statement:

> We have just made an important decision; namely to build a permanent air base at Faya (Largeau), which will essentially be for civilian and economic purposes, to enable northern Chad to be developed. But as a permanent air base with a long runway, one can also imagine fighter aircraft and I believe Colonel al-Qadhdhafi will understand very clearly that this is dissuasive.[69]

At the heart of Libya's conflict with Chad was Qadhdhafi's fear that forces hostile to his regime could threaten Libya from its very vulnerable southern borders. Qadhdhafi therefore adopted a foreign policy that kept him in control of at least part of the northern Chadian territory to prevent any external incursion into Libya. As long as the French maintained their position south of the 16th parallel, Qadhdhafi could continue to play his games in northern Chad. The announcement of the air base at Faya-Largeau, however, changed the situation very significantly. The threat to Libya was perceived as imminent, and the People's Bureau for Foreign Liaison declared, "These military preparations confirm that France and Habre now have a free hand to launch an aggression against the Jamahiriyah's territory."[70]

The impending threat was real. The Libyan armed forces had just suffered a serious setback, in part because of French logistic support to the Chadians. Furthermore, that defeat and the high casualty rate suffered by the Libyan army were creating dissatisfaction in its ranks and led many officers and pilots to defect to Egypt seeking political asylum.[71] Domestically, Libyans felt very unhappy about the results of this little understood war and the price they had to pay for it.[72]

Tactically, therefore, Qadhdhafi's conciliatory action vis-à-vis the Chadian government was a predictable reaction to external threats to Libya's territory and domestic threats to his own regime. Strategically, however, the action was part of a larger regional foreign policy that involved a move to mend fences with all North African states and the adoption of a less radical position on political matters that concerned the whole region.

Although both sides agreed to resume diplomatic relations, the ongoing conflict over the issue of the Aouzou strip is by no means over. On a television program aired a week after both states made the announcement about opening embassies in each other's capitals, Qadhdhafi was seen addressing the General Assembly of the People's Court. In his speech he said, "Now we are fighting for the Gulf of Sidra or for Aozou— these are parts of the homeland which were compromised."[73] In July 1989 Qadhdhafi was reportedly still scheming to overthrow the Chadian government of Hissene Habre and had armed forces operating in the Darfur province of Sudan to carry out the coup. Apparently his plans had gone awry when those forces turned against a Sudanese tribe instead and went on a killing rampage that left thousands dead.[74]

## Trends and Prospects

In the wake of the U.S. bombing of Libya, Qadhdhafi found himself isolated in the region, with little political support in the Arab world or elsewhere. To survive domestically and reduce the threat of further external intervention, he resorted to the same practices that had proved successful in earlier periods when he had found himself cornered.

His strategy was fundamentally conciliatory. In fact, this phase was characterized by an almost complete lack of conflictual policies vis-à-vis his neighbors. Even with respect to Egypt Qadhdhafi modified his stand. Despite the fact that he refused to resume diplomatic relations with Egypt when most Arab states did, Qadhdhafi has tried to effect a reconciliation between Mubarak and himself. The Egyptian leader admitted that a number of Libyan delegations were sent to Egypt to open a dialogue between the two heads of state and that both Tunisia and the United Arab Emirates acted as mediators between the two nations.[75] As a gesture of goodwill, Libya agreed in late October 1988 to talks with Egypt on settling arrears and paying compensations to Egyptian workers who had been laid off by Libyan firms in 1986.[76] On

May 23, 1989, Qadhdhafi attended the Arab summit in Casablanca and met with Mubarak. They embraced publicly and set up a quadripartite minisummit with President Asad of Syria and President Bin Jadid of Algeria to thrash out their differences. In July 1989 Libya and Egypt began planning the reestablishment of diplomatic ties after more than a decade of acrimonious relations.

Ideologically Qadhdhafi has adopted a more low key approach to foreign policy. He has resumed cordial relations with PLO chief Yasir 'Arafat and has moved away from support of Iran in the war against Iraq and toward the position of mainstream Arab states. He has moderated his position toward the West and has attempted to improve Libya's relations with the United States. He has also been instrumental in the release of a Belgian physician held hostage in Beirut.

It is difficult to predict how far Qadhdhafi will go in moderating his views on the regional level or on liberalizing the economy on the domestic level. Suffice it to say that those policies have worked to bring him back to center stage and have given new life to a system that was becoming moribund.

### Notes

1. *The Washington Post*, 9 January 1986, p. A1, A15. It was later proved that those terrorist attacks had been carried out by Abu Nidal's group, an extremist Palestinian organization, and was backed primarily by Syria. See Eamonn McCann, "Diverse Reports," London ITV, 11 February 1987, in FBIS-MEA, 12 February 87, Q3. See also Bob Woodward, *Veil: The Secret Wars of the CIA, 1981–1987*, Simon and Schuster, New York, 1987, p. 431.

2. See Blundy and Lycett, p. 6.

3. *The New York Times*, 29 March 1986, p. 3.

4. *The Washington Post*, 26 March 1986, p. A22.

5. *The Washington Post*, 22 April 1986, p. A1.

6. *The Washington Post*, 15 April 1986, p. A1.

7. *The Washington Post*, 16 April 1986, p. A23.

8. *The Washington Post*, 17 April 1986, p. A21.

9. Ibid.

10. *Al-Inqadh*, No. 21, March 1987, p. 3.

11. Informal talk with some opposition members in Washington, D.C., in April 1986.

12. *Al-Tadamun*, London, 21 April 1988, pp. 7–10, in FBIS-NES, 7 April 1988, 5.

13. *The Washington Post*, 11 September 1988, p. A33.

14. Mary-Jane Deeb, "Religion and Politics in Libya," in Stuart Mews, *Religion in Politics: A World Guide*, Longman, Essex, England, 1989.

15. Rouleau, "Sudans's Revolutionary Spring," p. 9.

16. Ibid.

17. Lesch, "Rebellion in Southern Sudan," p. 15.

18. *The Washington Post*, 28 March 1986, p. A17.

19. *The New York Times*, 4 May 1986, p. E3; *The Washington Post*, 7 April 1986, p. A10.

20. *The Washington Post*, 17 April 1986, p. A21.

21. *The Wafd*, Cairo, 4 July 1987, p. 3.

22. *The Washington Post*, 28 March 1986, p. A17.

23. Ibid,. p. A20.

24. *The Washington Post*, 13 April 1986, p. A25.

25. The Egyptian press reported that the Sudanese admitted the presence of Libyan troops in Kulb, Tina, Fort Branza, and Bayda in northeast Sudan. *Al-Wafd*, Cairo, 10 September 1987, p. 1.

26. *The Washington Post*, 7 April 1986, A10.

27. From an interview with Sadiq al-Mahdi, *The Washington Post*, 24 April 1986, p. A33.

28. *The Washington Post*, 17 April 1986, pp. A21, A23.

29. Ibid., p. A23.

30. *The New York Times*, 14 November 1988, p. A10.

31. Ibid.

32. *Al-Nahar*, Beirut, 12 November 1988, p. 8.

33. *The New York Times*, 4 March 1989, p. A18.

34. See King Hasan's address to the nation in which he abrogates the union treaty with Libya, Rabat Domestic Service, 29 August 1986, in FBIS-MEA, 2 September 86, Q22–23.

35. *The New York Times*, 5 March 1989, p. 15.

36. *The Washington Post*, 9 July 1989, p. 22.

37. *The New York Times*, 30 August 1986, p. 3. See also Mary-Jane Deeb, "Inter-Maghribi Relations Since 1969: A Study of the Modalities of Unions and Mergers," in *The Middle East Journal*, Winter 1989, Vol. 43, No. 1.

38. Ibid.

39. *Al-Nahar*, Beirut, 14 August 1986, p. 8.

40. Informal conversation with Tunisian ambassador Habib Bin Yahya, Washington, D.C., October 1986.

41. Qadhdhafi's speech at the General People's Congress, Tripoli Television Service, 2 March 1987, in FBIS-MEA, 3 March 87, Q4.

42. Rabat MAP, 31 October 1988, in FBIS-NES, 2 November 88, 17.

43. Rabat Domestic Service, 27 November 1988, reportage on interview with King Hasan by an ABC correspondent in Madrid, in FBIS-NES, 30 November 88, 13.

44. See chronology of "Libya" in *The Middle East Journal*, Spring 1987, Vol. 41, No. 2, p. 272.

45. Qadhdhafi's address to the People's National Assembly in Algiers on 29 June 1987, Tripoli Television Service, in FBIS-MEA, 1 July 87, A1.

46. Ibid., p. A2.

47. Ibid., p. A4.

48. Rabah Bitat's statement in Algiers, APS, 30 June 1987, in FBIS-MEA, 2 July 87, A1.

49. Ibid.

50. *The Washington Post*, 7 October 1987, A26.

51. *The Washington Post*, 7 February 1988, A25–A26.

52. Text of press statement issued in Algiers on 28 June 1988, in FBIS-NES, 30 June 88, 10–11.

53. *Al-Nahar*, Beirut, 26 November 1988, p. 1.

54. See speech of the Secretary of the General People's Committee, JANA, 4 April 1988, in FBIS-NES, 5 April 88, 11.

55. Qadhdhafi's speech at Ra's Jadir, Tripoli Television Service, 7 April 1988, in FBIS-NES, 8 April 88, 8.

56. Ibid.

57. *The Washington Post*, 30 October 1988, p. A43.

58. Tunis Domestic Service, 10 October 1988, in FBIS-NES, 4 October 88, 10.

59. For an analysis of the new Maghriban union see Mary-Jane Deeb, "The Arab Maghrib Union in the Context of Regional and International Politics," in *Middle East Insight*, Vol. 6, No. 5, Spring 1989, pp. 42–46; and idem., "A New Era in the Maghreb?" in *The World and I: A Chronicle of Our Changing Era*, Vol. 4, No. 7, July 1989, pp. 107–112.

60. Between 1,500 and 2,000 fighters who had been loyal to Ouedeye rallied around Habre's government. Paris AFP, 24 March 1987, in FBIS-MEA, 25 March 87, S2.

61. *Al-Inqadh*, No. 21, March 1987, p. 18. Clashes were reported between Libyan forces and those of Ouedeye, and Ouedeye himself was wounded and imprisoned in Tripoli.

62. Ibid., p. 19.

63. Ibid.

64. Ndjamena Domestic Service, 25 March 1987, in FBIS-MEA, 25 March 87, S1.

65. Ibid.

66. Statement by French cooperation minister Michel Aurillac to Agence France Presse, AFP 24 March 1987, in FBIS-MEA, 25 March 87, S2.

67. FBIS-NES, 7 April 1988, 5.

68. *New York Times*, 27 May 1988, p. 2.

69. Paris International Service, 3 May 1988, in FBIS-NES, 5 May 88, 6.

70. Tripoli, JANA, 7 May 1988, in FBIS-NES, 9 May 88, 12.

71. *Al-Nahar*, Beirut, 20 July 1987, p. 1.

72. *The New York Times*, October 4, 1988, A8.

73. Tripoli Television Service, Qadhdhafi's address to the General Assembly of the People's Court, 10 October 1988, in FBIS-NES, 12 October 88, 19.

74. *The Washington Post*, 9 July 1989, p. 22.

75. *Al-Majallah*, London, 28 September–4 October 1988, p. 8, in FBIS-NES, 4 October 88, 5.

76. *Al-Sharq al-Awsat*, London, 27 October 1988, p. 1.

# 9

# Conclusion

Foreign policy, one of the most complex aspects of policymaking in advanced industrialized societies, is difficult to trace to any particular agency, group, or individual because so many interest groups and institutions are involved in the decisionmaking process. By contrast, the foreign policy of small Third World nations is often determined by an individual or a small clique. It is therefore easier to follow the evolution of foreign policy in such instances and discover the rationale and the patterns that shape it.

On the other hand, because the foreign policy of small Third World nations is so often the brainchild of a very small number of people, it is subject to much greater fluctuations than is the external policy of an advanced industrialized nation. Changes occur primarily when the leadership of that country is overturned or loses power in some other fashion.

The difference between one regime's policy and that of another can be fundamental, based on ideological principles aimed at transforming that nation's ties to the rest of the world; or it can be more one of style than of content in the conduct of foreign affairs. That country's relation to the superpowers (a move away from the West toward the East bloc of states or vice versa) may be one of the first noticeable changes in foreign policy. It is often followed by increased or diminished involvement in the affairs of the regional system of states to which the small Third World nation belongs.

Despite changes in the foreign policy of one regime in contrast to that of another, many of the ultimate objectives remain the same because the primary determinants of the policy remain constant. Of those, the geographic determinants are the most permanent. A state's neighbors will not change, nor, in general, will the country's size and natural resources (in the case of oil-producing countries, however, new resources have meant a dramatic transformation in their relations to the outside world). Historical links between neighbors will also affect their ties, and regional conflicts based on ethnic, religious, or cultural differences may be perpetuated for centuries irrespective of the regimes in power. A state's relative power position within a system of states may be very difficult to change, with major powers maintaining greater influence over the system than minor ones do. Social structure transformations occur more slowly than regime changes in the Third World. The religious establishment, the tribal leadership, the urban notability, may be fixtures of the political system irrespective of who is actually in power. Thus, a new regime may have to take into consideration the interests of social institutions even in foreign policy matters or else risk antagonizing them and creating a domestic opposition that is difficult to eradicate.

The foreign policy of a small developing nation is also affected by events outside its control. Revolutions, coups, reforms, and the emergence of new ideologies in neighboring states have immediate repercussions on the small state's political system. A change in the regime of a regional power may herald new realignments in the state system that lead to a new balance of power and the necessity to rethink previous alliances. Reforms, including the liberalization of the economy of an erstwhile socialist neighbor, may lead to domestic pressure for a similar program and changes in trading patterns with external powers. Increased external socialist measures may force a small state to reconsider its economic and political ties with the major industrialized nations or with its main trading partners inside or outside the regional system.

## Libya's Patterns of Foreign Policy Behavior

Libya's foreign policy since independence in 1951 has been shaped first by King Idris I and his cabinets and then by Qadhdhafi. It is therefore fairly easy to analyze the evolution of that policy and distinguish those issues that have remained of primary importance to Libya's national interest and those that have been a product of the interests of the regime in power.

Qadhdhafi came to power by means of a coup that unseated a legitimate traditional ruler who, despite his lack of popularity, represented a genuine indigenous form of leadership: that of the Sanussiya movement. Qadhdhafi was never able to build a solid power base and acquire the legitimacy needed to govern the country unchallenged. Instead, he faced fundamental opposition to his rule from the very beginning and had to rely on outside forces and coercion to stay in power. The threats to his regime were real, and his foreign policy was often formulated with an eye on the domestic impact it would have in enhancing his popularity and increasing his legitimacy. His foreign policy was also affected by the existence of a vocal Libyan opposition in neighboring states that called for the overthrow of his regime.

The threat to Libya's borders may have been more apparent than real. It may have been used to mobilize the Libyan population around its leader in the absence of more positive incentives to do so. The fact remains that both Qadhdhafi and King Idris saw Libya as weak and vulnerable to external interference, if not to direct military and political intervention. Both sought to protect Libya by means of alliances with regional and/or external powers. After Libya's external revenues rose sharply with the oil exports, King Idris and later Qadhdhafi sought to build a military force capable of deterring attacks on Libyan territory, and both used generous financial aid to pacify Libya's neighbors. But whereas Idris chose a neutral foreign policy with respect to intraregional conflicts in order to safeguard Libya's independence, Qadhdhafi chose complete involvement in Arab politics primarily to secure the recognition and support of Arab leaders and to deter attacks against Libya's borders. Neither course of action was completely successful. It has been this perception of weakness, coupled with the fear that Libya's very substantive oil wealth was a major inducement to regional powers with hegemonic ambitions, that has formed the basis of Libya's foreign policy since independence.

To counter both real and perceived threats, Qadhdhafi manipulated ideology (pan-Arab, pan-Islamic, and revolutionary); sought to create unions, mergers, and alliances with neighboring states and with states outside the region; and combined conciliatory with conflictual foreign policy actions (mediation, conciliation, economic assistance, and military aid, on the one hand, with sabotage, assassinations, and military interventions, on the other).

Qadhdhafi's foreign policy actions form clearly identifiable patterns of behavior. Libya's various attempts at setting up unions and mergers with neighboring states fall into one such pattern. Those attempts have taken place when Qadhdhafi felt threatened externally or isolated regionally. He would first try to merge or unite Libya with a major regional power in order to protect it from those external threats. During most of the period under study, Libya has been allied to one of the three major powers of North Africa: Egypt up to the end of 1973, Algeria from 1975 to 1981, and Morocco from 1984 to 1986. Since February 1989 Libya has been part of a larger bloc that includes Morocco, Algeria, Tunisia, and Mauritania.

When Qadhdhafi failed to find a major regional power to act as protector, he sought a merger with a minor regional power, such as Tunisia or Chad, to strengthen Libya's position regionally. When neither major nor minor regional powers were interested in allying themselves to Libya, as in the period following the October 1973 Arab-Israeli War, Qadhdhafi sought the protection of an external power—in that case, the Soviet Union. It is significant that when such alliances took place between two or more states in the region and did *not* include Libya, Qadhdhafi condemned the alliance as serving the interests of imperialist powers and fragmenting the Arab world into petty antagonistic blocs. When Libya joined such alliances, they became, in Qadhdhafi's words, the first step in the direction of complete unity of the Arab world.

Whenever Qadhdhafi perceived the survival of his regime or Libya's territorial integrity to be threatened, he resorted to ideology in order to mobilize support for himself and his policies. Whenever he felt secure domestically and regionally, there was a marked decline in his use of ideology as a tool of policy. In the name of Arab unity, for instance, he could justify any alliance he chose to make with Arab states; yet in the name of revolutionary socialism and anti-imperialism he could justify any confrontation with his neighbors or with Arab states such as Egypt or Saudi Arabia. Under the slogan of Islam, he could attack the Western powers as being crusaders and the Saudis as being pro-Western. But in the name of Islam, he could also praise the Saudis if he needed them and call for the spiritual union of all Islamic peoples.

Ideology also served to build up his image as a charismatic leader who braved incredible odds to defend Libya, its honor, and its people. He pitted himself against Egypt in the 1970s and against the United States in the 1980s, playing David to their Goliath. This posturing was a very important part of his ideology. His image, which had been created by Heikal in 1969, was as an immediately recognizable, strong public personality of heroic proportions for some and criminal dimensions for others. Ideology was thus used to explain events and policies, justify the choice of allies and enemies, outline long-range foreign policy objectives, and most important, enhance Qadhdhafi's own legitimacy and leadership.

In terms of his style of conducting foreign policy, each time Qadhdhafi felt his regime or Libya's borders to be threatened by external forces, he engaged in a conflictual pattern of behavior. This included subversive activities, military interventions, support for opposition groups, and abusive mass media campaigns against the state or states he perceived were threatening his security. When the threats became overwhelming, and both his regime and Libya's borders were endangered simultaneously, he retracted and became conciliatory. He diffused the threats by trying to resolve his differences with Libya's neighbors, by entering into negotiation with them on economic and political matters, and by offering them substantive economic or military aid.

When Qadhdhafi felt secure domestically and regionally, he assumed the role of a statesman in contrast to that of the revolutionary he played when threatened. He offered his services to mediate intraregional as well as extraregional conflicts. He hosted large regional conferences and meetings and paid ostentatious visits to other Arab heads of state. His ideological rhetoric became conciliatory, and his calls for revolution all but disappeared. He also became critical of the Arab "masses" whose erstwhile defender he had been.

The difference between his attitude when under overwhelming stress and when secure was twofold: one of visibility and one of content. When faced by imminent threats of attack or of a coup, Qadhdhafi withdrew into the shadows, and his conciliatory policy was carried out through envoys with very little publicity. When Qadhdhafi felt secure, his actions were carried out by himself publicly. When seriously threatened, Qadhdhafi's policies were conciliatory in the sense that he retreated from certain previously held positions; he appeared to give in to the demands of other powers. When he was secure, he acted more positively. He mediated the conflicts of others; he devised new ways of doing business with his neighbors; he started completely new projects. These differences however, were often more a matter of degree than of substance.

## Some Implications of This Analysis

Rather than try to identify those factors in Qadhdhafi's personality that have influenced his foreign policy in North Africa, this book has focused primarily on patterns of behavior that are recurrent, easily recognizable, and therefore predictable. It is undeniable, however, that the choice of foreign policy actions to achieve certain ends are a function of a leader's personality. The decision to undertake subversive actions against states that are perceived as threatening, for instance, or to be conciliatory under pressure, reflects individual preferences that may be unique to a particular leader. Under similar circumstances other heads of state may react quite differently. Thus, without denying the importance of the role of personality in foreign policy, I have emphasized those aspects that can form an objective basis for research.

At the state level of foreign policymaking, one must view the world from an insider's perspective—that is, adopt a leader's point of view as well as that of a country's mass media, opposition factions, and neighboring heads of state. This approach helps the researcher to understand the way a state perceives its own interests, the way it interprets the intentions and actions of other nations, and the way it justifies and rationalizes policies. Only by understanding a state's self-perception and perception of others can one interpret foreign policy actions in a meaningful way.

Libya was studied as part of a larger system of states linked by geographical proximity, cultural affinity, and a sense of identity. This approach ensures that foreign policy actions are understood in the context in which they are made. A state cannot be isolated from its geopolitical sphere of action, and foreign policy behavior cannot be understood only in terms of a state's interests or articulated policy. One must take into consideration what those actions will mean for the system as a whole and analyze their meaning in terms of the region as well as the individual state's motivations.

Libya's foreign policy objectives were identified primarily in terms of the security of the regime and the country's independence and territorial sovereignty. In this postcolonial era when Western powers are no longer policing the world, regional powers in Africa and Asia often attempt to expand their influence and at times their borders as well. The security of small states is a legitimate matter of concern for their leaders, especially when they lack the resources to defend their territorial sovereignty or the domestic legitimacy to mobilize support for the regime.

Another advantage of the approach used in this book is that it operationalizes certain theoretical concepts that can then be used to analyze the foreign policies of other small Third World countries. When power is defined as capabilities, for instance, it becomes easier to compare smaller, less powerful states in a region in terms of their population, their size, their economic level of development, their military resources, and so forth. When foreign policy actions are defined as the dependent variable of foreign policy and are broken down into discrete and identifiable actions, it becomes possible to select, categorize, and eventually organize those actions into patterns. The patterns reveal the nature of the relations among states and help predict how specific states will behave under certain conditions. The patterns will, however, vary from state to state and from leader to leader within the same state.

The organization of foreign policy actions into patterns can prove useful in understanding what is often described as the irrational, erratic, or unpredictable behavior of some of the leaders of Third World nations. With this approach, their behavior can be systematized to give us a more accurate picture of their policies. A demystification of the personality factor occurs when actions are identified and organized. This process often reveals a very rational pattern of behavior, despite apparent theatrical performances aimed at projecting images of power and authority. Although the particular pattern of foreign policy behavior that emerges from the study of a particular state will remain unique in terms of the state and its leaders, the framework itself can be applied across the border and over different time spans.

Ideology also provides a useful tool in understanding the foreign policy of a state. Rather than try to explain the many different ways ideological concepts are used in foreign policy, and reconcile the contraditions between ideological statements of policy and actual foreign policy actions, this approach views ideology in terms of its generalized functions. These include the justification, explanation, and rationalization of foreign policy as well as the enhancement of a leader's legitimacy and authority. It then becomes easier to deal with the apparent contradictions between stated and actual policies and between the general and the specific contexts within which policymaking takes place.

## Future Trends

Whereas King Idris I viewed Britain and the United States as allies and protectors of Libya's sovereignty and supporters of his regime, Qadhdhafi feared the West and saw it as a potential threat to Libya's security and to that of the Arab world. The king realized, too late, that the West could not or would not stand by him when he was overthrown by the military coup of 1969. By the late 1980s Qadhdhafi probably came to a similar conclusion about the Soviet Union, which he had perceived as the protector and defender of Libya's territorial sovereignty but which could not prevent the U.S. bombing of April 1986.

The Arab Maghribi Union of February 1989 may represent, among other things, a new realization about the limits of the power of the Western and Eastern blocs of nations to mediate regional conflicts, to impose solutions, or to extricate North Africa from its intractable economic problems. The member states, including Libya, may have reached a new maturity and may be turning toward each other to find solutions.

The trend in Libya's foreign policy is toward greater accommodation with the states of both the Maghrib and the Mashriq. With few exceptions the Arab states themselves are no longer divided along radical and moderate lines. Socialist states are opening up their economies and their political systems after having failed to create the just and prosperous societies they had promised. There also appears to be a decline in ideological rhetoric now that the Islamic forum is monopolizing the states' political dialogue with its citizens. A new pragmatism is emerging to confront the dual threat of a deteriorating economy and a vocal and radical Islamic opposition, and Qadhdhafi is following suit.

# Bibliography

## Documents, Official Publications, and Pamphlets

Algeria (Democratic and Popular Republic of), Direction des Statistiques, *Annuaire statistique de l'Algerie*, Algiers, 1976.

American University of Beirut, *Al-Watha'iq al-'Arabiya, 1970*, Beirut, n.d.

———, *Al-Watha'iq al-'Arabiya, 1972*, Beirut, n.d.

Egypt (Arab Republic of), Ministry of Information, State Information Service, *Speeches and Interviews by President Anwar El-Sadat, September 1970–December 1971*, Cairo, n.d.

Libya (Libyan Arab Republic), *Min Ahadith al-'Aqid Mu'ammar al-Qadhdhafi fi al-Sahafa al-'Arabiya wal-'Alamiya*, Arab Revolution Printing Press, Tripoli, n.d.

———, *Mustafa Khawjat, Tarikh Fazzan*, eighteenth century manuscript, edited by the Center of Libyans' Jihad, Tripoli, 1979.

———, *The Official Gazette*, Tripoli, 1970.

———, Al-Qadhdhafi, Mu'ammar, *Al-Kitab, al-Akhdar, al-Fasl al-Awal Hal-Mushkilat al-Dimuqratiya, Sultat al-Sha'b*, n.p., n.d.

———, Al-Qadhdhafi, Mu'ammar, *Al-Kitab al-Akhdar, Hal al-Mashkal al-Iqtisadi, al-Ishtirakiya*, Tripoli, al-Sharikat al-'Amma lil-Nashr, wal-Tawzi' wal-'I'lan, n.p., 1977.

———, Al-Qadhdhafi, Mu'ammar, *Al-Sijl al-Qawmi, Bayanat wa Khutab wa Ahadith, 1970–1971*, Vol. 2, n.p., n.d.

———, Al-Qadhdhafi, Mu'ammar, *Al-Sijl al-Qawmi, Bayanat wa Khutab wa Ahadith, 1973–1974*, Vol. 5, Arab Revolution Printing Press, Tripoli, n.d.

———, Al-Qadhdhafi, Mu'ammar, *Al-Sijl al-Qawmi, Bayanat wa Khutab wa Ahadith al-'Aqid Mu'ammar al-Qadhdhafi, 1976–1977*, Vol. 8, The Arab Revolution Printing Press, Tripoli, n.d.

———, (Socialist People's Libyan Arab Jamahiriya), Secretariat of Planning, Census and Statistics Department, *Nata'ij al-Ta'dad al-'Am lil-Sukan*, Government Press, Tripoli, 1977.

## Libyan Opposition Publications

Committee for the Day of Solidarity with the Libyan People, *Watha'iq Tudin al-Qadhdhafi*, pamphlet, n.p., n.d.

*Al-Inqadh*, n.p., 1982–1987.

Al-Maqarif, Muhammad Yusuf, *Mudhakkara Muqaddama ila Mu'tamar al-Qimat li-Munadhama al-Wihda al-Afriqiya al-Mun'aqad bi Madinat Nairobi-Kenya*, pamphlet, Nairobi, June 1981.

National Front for the Liberation of Libya, *Akhbar Libya*, n.p., 1984–1987.

———, *Libya: Daring to Hope Again*, pamphlet, Munich, April 1974.

———, *Memorandum Presented to the 69th Annual Session of the International Labor Organization*, pamphlet, Geneva, June 1983.

———, *The National Front for the Salvation of Libya: A Program of Struggle to Topple the Gadhafi Regime and Lay the Foundation for Constitutional Democratic Rule in Libya*, pamphlet, Chicago.

———, *News Letter*, 1982–1987.

Tunisia, Institut Nationale de la Statistique, *Annuaire Statistique de la Tunisie, 1976–1977*, Tunis, n.d.

———, Ministry of Foreign Affairs, *Recent Developments in the Relations Between Libya and Tunisia*, pamphlet, Tunis, June 1986.

United States, Congress, House, Subcommittee on Africa of the Committee on Foreign Affairs, *Libya-Sudan-Chad Triangle: Dilemma for United States Policy*, Hearings, 97th Congress, 1st session, October 29 and November 4, 1981, U.S. Government Printing Office, Washington, D.C., 1982.

———, Congress, House, Subcommittee on Europe and the Middle East of the Committee on Foreign Affairs, *Review of Recent Developments in the Middle East 1979*, Hearings, 96th Congress, 1st session, July 26, 1979, U.S. Government Printing Office, Washington, D.C., 1979.

———, Department of Commerce, *Joint Publications Research Service, Near East and North Africa*, 1969–1987.

———, Department of Defense, *Congressional Presentation: Security Assistance Program*, FY 1983, Washington, D.C., 1982.

———, Department of State, Bureau of Public Affairs, *The Libyan Problem*, Special Report, No. 111, October 1983.

———, Department of State, *United States Treaties and Other International Agreements*, Vol. 5, Part 3, 1954, U.S. Government Printing Office, Washington, D.C., 1956.

———, Foreign Broadcast Information Service, *Daily Report: Middle East and Africa*, 1969–1987.

———, National Archives and Records Administration, Despatch from Jefferson Caffery, Cairo, to the Department of State, Washington, D.C., 673.7431/9-1450 XR320. "Egyptian-Libyan Border Question at General Assembly," September 14, 1950.

———, National Archives and Records Administration, Despatch from Marion J. Rice, Benghazi, to the Department of State, Washington, D.C., 673.74/9-551. "Egyptian Influence in Cyrenaica," September 5, 1951.

———, National Archives and Records Administration, Despatch from Henry Villard, Tripoli, to the Department of State, Washington, D.C., 673.74/9-12532 XR 641.73. "Prime Minister's Comment on Egyptian Influence in Libya," September 12, 1953.

——, National Archives and Records Administration, Despatch from Peter R. Chase, Benghazi, to the Department of State, Washington, D.C., 673.82/7-2254 XR 773.13. "Libya's Relations with Turkey," July 22, 1954.

## Books and Articles

Abdi, Nourredine, "Common Regional Policy for Algeria and Libya: From Maghribi Unity to Saharan Integration," in E.G.H. Joffe and K.S. McLachlan (eds.), *Social and Economic Development of Libya*, MENAS, Cambridgeshire, 1982.

Abu al-Majd, Sabri, *Bayn Misr wa Libya, Da'iman 'Ilaqat Qawiya 'Azliya Muzdahira*, n.p., n.d.

Alexander, Nathan (pseud.), "The Foreign Policy of Libya: Inflexibility Amid Change," *Orbis*, Vol. 24, No. 4, Winter 1981.

Allan, J. A., "Libya Accommodates to Lower Oil Revenues: Economic and Political Adjustments," *International Journal of Middle East Studies*, Vol. 15, No. 3, August 1983.

—— (ed.), *Libya Since Independence*, St. Martin's Press, New York, 1982.

Aluko, Olajide, *Nigerian Foreign Policy Alternative Perceptions and Projections*, St. Martin's Press, New York, 1983.

—— (ed.), *The Foreign Policies of African States*, Hodder and Stoughton, London, 1977.

Amoretti, B. Scarcia, "Libyan Loneliness in Facing the World: The Challenge of Islam?" in Adeed Dawisha (ed.), *Islam in Foreign Policy*, Cambridge University Press, London, 1983.

Anderson, Lisa, "Qadhdhafi and His Opposition," *The Middle East Journal*, Vol. 40, No. 2, Spring 1986.

——, "Qadhdhafi and the Kremlin," *Problems of Communism*, September-October 1985.

——, *The State and Social Transformation in Tunisia and Libya, 1830–1980*, Princeton University Press, Princeton, N.J., 1986.

Ansell, M. O., and T. M. Arif (eds.), *The Libyan Revolution: A Sourcebook of Legal and Historical Documents*, Oleander Press, Harrow, England, 1972.

Barakat, Halim (ed.), *Contemporary North Africa: Issues of Development and Integration*, Center for Contemporary Arab Studies, Washington, D.C., 1985.

Bearman, Jonathan, *Qadhdhafi's Libya*, Zed Books, London, 1986.

Bechtold, Peter K., "The Contemporary Sudan," *American-Arab Affairs*, No. 6, Fall 1983.

——, "New Attempts at Arab Cooperation: The Federation of Arab Republics, 1971– ," *The Middle East Journal*, Vol. 27, No. 2, Spring 1973.

Belaid, Sadok, "L'Operation de Gafsa de Janvier 1980 et ses enseignements," *Revue Tunisienne de Droit*, Vol. 11, 1979, Numero Special.

Ben Adjmia, "Structure des villages et origine de leur population dans le Sahel Septentrional," *Cahiers de Tunisie*, Vol. 12, 1964.

Berrie, Y., and S. Kebzabo, "Que fait Khaddafi au Tchad?" *Jeune Afrique*, No. 768, September 26, 1975.

Bianco, Mirella, *Gadafi: Voice From the Desert*, Longman, London, 1975.

Bilal, 'Abdallah, *Qira'at fi Hadhihi al-Tahawwulat*, The General Company for Publication, Distribution and Advertisement, n.p., 1979.

Blundy, David, and Andrew Lycett, *Qaddafi and the Libyan Revolution*, Little, Brown, Boston, 1987.

Boutros-Ghali, Boutros, "La diplomatie Egyptienne durant la periode post-Sadatienne," *Studia Diplomatica*, Vol. 36, No. 1, 1983.

Brewer, William D., "The Libyan-Sudanese 'Crisis' of 1981: Danger for Darfur and Dilemma for the United States," *The Middle East Journal*, Vol. 36, No. 2, Spring 1982.

Brown, L. Carl, *International Politics of the Middle East: Old Rules, Dangerous Game*, Princeton University Press, Princeton, N.J., 1984.

Carr, Edward H., *The Twenty Years' Crisis, 1919–1939: An Introduction to the Study of International Relations*, Harper and Row, New York, 1964.

Carvely, Andrew, "Libya: International Relations and Political Purposes," *International Journal*, Vol. 28, No. 4, Autumn 1973.

Cecil, Charles O., "The Determinants of Libyan Foreign Policy," *The Middle East Journal*, Vol. 19, No. 1, Winter 1965.

Clarke, J., "Some Observations on Libyans in Tunisia," *Cahiers de Tunisie*, Vol. 21, No. 2, 1958.

Claude, Iris L., *Power and International Relations*, Random House, New York, 1962.

Cohen, Bernard C., and Scott A. Harris, "Foreign Policy," in Fred I. Greenstein and Nelson W. Polsby (eds.), *Handbook of Political Science*, Vol. 6, Addison-Wesley, Reading, Mass., 1975.

Cooley, John K., *Libyan Sandstorm: The Complete Account of Qaddafi's Revolution*, Holt, Rinehart and Winston, New York, 1982.

Dahmani, Abdelaziz, "Algerie: La nouvelle diplomatie," *Jeune Afrique*, No. 1093, December 16, 1981.

Damis, John, *Conflict in Northwest Africa: The Western Sahara Dispute*, Hoover Institution Press, Stanford, Calif., 1983.

———, "Mauritania and the Sahara," *Middle East International*, No. 71, May 1977.

Deeb, Marius, "Islam and Arab Nationalism in al-Qadhdhafi's Ideology," *Journal of South Asian and Middle Eastern Studies*, Vol. 2, No. 2, December 1978.

———, "Radical Political Ideologies and Concepts of Property in Libya and South Yemen," *The Middle East Journal*, Vol. 40, No. 3, Summer 1986.

Deeb, Marius, and Mary-Jane Deeb, "Libya: Internal Developments and Regional Politics," in David H. Partington (ed.), *The Middle East Annual*, Vol. 4, 1984, G. K. Hall and Co., Boston, 1985.

———, *Libya Since the Revolution: Aspects of Social and Political Development*, Praeger, New York, 1982.

Deeb, Mary-Jane, "The Arab Maghrib Union in the Context of Regional and International Politics, *The Middle East Insight*, Vol. 6, No. 5, Spring 1989.

———, "Idris I," in Bernard Reich (ed.), *Political Leaders of the Contemporary Middle East and North Africa*, Greenwood Press, New York, 1990.

———, "Inter-Maghribi Relations Since 1969: A Study of the Modalities of Unions and Alliances," *The Middle East Journal,* Vol. 43, No. 1, Winter 1989.

———, "Libya," in Stuart Mews (ed.), *Religion in Politics: A World Guide,* Longman Group, London, 1989.

———, "Libya's Economic Development, 1969–1986: Social and Political Implications," *Maghreb Review,* Vol. 11, Nos. 1–2, January-April 1987.

———, "New Thinking in Libya," *Current History,* Vol. 89, No. 546, April 1990.

———, "Qaddafi's Calculated Risks," *SAIS Review,* Vol. 6, No. 2, Summer-Fall 1986.

Dougherty, James E., and Robert L. Pfaltzgraff, Jr., *Contending Theories of International Relations,* J.B. Lippincott, Philadelphia, 1971.

Erikson, Erik H., *Young Man Luther, A Study in Psychoanalysis and History,* W. W. Norton, New York, 1958.

Evans-Pritchard, E. E., *The Sanusi of Cyrenaica,* Clarendon Press, Oxford, 1949.

Fahmy, Ismail, *Negotiations for Peace in the Middle East,* The Johns Hopkins University Press, Baltimore, Md., 1983.

El-Fathaly, Omar, and Richard Chakerian, *Political Development and Bureaucracy in Libya,* Lexington Books, Lexington, Mass., 1977.

El-Fathaly, Omar, and Monte Palmer, *Political Development and Social Change in Libya,* Lexington Books, Lexington, Mass., 1980.

Feldman, Mark B., "Tunisia-Libya Continental Shelf Case: Geographic Justice or Judicial Compromise?" *American Journal of International Law,* Vol. 77, April 1983.

First, Ruth, *Libya: The Elusive Revolution,* Penguin Books, Baltimore, Md., 1974.

Freedman, Robert O., *Soviet Policy Toward the Middle East Since 1970,* Praeger, New York, 1982.

Ghanem, Shukri, "The Libyan Economy Before Independence," in E.G.H. Joffe and K. S. McLachlan (eds.), *Social and Economic Development of Libya,* MENAS, Cambridgeshire, 1982.

Grimaud, Nicole, *La politique exterieure de l'Algerie,* Editions Karthala, Paris, 1984.

Haas, Ernst B., "The Balance of Power: Prescription, Concept or Propaganda," *World Politics,* Vol. 5, July 1953.

Haig, Alexander M., Jr., *Caveat, Realism, Reagan and Foreign Policy,* Macmillan, New York, 1984.

Haley, Edward, *Qadhdhafi and the United States Since 1969,* Praeger, New York, 1984.

Hamid, Muhammad Bashir, "The 'Findlandization' of Sudan's Foreign Policy: Sudanese-Egyptian Relations Since the Camp David Accords," *Journal of Arab Affairs,* Vol. 2, No. 2.

Harris, Lillian Craig, *Libya: Qadhafi's Revolution and the Modern State,* Westview Press, Boulder, Colo., 1986.

Heikal, Mohamed, *The Road to Ramadan,* Times Book Co., New York, 1975.

Heller, Mark (ed.), *The Middle East Military Balance, 1983,* Jaffee Center for Strategic Studies, Tel Aviv University, Tel Aviv, 1983.

Heller, Mark, Dov Tamari, and Zeev Eytan (eds.), *The Middle East Military Balance, 1984*, Jaffee Center, Tel Aviv University, Tel Aviv, 1984.

Herman, Lawrence L., "The Court Giveth and the Court Taketh Away: An Analysis of the Tunisia-Libya Continental-Shelf Case," *International and Comparative Law Quarterly*, Vol. 33, No. 4, October 1984.

Holsti, Kal J., *International Politics: A Framework for Analysis*, Prentice-Hall, Englewood Cliffs, N.J., 1972.

Hottinger, Arnold, "L'expansionisme Libyen: Machrek, Maghreb et Afrique Noire," *Politique Etrangère*, Vol. 46, No. 1, March 1981.

Howell, John, "An Analysis of Kenyan Foreign Policy," *The Journal of Modern African Studies*, Vol. 6, No. 1, 1968.

Al-Hundiri, Sa'id 'Abd al-Rahman, *Al-'Ilaqat al-Libiya al-Tchadiya, 1843–1975*, Markaz Jihad al-Libiyin, Tripoli, 1983.

International Institute for Strategic Studies, *The Military Balance, 1982–1983*, IISS, London, 1982.

"Interview with Boutros-Boutros Ghali," *American Arab Affairs*, No. 6, Fall 1983.

Itzkowitz, Norman, and Volkan Vanik, *The Immortal Attaturk: A Psychobiography*, University of Chicago Press, Chicago, 1984.

Kennan, George F., *Realities of American Foreign Policy*, W. W. Norton & Co., 1966.

Keohane, Robert C. (ed.), *Neorealism and Its Critics*, Columbia University Press, New York, 1986.

Khadduri, Majid, *Modern Libya: A Study in Political Development*, The Johns Hopkins University Press, Baltimore, Md., 1963.

Korany, Bahgat, and Ali E. Hillal Dessouki (eds.), *The Foreign Policies of Arab States*, Westview Press, Boulder, Colo., 1984.

Laipson, Ellen, "U.S. Policy in Northern Africa," *American-Arab Affairs*, No. 6, Fall 1983.

Lanne, Bernard, *Tchad-Libye: La Querelle des Frontières*, Editions Karthala, Paris, 1982.

Leca, Jean, "Le traité instituant l'union Arabo-africaine," *Maghreb-Machrek*, No. 106, October-December 1984.

Lemarchand, René, "Libyan Goals, Objectives and Prospects in Africa," paper prepared for the Defense Academic Research Support Program Conference on Prospects for Africa, U.S. European Command, Stuttgart, West Germany, April 1986.

Lesch, Ann Mosely, "Rebellion in the Southern Sudan," *Universities Field Staff International, Inc., Reports*, No. 8, Africa, 1985.

_____ , "The Fall of Nimeiri," *Universities Field Staff International, Inc., Reports*, No. 9, Africa, 1985.

_____ , "Transition in the Sudan: Aspirations and Constraints," *Universities Field Staff International, Inc., Reports*, No. 20, Africa, 1985.

Le Tourneau, Roger, "Libyan Education and Its Development," in UNESCO, *Report of the Mission to Libya*, Johannes Weisbecker, Frankfurt, 1952.

"Libya-Morocco: Treaty Instituting the Arab-African Union of States," *International Legal Materials*, Vol. 23, No. 5, September 1984.

"Libya-Tunisia: Agreement to Submit Question of the Continental Shelf to the International Court of Justice," *International Legal Materials*, Vol. 18, No. 1, January 1979.

"La Libye regarde vers l'ouest," *Maghreb-Machrek*, No. 70, October-December 1975.

Macdonald, Robert W., *The League of Arab States: A Study in the Dynamics of Regional Organization*, Princeton University Press, Princeton, N.J., 1965.

Mack, John E., *A Prince of Our Disorder: The Life of T. E. Lawrence*, Little, Brown, Boston, 1976.

———, "T. E. Lawrence and the Uses of Psychology in the Biography of Historical Figures," in L. Carl Brown and Norman Itzkowitz (eds.), *Psychological Dimensions of Near Eastern Studies*, Darwin Press, Princeton, N.J., 1977.

Mammeri, H. "Le colonel Kadhdhafi et la question Tchadienne," *Maghreb-Machrek*, No. 80, April-June 1978, pp. 11–13.

Mansur, 'Ali 'Ali, *Khutwa Ra'ida Nahwa Tatbiq Ahkam al-Shari'a al-Islamiya fi al-Jumhuriya al-'Arabiya al-Libiya*, Dar al-Fatwa, Beirut, 1972.

Martin, Michael et al., "Les armées et la defense," *Annuaire de l'Afrique et du Moyen Orient*, Editions Jeune Afrique, Paris, 1981.

Morgenthau, Hans J., *Politics Among Nations: The Struggle for Power and Peace*, 6th ed., Alfred Knopf, New York, 1985.

———, *The Purpose of American Politics*, Alfred Knopf, New York, 1960.

Muscat, Frederic, *Ra'isi Ibni*, Adam Publishers, Valetta, Malta, n.d.

Nelson, Harold D. (ed.), *Area Handbook for Chad*, U.S. Government Printing Office, Washington, D.C., 1972.

———, *Libya: A Country Study*, Foreign Area Studies Series, U.S. Government Printing Office, Washington, D.C., 1979.

Neuberger, Benyamin, *Involvement, Invasion and Withdrawal: Qadhdhafi's Libya and Chad, 1969–1981*, Occasional Papers, No. 83, Tel Aviv University, Tel Aviv, 1982.

N'Gangbet, Michel, *Peut-on encore sauver le Tchad?* Editions Karthala, Paris 1984.

Niebuhr, Reinhold, *Christian Realism and Political Problems*, Charles Scribner's Sons, New York, 1953.

Nyrop, Richard et al., *Area Handbook for Libya*, U.S. Government Printing Office, Washington, D.C., 1973.

Ogunbadejo, Oye, "Qadhdhafi's North African Design," in *International Security*, Vol. 8, No. 1, Summer 1983.

Otayek, Rene, "La Libye revolutionnaire au Sud du Sahara," *Maghreb-Machrek*, No. 94, October-December 1981.

Parker, Richard B., "Appointment in Oudja," *Foreign Affairs*, Vol. 63, No. 5, Summer 1985.

———, *North Africa: Regional Tensions and Strategic Concerns*, Praeger, New York, 1984.

Pelt, Adrian, *Libyan Independence and the United Nations: A Case of Planned Decolonization*, Yale University Press, New Haven, Conn., 1970.

Pincher, Chapman, "Egypt Gets Libyan Planes," *Daily Express*, London, April 10, 1973.

Quandt, William B., *Saudi Arabia in the 1980's: Foreign Policy, Security and Oil*, The Brookings Institution, Washington, D.C., 1981.

Rondot, P., "Libye une politique etrangère independente," *Revue Francaise d'Etudes Politiques Mediterranéênes*, No. 16, April 1976.

Rouleau, Eric, "Sudan's Revolutionary Spring," *Middle East Research and Information Project Reports*, No. 135, September 1985.

Ruedy, John, "Historical Influences on Intra-Regional Relations in the Maghrib," in Halim Barakat (ed.), *Contemporary North Africa: Issues of Development and Integration*, Center for Contemporary Arab Studies, Washington, D.C., 1985.

El-Sadat, Anwar, *In Search of Identity: An Autobiography*, Harper and Row, New York, 1978.

Salameh, Ghassan, *Al-Siyasa al-Kharijiya al-Sa'udiya Mundhu 'Am 1945: Dirasat fi al-'Ilaqat al-Dawliya*, Institute of Arab Development, Beirut, 1980.

Sanger, Richard H., "Libya: Conclusions on an Unfinished Revolution," *The Middle East Journal*, Vol. 29, No. 4, Autumn 1975.

Santucci, J. C., "L'Unification maghrébine: Realisations institutionelles et obstacles politiques," in Roger Le Tourneau et al., *L'unite Maghrebine dimensions et perspectives*, C.N.R.S., Paris, 1972.

Schatzberg, Michael, "Zaire," in Timothy M. Shaw and Olajide Aluko (eds.), *The Political Economy of African Foreign Policy: Comparative Analysis*, St. Martin's Press, New York, 1983.

Seale, Patrick, and Maureen McConville, *The Hilton Assignment*, Praeger, New York, 1973.

Selhami, Mohamed, "Libye: Ce qui a changé," *Jeune Afrique*, No. 1082, September 30, 1981.

El-Shazly, Saad, *The Crossing of the Suez*, American Mideast Research, San Francisco, 1980.

Shukri, Fu'ad, *Milad Dawlat Libya al-Haditha: Watha'iq Tahririha wa Istiqlaliha*, Matba'at al-I'timad, Cairo, 1957.

Sicker, Martin, "The Libyan Opposition to Qadhdhafi," *Global Affairs*, Vol. 1, No. 3, Summer 1986.

Slim, Habib, "Le comité permanent consultatif du Maghreb entre le passé, le present et l'avenir," *Revue Tunisienne de Droit*, Vol. 12, 1980.

Spykman, Nicholas J., *American Strategy and World Politics*, Harcourt, Brace, New York, 1942.

St. John, Ronald Bruce, "The Determinants of Libyan Foreign Policy, 1969–1983," *The Maghreb Review*, Vol. 8, Nos. 3-4, 1983.

———, "The Ideology of Mu'ammar al-Qadhdhafi: Theory and Practice," *International Journal of Middle East Studies*, Vol. 15, No. 4, November 1983.

———, "Libya's Foreign and Domestic Policies," *Current History*, Vol. 80, No. 470, December 1981.

———, *Qaddafi's World Design: Libyan Foreign Policy, 1969–1987*, Saqi Books, Worcester, England, 1987.

Al-Tawila, 'Abd al-Sattar, *Al-'Aqid al-Qadhdhafi wa Misr*, Ruz al-Yusuf Publications, Cairo, 1977.

Tessler, Mark, "Continuity and Change in Moroccan Politics, Part I: Challenge and Response in Hasan's Morocco," *Universities Field Staff International, Inc., Reports*, No. 1, Africa, 1984.

_____ , "Continuity and Change in Moroccan Politics, Part II: New Troubles and Deepening Doubts," *Universities Field Staff International, Inc., Reports*, No. 2, Africa, 1984.

Tripp, Charles, "La Libye et L'Afrique," *Politique Etrangère*, No. 2, Summer 1984.

Vatikiotis, Panayotis J., *Nasser and His Generation*, Croom Helm, London, 1978.

Villard, Henry S., *Libya: The New Arab Kingdom of North Africa*, Cornell University Press, Ithaca, N.Y., 1956.

Waltz, Kenneth N., *Theory of International Politics*, Addison-Wesley, Reading, Mass., 1979.

Weinstein, Franklin, *Indonesian Foreign Policy and the Dilemma of Dependence: From Sukarno to Soeharto*, Cornell University Press, Ithaca, N.Y., 1976.

_____ , "The Uses of Foreign Policy in Indonesia: An Approach to the Analysis of Foreign Policy in the Less Developed Countries," *World Politics*, Vol. 24, April 1972.

Well, Rick, "Nimeiry Under Seige," *Africa Report*, May-June 1984.

Whitworth, William, *Naive Questions About War and Peace*, W. W. Norton, New York, 1970.

Wilkinson, Ben, "Shifting Alignments in the Maghreb," *The Middle East*, May 1984.

Woodward, Bob, *Veil: The Secret Wars of the CIA, 1981–1987*, Simon and Schuster, New York, 1987.

Wright, John, "Chad and Libya: Some Historical Connections," *The Maghreb Review*, Vol. 8, Nos. 3-4, 1983.

_____ , *Libya: A Modern History*, Johns Hopkins University Press, Baltimore, Md., 1982.

Zartman, I. William, "Arms Imports: The Libyan Experience," *World Military Expenditures and Arms Transfers, 1971–1980*, U.S. Arms Control and Disarmament Agency, Washington, D.C., 1983.

_____ , "Conflict in the Sahara," Middle East Problem Paper, No. 19, Middle East Institute, Washington, D.C., 1979.

_____ , "Foreign Relations of North Africa," in *Annals*, AAPSS, No. 489, January 1987.

_____ , *International Relations in the New Africa*, Prentice-Hall, Englewood Cliffs, N.J., 1966.

_____ , "National Interest and Ideology," in Vernon McKay (ed.), *African Diplomacy: Studies in the Determining of Foreign Policy*, Praeger, New York, 1967.

_____ , *Ripe for Resolution: Conflict and Intervention in Africa*, Yale University Press, New Haven, 1985.

_____ , "What's at Stake in Chad," *World View*, Vol. 26, No. 11, November 1983.

_____ (ed.), *Man, State and Society in the Contemporary Maghreb*, Praeger, New York, 1971.

Zartman, I. William, and A. G. Kluge, "Heroic Politics: The Foreign Policy of Libya," in Baghat Korany and Ali Hillal Dessouki (eds.), *The Foreign Policies of Arab States*, Westview Press, Boulder, Colo., 1984.

———, "Qaddafi's Foreign Policy," *American Arab Affairs*, No. 6, Fall 1983.

Zartman, I. William, and Yassin el-Ayouty, *The OAU After Twenty Years*, Praeger, New York, 1984.

Zartman, I. William, and Aureniano Buendia, "La politique étrangère Libyenne," in Maurice Flory (ed.), *La Libye nouvelle*, C.N.R.S., Paris, 1975.

——— et al. (eds.), *Political Elites in Arab North Africa*, Longman, New York, 1982.

Ziadeh, Nicola A., *Sanusiyah: A Study of a Revivalist Movement in Islam*, E. J. Brill, Leiden, 1968.

## Dissertations

Ben Salem, Ahmed, "L'affaire de la borne 233 et le droit international public," dissertation for the Diplome d'Etudes Supérieures en Droit Public, School of Law, Political Science and Economics, University of Tunis, Tunis, 1972.

Ben Yedder, Neziha, "Le réglement pacifique des conflits inter-maghrebins," dissertation for the Diplome d'Etudes Supérieures en Droit Public, School of Law, Political Science and Economics, University of Tunis, Tunis, 1975.

Charfi, Lotfi Karim, "Des équilibres diplomatiques et militaires au maghreb (1960–1985)," dissertation for the Diplome d'Etudes Supérieures, Institut d'Etudes des Relations Internationales, Paris, 1985.

Fituri, Ahmed Said, "Tripolitania, Cyrenaica and Bilad as-Sudan: Trade Relations During the Second Half of the Nineteenth Century," dissertation for the University of Michigan, Ann Arbor, 1982.

El-Horeir, Abdulmola S., "Social and Economic Transformations in the Libyan Hinterland During the Second Half of the Nineteenth Century: The Role of Ahmad Al-Sharif Al-Sanusi," dissertation for the University of California, Los Angeles, 1981.

## Newspapers and Periodicals

*L'Action* (Tunis)
*Afrique Contemporaine* (Paris)
*Al-Ahram* (Cairo)
*Al-Akhbar* (Cairo)
*Al-'Alam* (Rabat)
*American-Arab Affairs*
*Annuaire de l'Afrique du Nord* (Paris)
*Arab Report and Record*
*Cahiers de Tunisie* (Tunis)
*Current History*
*Defense and Foreign Affairs*
*Al-Dustur* (Amman)

*L'Express* (Paris)
*Facts on File*
*Le Figaro* (Paris)
*Foreign Affairs*
*Foreign Policy*
*Global Affairs*
*Al-Inqadh*
*International Journal of Middle East Studies*
*Jeune Afrique* (Paris)
*Journal of Arab Affairs*
*The Journal of Modern African Studies*
*The Journal of South Asian and Middle Eastern STudies*
*Keesings Contemporary Archives*
*Maghreb-Machrek* (Paris)
*Maghreb Review* (London)
*Le Matin* (Casablanca)
*Middle East* (London)
*Middle East Economic Digest* (London)
*Middle East International* (London)
*Middle East Journal*
*Middle East Research and Information Projects Reports*
*Le Monde* (Paris)
*Al-Nahar* (Beirut)
*New York Times*
*Orbis*
*Politique Etrangère* (Paris)
*Revue Française d'Etudes Politiques Mediterranéènes* (Paris)
*Revue Tunisienne de Droit* (Tunis)
*Al-Safir* (Beirut)
*SAIS Review*
*Al-Sharq al-Awsat* (London)
*Studia Diplomatica* (Rome)
*Al-Wafd* (Cairo)
*Washington Post*
*World Politics*
*World View*

# Index